Ecumenical Dynamic

Ecumenical Dynamic

Living in More than One Place at Once

Keith Clements

**World Council
of Churches**
Publications

ECUMENICAL DYNAMIC
Living in More than One Place at Once

Copyright © 2013 WCC Publications. All rights reserved. Except for brief quotations in notices or reviews, no part of this book may be reproduced in any manner without prior written permission from the publisher. Write: publications@wcc-coe.org.

WCC Publications is the book publishing programme of the World Council of Churches. Founded in 1948, the WCC promotes Christian unity in faith, witness and service for a just and peaceful world. A global fellowship, the WCC brings together more than 349 Protestant, Orthodox, Anglican and other churches representing more than 560 million Christians in 110 countries and works cooperatively with the Roman Catholic Church.

Opinions expressed in WCC Publications are those of the authors.

Scripture quotations are from the New Revised Standard Version Bible, © copyright 1989 by the Division of Christian Education of the National Council of the Churches of Christ in the USA. Used by permission.

Cover design: Josh Messner
Cover image: *Pacem in terris*, Hans Erni, copyright by the artist, used by permission.
Book design and typesetting: Josh Messner

ISBN 978-2-8254-1596-2

World Council of Churches
150 route de Ferney, P.O. Box 2100
1211 Geneva 2, Switzerland
http://publications.oikoumene.org

Contents

Preface   vii

Abbreviations   xi

Part One. The Dynamic Encountered

1. Living in More than One Place at Once: What Does It Mean   3
   to Be "Ecumenical"? A Parable

2. I Had a Dream: To Be Ecumenical   23

3. Where Do We Live? The Biblical Paradigm   37

Part Two. The Dynamic Illustrated

4. First to See the Future: The Anglo-German Churches'   57
   Peace Exchanges 1908–1909

5. Creative Disempowerment: The Real Legacy of Edinburgh 1910   77

6. Beginning All Over Again: Barmen 1934   91
   and the Ecumenical Movement Questioned

7. Apostle of Unity: Why Bishop George Bell Is Important   107

8. "Perfectly Mad Adventure": J.H. Oldham's "Moot"   125
   and the End of Christendom

9. European Journey of Hope: From Creed to Charter   141

Part Three. The Dynamic Continues

10. Community: Promise or Danger?   157

11. Translating Faith into Public Policy: "Middle Axioms" Revisited 177

12. Who Are We? Continuing Ecumenical Quest   195

Index   215

*In grateful remembrance
of Morris West, Elizabeth Salter and Ion Bria,
guides ahead of me on the ecumenical way*

Preface

These days a book on ecumenism is likely to encounter three types of potential reader. First, there are the ecumenical enthusiasts who will eagerly seize upon any treatment of a subject so dear to their heart and will not ask for any explanation or justification for another book on the subject. Indeed, in the current "ecumenical winter," they will warmly welcome any positive presentation from any quarter. Second, there are the diehard opponents, who see the ecumenical movement of the last hundred years or so as the great distraction or indeed betrayal of the Christian cause, whether that cause be identified with "evangelism" narrowly understood or the maintenance of the unchanging tradition of their own particular church as the only true version of the gospel. Third, and probably in the great majority, there are those who claim to be no longer interested, if ever they were, in a movement which for better or worse has now run its course: classic, institutional, organized, or however else they wish to disparage the ecumenism of the recent past.

I hope this book will make all three types of reader think again, not least the third category. The dismissal of the modern ecumenical story as a story of organizations and structures or one of attempts at organic union—all of which, according to the story, have been misguided or had their day—carries with it valid points of criticism. But one can too easily dismiss the story by ignoring the inner dynamic which impelled it from the beginning. It is a vital element of that dynamic, which I identify as "living in more than one place at once," which I attempt to highlight as *not* over and done with.

As for the second category of readers, I scarcely dare hope to make any converts from among them, but I will be satisfied if they can at least recognize the seriousness of the claim I make: that this ecumenical dynamic, far from being peripheral to the gospel, expresses its heart—love which goes out of itself and its own place and lives where the other lives, as God in Jesus Christ did for us all. Ecumenism involves deep conviction, not the suspension of convictions under compromise.

And the first category, the enthusiasts who need no persuading? They too need to ponder more deeply what it is they wish to promote as ecumenism. In particular, they need to reconsider just what *is* the ecumenical story; they need to consider the dynamic that has been at the heart of the ecumenical journey and that will need to be carried into its future. As the reader will soon see, this leads me to query some of the conventional wisdom about modern ecumenical history, for example that it all began at Edinburgh in 1910.

The book is structured in three parts. In Part I, *The Dynamic Encountered*, the ecumenical dynamic is treated in a general survey of the recent and contemporary scene, then in terms of my own ecumenical formation, and thirdly as a major biblical theme which underlies all else that I say about "living in more than one place at once." Part II, *The Dynamic Illustrated*, looks at five episodes and one key figure in the modern ecumenical story. The fact that the focus here is largely upon Europe does not mean that I think only Europe matters in the story. Far from it: while my own most intense involvement has certainly been in Europe, over the years ecumenical activity has taken me to the Middle East, Africa, Australasia, North America, Central and Latin America, and East Asia, including the land of my birth, China. It is simply that Europe is where my studies have most closely focused or (in the case of chapter 9) where I have been most directly involved, and rather than lapse into generalities I feel more confident in using these European stories as particular illustrations of the ecumenical dynamic. Of course there are other stories to be told, and readers in other parts of the world may well wish to draw comparisons and find resonances in their own contexts, which will be all to the good. Finally, in Part III, *The Dynamic Continues*, I look at three contemporary areas where the dynamic still needs to be applied, both drawing from the past story and engaging with the new challenges before us.

Four of the chapters are adaptations of papers that have previously appeared: chapter 4, as "The Anglo-German Churches' Exchange Visits of 1908-09" in *The Ecumenical Review* 59, no. 2-3 (April-July 2007); chapter 6, as "Barmen and the Ecumenical Movement" in *The Ecumenical Review* 61, no. 1 (March 2009); chapter 7, as "George Bell: An Apostle for Unity" in *Crucible* (April-June 2010); and chapter 9 as "Two Decades of Ecumenism in Europe: A Promising Past with an Uncertain Future" in Anna M. Robbins, ed., *Ecumenical and Eclectic: The Unity of the Church in the Contemporary World; Essays in Honour of Alan P.F. Sell* (Paternoster, 2007). To the editors of each of these publications grateful acknowledgment is made for their permission to use the material.

My special thanks go to Michael West, World Council of Churches publisher, for his ready encouragement and advice in preparing the text for publication. There are many others to whom I owe gratitude, from all over the world, whose thoughts and experiences have found their way into these pages, whether they are aware of it or not. Finally, I hope that the three names found on the dedication page—Baptist, Quaker, and Russian Orthodox respectively—testify how "living in more than one place at once" has been personally exemplified to me by friends from widely differing traditions who have gone ahead on the ecumenical path. It is my hope that in turn this book will help keep that way open for the coming generation.

Keith Clements
Portishead, England

Abbreviations

ACTS	Action of Churches Together in Scotland
BBC	British Broadcasting Corporation
BCC	British Council of Churches
BCE	Before Christian Era
BMS	Baptist Missionary Society
CCBI	Council of Churches for Britain and Ireland
CCEE	Council of Catholic Episcopal Conferences in Europe
CE	Christian Era
CEC	Conference of European Churches
CICCU	Cambridge Inter-Collegiate Christian Union
CIMADE	Comité inter-mouvement aupres des evacués
COMECE	Commission of Episcopal Conferences in the European Union
CSCE	Conference on Security and Cooperation in Europe
CTBI	Churches Together in Britain and Ireland
CTE	Churches Together in England
Cytun	Churches Together in Wales
GDR	German Democratic Republic
IMC	International Missionary Council
IRM	International Review of Missions
JPIC	Justice, Peace and the Integrity of Creation
LEP	Local Ecumenical Project
MCFC	Metropolitan Free Church Federation
NATO	North Atlantic Treaty Organization
NGO	Non-governmental organization
SCM	Student Christian Movement
TRC	Truth and Reconciliation Commission (South Africa)
UN	United Nations
UNESCO	United Nations Educational, Scientific and Cultural Organization
WCC	World Council of Churches
WSCF	World Student Christian Federation
YMCA	Young Men's Christian Association

Part One
The Dynamic Encountered

Chapter 1

Living in More than One Place at Once

What Does It Mean to Be "Ecumenical"? A Parable

It is the autumn of 1940. On the French plateau of Gurs close to the northern slopes of the Pyrenees, enclosed in barbed wire stands a rather shabby collection of huts. It is "home" to some 16,000 thousand men, women, and children of various nationalities, all of them refugees either from the part of France to the north that has fallen to occupation by the forces of Nazi Germany, or from Germany itself. With the onset of the winter rains, cold and mud are adding to the misery of hunger, sickness, and fear for the future. A young French woman is calling at the camp, bringing as many supplies of medicines and toiletries as she can carry. The French police eye her warily. The large number of so many people who are escapees from the Germans makes the camp's presence in Vichy France, that part of France which has made its humiliating peace with Nazi Germany, a sensitive issue. The French do not wish to give the Nazi authorities any grounds for suspecting that they are harbouring actual enemies—especially Germans—of the regime, still less allowing support for them from outside the camp. But the young woman has been to the camp several times before and is allowed in. Once she is inside, her supplies are gratefully received. On this day, however—a Sunday—she causes surprise by announcing that she would also like to hold a worship service. A member of the French Reformed Church, she is neither a pastor nor a professional theologian, but certainly theologically aware, and her long experience of Christian youth work means she is no stranger to leading prayer services and Bible studies. The authorities give her permission and offer her the use of the shower block, which is not used on Sundays. They expect about 50 people to come. In fact 600 turn up, crowding to the doors. So the service begins, the only light a candle by which the young woman reads. She is reading a psalm when suddenly a loud cry erupts from the darkness at the back of the room, and a tall bearded man wrapped in a blanket rushes down the aisle towards her shouting "Madeleine! Madeleine!" Others grab him, and he is hustled away and out through the door in some distress. Madeleine Barot, for that is her name, is puzzled: although she does not for the moment recognize the man, he clearly thought he knew her. But what would happen if the authorities suspected she was visiting the camp in order to find someone?

3

Afterwards, she asks about this man. He is German, Herbert Jehle by name, and because of his outburst they have put him in solitary, a barbed wire enclosure in a field to which they now take her. On seeing her, evidently realising the possible danger in which they both find themselves, he turns his back and simply writes with his finger in the sand: *Amsterdam*. The penny begins to drop. A week later Jehle is released for good behaviour, Barot meets him again, and they feel able to talk freely. Amsterdam was where in July 1939, just weeks before war broke out, the World Conference of Christian Youth was held. Both Madeleine Barot and Herbert Jehle were among the 1500 delegates who gathered there to pray, study, and celebrate together their fellowship in the gospel. Those young people knew what, humanly speaking, the future held (some would soon die), but declared in their conference message: "The nations and peoples of the world are drifting apart. The Churches are coming together. There is a growing conviction of the essential togetherness of all Christians. In war, conflict and persecution we must strengthen one another and preserve our Christian unity unbroken."[1] A physicist by training and a Quaker pacifist, Herbert Jehle had had to flee his native Germany, but at Amsterdam had found himself in the wider family of the household of faith. Interned at Gurs and suddenly recognising Madeleine Barot at the service, he could not contain his surprise and joy, which for a moment flung all inhibiting sense of danger to the winds. Together Barot and Jehle were now to incarnate the Amsterdam conference message, as with others they formed a prayer cell in the camp. In due course, Madeleine Barot, with several friends, organised Herbert Jehle's escape from Gurs and his flight to permanent and safer refuge in the USA.

For her part, Madeleine Barot, nurtured in the World Student Christian Federation, had been working in fascist Italy when the war broke out, but at once returned to France to work for refugees. She was a founding member and general secretary of CIMADE, the French Protestant churches' agency for refugee and relief work, and when Vichy France too was occupied in 1942, she became active in the resistance network helping Jews and others escape into Spain and Switzerland. In all this, she worked closely with equally committed Catholic priests. After the war she was to work devotedly for the new World Council of Churches in the areas of youth and women. Meanwhile, in the safety of the USA, Herbert Jehle had not forgotten her, and once France was liberated he organised the sending of food parcels to Barot and her CIMADE colleagues.[2]

---

1. See Ruth Rouse and Stephen Neil, eds., *A History of the Ecumenical Movement 1517-1948* (London: SPCK, 1986), 708 and W.A. Visser 't Hooft, *Memoirs* (Geneva: WCC Publications, 1987), 101.
2. For the biography of Barot, including this story, see André Jacques, *Madeleine Barot* (Geneva: WCC Publications, 1991).

This particular story of encounter and re-encounter in very changed circumstances will not of itself feature prominently in official histories of what we call "the ecumenical movement." But nothing expresses more clearly what that history, the big story, is all about: encounters that generate relationships—relationships that can suddenly assume a new significance in unexpected ways, where they are tested and put to further use in yet deeper trust and commitment, to the point where people realise that they no longer hope for but *are* a new community of shared belief, acceptance, endeavour, and mutual service. Again and again, the initial encounter is one which opens eyes to a wider and very different world than known before, seen through the eyes of the other, a world which in turn prompts the newcomer to a new kind of self-awareness too.

This was so for many at Amsterdam in 1939. Among the British delegates was a young Scottish Baptist, David Russell. It was the first time he had been any distance from his native Glasgow, let alone abroad, and it provided his first encounter with everything from American hot-gospellers to Eastern Orthodox: "I had lived in such a confined environment. I began to realise that my God—my God—my Scottish Baptist God—was too small and that Scotland itself, for all its worth, was not after all the centre of the earth."[3] Russell, in later life, was to be not only a noted biblical scholar and general secretary of the Baptist Union of Great Britain, but a tireless international ecumenical worker for human rights and religious freedom. He habitually ascribed his later commitments to the transformative effect of that first experience at Amsterdam and the friendships which he began to make there.

"I had lived in such a confined environment." Russell found himself *invited now to live*, mentally, in more than one place at once, realising that he belonged to a bigger world and a larger community of faith than he previously reckoned on. Jehle was, as a refugee, *having to live* in more than once place at once (or at any rate in several places in quick succession), his native Germany and wherever else he could find safety. Barot *chose to live* another kind of double life: as well as the anxious life of a citizen of a defeated and occupied country, the strenuous and dangerous life of a relief worker and resistance agent on behalf of people in even greater danger than herself. These people and their experiences, in their different ways, illustrate what being "ecumenical" means: living in more than one place at once, or living with more than one group of people at once, across frontiers of nationality and religious tradition, and thereby witnessing to a new kind of community already in the making, which relativises our other identities and loyalties. Among Jehle's fellow-German friends was Dietrich Bonhoeffer, whose last recorded words on the day before his

---

3. See Keith Clements, "Profile: David Russell," *Epworth Review* 23, no. 3 (Sept. 1996): 24.

execution in 1945, a message to his English friend George Bell, bishop of Chichester, are a poignant testimony to the ecumenical conviction: "Tell him that … with him I believe in the principle of our Universal Christian Brotherhood which rises above all national interests, and that our victory is certain."[4]

The popular view is that "being ecumenical" means "to promote Christian unity" in terms of getting churches to relate more closely, if not actually unite, and to work together at national and international levels, through councils of churches or organisations of "churches together." "Being ecumenical" certainly can involve all these, but these are the outcomes of something deeper, an actual way living, thinking and believing. Our English term "ecumenical" is the transliteration of the Greek word *oikoumene*, which derives from the verb *oikein*, "to inhabit" and the noun *oikos*, "household." In the time of the early church *oikoumene* denoted "the [whole] inhabited earth." The first gatherings of the bishops of the whole church were known as "ecumenical councils" because they were representing the churches of what was then the whole known inhabited world: not only from the great centres of Jerusalem, Antioch, Rome, and Alexandria but from the furthest borders of the Roman Empire, from northernmost York to southerly Carthage, from Atlantic Spain to the Black Sea. Even within the confines of what was essentially the one empire, being ecumenical meant being prepared to sit with, listen to, speak with, pray with, learn from, and decide with people who might be from far away and of very different context, culture, language and expression of the faith. Being ecumenical means recognising that there is only one *oikoumene*, one inhabited earth, but that it is of diverse habitations. None of us can live in every habitation, every place. But neither do we appreciate the fact of the *oikoumene* if in mind and heart we inhabit *only* one place all the time. Being ecumenical means living in more than one place at once: at home and where we are not at home or not quite at home, with the familiar and with the strange, because we are part of a new community being created which relativises the significance of our particular place. As the unknown writer of the *Letter to Diognetus* said of Christians sometime in the second or third century, "every strange city is their home-town and every home-town is strange to them."[5]

A Great Story

"The ecumenical movement" has generally come to mean the story of how the churches of the world, divided since the Great Schism between East and West in the 11th century, the Reformation of the 16th century and subsequent fragmentations,

---

4. Eberhard Bethge, *Dietrich Bonhoeffer*, rev. ed. (Minneapolis: Fortress, 2000), 1022 n. 54.
5. See Hans Lietzmann, *A History of the Early Church*, vol. 2 (London: Lutterworth, 1961), 188.

and spread throughout the world by migration, colonial expansion, and missionary enterprise, have since the opening decade of the 20th century been discovering each other across the diversity of traditions, confessions and national and cultural contexts, with the aim of seeking that unity which God wills and enables: as it is most universally expressed, to fulfil the "high priestly" prayer of Jesus "that they may all be one" (John 17:20). At its core is the goal of seeking "visible unity," however variously that unity may be conceived. For some that goal means organic union between hitherto separated churches, even if for the present the means to that union cannot be envisaged. For others it means a full mutual recognition and acceptance by each church of each other as expressions of the one body of Christ, witnessed above all in communion at the Lord's table, the eucharist. For others the emphasis on visible unity lies in cooperating as closely as possible in life and mission, in evangelism, prophetic witness for justice and peace, and serving human need. For many, including myself, it means all these emphases drawn together in one vision of God's purpose in Christ "as a plan for the fullness of time, to gather up all things in him, things in heaven and things on earth" (Eph. 1:10). But at the heart of the story of the ecumenical movement are the stories of how, repeatedly, people of faith have dared to live not only in the here and now of their own tradition, their own place, their own time, but also in the thought-world of the other tradition, in another place and indeed another time yet to come.

This inner aspect is the enlivening current which runs through the main streams normally identified as making up the modern "ecumenical movement." I choose my words carefully, for it has to be said that a bare recital of the conferences, the assemblies and the founding of organisations—typically beginning with the Edinburgh World Missionary Conference of 1910—which are normally listed as "landmarks" in the story hardly makes for an exciting read. It is not surprising that much of the "ecumenical story" resonates less and less with today's Christian generation for whom that past is just that: past, and irrelevant to present interests and challenges. Even the so-called "River Chart" produced by the World Council of Churches[6] to portray in graphic form the 100-year story does no more than give some information about the past in terms of dates, places, gatherings and institutions. It portrays these as static buildings on the banks of the river, but gives no clues on what *actually being in the river, caught by the flow*, was like, still less whether that lively current is still running.

In all fairness, though, some main turns and confluences of the flow have to be noted to mark the direction. Depending on the particular standpoint of the observer,

---

6. Available online at http://www.oikoumene.org/fileadmin/images/wcc-main/programmes/riverchart_brochure-web.pdf by way of http://www.oikoumene.org/programmes/the-wcc-and-the-ecumenical-movement-in-the-21st-century.html. See also below, chapter 5.

a whole variety of points in the story at world level compete for attention as high-lights. To name but a few:

- The (often disregarded) pioneering letter of appeal from the Ecumenical Patriarchate in 1920 "unto all the Churches of Christ wheresoever they be" to form a league of the churches for mutual assistance, dialogue and the promotion of peace in the world; and in the same year the "Appeal to All Christian People" for reunion, made by the Lambeth conference.
- The solidarity shown to the Confessing Church of Germany in the 1930s by the churches represented in the "Life and Work" movement, and the declaration of repentance and reconciliation by leaders of that church to the ecumenical delegation at Stuttgart in 1945.
- The inaugural assembly of the WCC in the aftermath of world war, in 1948 at Amster-dam, where the churches resolved: "We intend to stay together."
- The principle set out in 1952 by the third world conference on Faith and Order at Lund, Sweden, asking the churches "whether they should not act together in all matters except those in which deep differences of conviction compel them to act separately?"[7]
- The Second Vatican Council's groundbreaking Decree on Ecumenism *Unitatis Red-integratio* (1964), joyfully recognising that "among our separated brethren also there increases from day to day a movement, fostered by the grace of the Holy Spirit, for the restoration of unity among all Christians"[8] and committing the Roman Catholic Church to serious ecumenical dialogue.
- The steps taken in the 1970s by the WCC Programme to Combat Racism which faced huge controversy, in Europe especially, for the support given by its Special Fund to liberation movements in southern Africa, marking a decisive shift of ecumenical solidarity towards the global south;
- The 1982 Faith and Order "convergence document" *Baptism, Eucharist and Minis-try* (the so-called "Lima Text" or "Lima Document")[9] which, gathering the fruits of decades of theological dialogue, showed how far, though certainly not completely, the Protestant, Anglican, Orthodox, and Roman Catholic churches had grown in agreement on these central matters of the faith.
- The conciliar process of "Justice, Peace and the Integrity of Creation" which, fol-lowing the WCC Vancouver assembly (1983), brought churches together to face the

7. See Morris West, "Lund Principle," in *Dictionary of the Ecumenical Movement* (Geneva: WCC 2002), 714 -15.
8. Decree on Ecumenism *Unitatis Redintegratio*, in *Vatican Council II: The Conciliar and Post-Conciliar Documents*, vol. 1, ed. Austin Flannery (Leominster: Fowler Wright, 1980), 452.
9. World Council of Churches, Commission on Faith and Order, "Baptism, Eucharist and Minis-try," Faith and Order Paper No. 111 (Geneva: WCC Publications, 1982).

issues of injustice, war, and ecological threats as matters not just of ethics but of confessing the faith, and was especially important to the European churches in a continent still divided by the Cold War.

• The encyclical *Ut Unum Sint* issued by Pope John Paul II (1995), summarising the fruits of three decades of ecumenical dialogue and encouraging further dialogue even on the most testing subjects such as the "petrine ministry" of the Pope.

There is no ground for triumphalism in a movement still so relatively young and still facing so many outstanding challenges, but neither is there cause to blush with shame despite the undoubted disappointments and mistakes along the way. Admittedly the modern ecumenical movement has always had its opponents and critics, not least in Britain, and by no means confined to biblical fundamentalists, anti-Papal zealots, Anglo-ultra-Catholics and theological illiterates. In the 1960s the notable Scottish theologian Ian Henderson delivered his violent polemic *Power Without Glory* against what he perceived to be a misguided attempt to bring about "One Church" through ecclesiastical power politics, in which the Church of England was the chief culprit: "Basically, Anglican diplomatic policy is the extermination of all Protestant (i.e. non-episcopally ordained) ministers."[10] This is what, claimed Henderson, had happened in the formation of the Church of South India in 1947, with a similar threat now hanging over the Church of Scotland if the Church of England were to have its way. Critics of Professor Henderson, including fellow-Scots, were not slow to allege that his ire was fed by his particular brand of Scottish nationalism as much as by concern for the Reformed faith. By contrast, the English church historian John Kent, a Methodist, was nothing if not dispassionate in his critique of ecumenism as "The Light that Failed," the title of a chapter in his astringent survey of the modern church in the eyes of the historian.[11] Kent's main complaint about the ecumenical movement was that it had basically failed in its objectives and, more seriously, habitually glossed over those failures with its own propaganda. Within four years of the formation of the WCC, Kent claims, "the original movement had run out of energy"[12] and by the 1980s "one was left with the impression that the enthusiasm of the churches for unity was about equal to the enthusiasm shown by the Great Powers for the avoidance of a Third World War with nuclear weapons."[13]

---

10. Ian Henderson, *Power Without Glory: A Study in Ecumenical Politics* (London: Hutchinson, 1967), 100.
11. John H.S. Kent, *The Unacceptable Face: The Modern Church in the Eyes of the Historian* (London: SCM, 1987).
12. Ibid., 203.
13. Ibid., 204.

As the Protestant movement slowed down, ecumenism for a time became fashionable in the Roman Catholic Church, but with no more success. As for the Church of South India, its creation "seems to have been a disaster." Kent, however, armed with sociological tools, also had penetrating questions to ask about the reasons for the failures of ecumenism, in particular the absence of Christian renewal accompanying schemes of union, and his final warning deserves to be heeded: "Ecumenism has suffered from excessive self-consciousness: its leaders were always telling each other and the world in general what the historical significance of the movement was, and attempting to create a school of historical interpretation by sheer assertion."[14]

Sociologists and historians are paid to be sceptical of stated values, motivations and versions of history and to propose explanations far more mundane for human enterprises than the official self-justifying (not to mention self-glorifying) accounts. That is salutary, and who can deny, for example, that a real factor in moves towards Christian unity may well have been the churches' destabilising fears for their status and security in a rapidly changing world, a world both secularising and increasingly pluralistic, in which the old Christendom was crumbling? But in dealing with any form of human relationships sheer suspicion, while uncovering all-too-human motivations, may miss what is nevertheless genuinely good and creative in that mix of ambition and aspiration, illusion and idealism. It would be unwarrantably cynical, for example, to assess a marriage *only* in terms of the psychological (and perhaps economic) pay-offs each partner gets out of it ("He's looking for another mother who will always say what a wonderful boy he is." "It's always been her dream to be joined to a powerful man—a cabinet minister or even a bishop would do.") and fail to recognise that even in all the ambiguities of that relationship there can be genuinely appreciative and self-giving love, each cherishing the other and generating yet more love in a new family. Whatever may be said against it the modern ecumenical movement overall is a great story of ventures into repentance and reconciliation following on from a past in which the Christian churches have not only been divided and antagonistic among themselves, but have often aided and abetted divisions among peoples and nations to the point of shedding blood. Against the immediate backdrop of a century of violence on a world scale, it reads particularly well. Moreover it does not *only* or even mainly comprise schemes, successful or otherwise, of organic union between churches whether in India or elsewhere. It is about entering into creative relationships and wider community.

---

14. Ibid., 215.

In Britain Too

Nor is the story confined to the somewhat rarefied heights of global ecclesiastical debate and diplomacy. It has found expression at all other levels from the national to the local, and not least in Britain. When one considers the situation of British church relations only a hundred years ago the change has been extraordinary. The years immediately prior to the 1914-18 war saw strident rivalry between the English Free Churches and the Church of England over the basic issue of establishment of the "national church," a continuing legacy of the slow and fitful removal of the disabilities suffered by non-Anglicans in the Victorian era. In particular there was bitter dispute over the issue of public funding for church schools. "Rome on the rates!" was the Dissenting war-cry of alarm sounded especially by Baptists and Congregationalists, many of whom were prepared to face confiscation of their goods and even imprisonment rather than pay their local taxes in violation of their conscience. In turn, on record are stories of teachers of Free Church allegiance being dismissed from Church of England schools. Sectarianism cut both ways. But as for Rome itself, it was hardly in the picture, let alone on the rates, its church still largely viewed as an alien intrusion into the land of Wycliffe, Cranmer, and Elizabeth I. The rejection by Parliament in 1926 of the proposed Revised Prayer Book on account of even mildly "catholic" elements in it was enough to demonstrate how deeply entrenched in the national psyche such partisan sentiments still lay.

Sixty years later, the climate was very different. The historian Adrian Hastings, concluding his account of the way the relationships between Anglicans, Roman Catholics and Free Churches had developed, and referring to the "great change" in the attitude to Christian unity since the end of the First World War, observed that by the mid-1980s,

> this "great change" had not only affected Anglicans and Free churchmen vastly more than it had in 1920 or 1940, but it now also included Catholics. A sense of one Christian community with a common mission and a common faith had become central to the experience of all the main churches in England in a way that it had never been previously. And that was a very great achievement.[15]

It was on this wave of gratitude and optimism that there was launched in 1985 a new ecumenical initiative, the Not Strangers but Pilgrims Inter-Church Process, involving study and discussion at every level, from national to local, and embracing just about all the church traditions in the British Isles—including the

---

15. Adrian Hastings, *A History of English Christianity 1920-1985* (London: Collins, 1986), 629.

Roman Catholics and the Black-led Pentecostal and Holiness Churches as well as those which had hitherto been members of the British Council of Churches (BCC), formed in 1942. Out of this was born a set of proposals for new "ecumenical instruments" to replace the BCC. The new bodies—one at four-nation level for the whole of the British Isles and four national bodies for England, Ireland, Scotland and Wales—would be more inclusive in their membership with Roman Catholic involvement a chief prize.[16] Equally significant, they would work in a new way, not as agencies "doing ecumenical work for the churches" but rather enabling the churches themselves to work closely together on the tasks which they identified as essential. The "churches together" model had arrived. This embodied the spirit of the Inter-Church Conference at Swanwick in September 1987 which gathered up the Not Strangers But Pilgrims process and set out the proposals to be put to the churches. The Swanwick Declaration rang with new hope and confidence:

> We now declare together our readiness to commit ourselves to each other under God. Our earnest desire is to become more fully, in his own time, the One Church of Christ, united in faith, communion, pastoral care and mission. . .
>
> It is our conviction that, as a matter of policy at all levels and in all places, our churches must now move from co-operation to clear commitment to each other, in search of the unity for which Christ prayed and in common evangelism and service of the world.[17]

Ecumenism not as an "extra," but as a dimension of all we do, was the watchword of the hour. The new instruments were launched in the autumn of 1990 in a spirit of great expectancy, although in some quarters there were fears that the desire for inclusivity and especially Roman Catholic participation might prove to be at the expense of the more prophetic voice that had been heard from the BCC. As one who was appointed to the staff of the four-nation body the Council of Churches for Britain

---

16. The Council of Churches for Britain and Ireland (CCBI) replaced the British Council of Churches. In due course it was renamed Churches Together in Britain and Ireland (CTBI). As well as being the overall coordinating body, it was designed to enable the churches at four-nation level to deal with international and public affairs and church life issues. New national bodies were set up for England (Churches Together in England—CTE), Scotland (Action of Churches Together in Scotland—ACTS) and Wales (Cytun), while in Ireland the Irish Council of Churches continued together with the Irish Inter-Church Meeting.

17. *Churches Together in Pilgrimage: Including Definitive Proposals for Ecumenical Instruments* ["The Marigold Book"] (London: British Council of Churches and Catholic Truth Society, 1989), 7. See also http://www.cte.org.uk/Articles/320032/Churches_Together_in/Local_Ecumenism/Resources/Revision/Churches_Together_in.aspx.

and Ireland (CCBI), I for one have no doubt that in the early days of the "new instruments," there was a real and sincere attempt by all concerned to make them embody and implement the new vision of ecumenism.

Decline—and Why?

All that was over twenty years ago. Today there is a wide consensus that, to put it variously, we are in an "ecumenical winter" both internationally and nationally, that the ecumenical movement has "run out of steam," that "ecumenism as we have known it has failed," that ecumenism is quite simply dead. It is not quite the case, yet, that relations have reverted outright to the antagonisms of the past, although at the global level the 1990s saw an outbreak of suspicion and verbal hostility between some parts of Eastern Orthodoxy and Western Christianity in both its Roman Catholic and Protestant forms, a hostility which is not yet fully healed despite conciliatory overtures from the Vatican and strenuous efforts by the WCC. In Britain it is already the case that—at least as far as England is concerned—we cannot speak as confidently as did Adrian Hastings in the 1980s of "one Christian community with a common mission and a common faith." Both the vision and the energy have gone. The death in 1999 of Cardinal Basil Hume, probably the most widely loved and respected Christian leader in Britain since the mid-1970s and a chief inspiration of the Inter-Church Process, symbolized if not marked the decline. The visit of Pope Benedict XVI to Britain in 2011 had many positive features but neither received nor generated anything like the universal excitement of John Paul II's pilgrimage in 1982. Everyone is anxious to say "there can be no going back," but no-one seems eager to move forward or to plot the future path. There being little interest in carrying the story onwards with anything like the energy of the former days, the danger is of the relations that have been built up over the past century unravelling through indifference and brooding suspicions.

Readers from a context other than the British Isles may wish to compare their situation with what I am now describing. Today, what is euphemistically called "a sober realism" prevails, illustrated by the remarks of five English church leaders— Anglican, Roman Catholic, and Free Church—who at the start of the Week of Prayer for Christian Unity in January 2009 were invited by the religious press to offer their visions and understandings of Christian unity. The result,[18] to anyone hoping for a fresh injection of energy into the ecumenical movement, was not exactly encouraging. The Archbishop of Canterbury, Rowan Williams, was alone in asking that the

---

18. As seen in, e.g., the *Baptist Times*, 22 January 2009. The interviewees were: the then Archbishop of Canterbury Rowan Williams; the then Archbishop of Westminster Cardinal Murphy O'Connor; and the General Secretaries of the Baptist Union (Jonathan Edwards), the Methodist Church (Martin Atkins), and the United Reformed Church (Roberta Rominger).

goal of visible unity be kept in view and prayed for. Otherwise the "visions" largely consisted of incontrovertible generalisations about "the unity of the Church for the sake of the kingdom of God" or "to put Jesus first and to be the Church that he has called us to be," while the overall impression was that "we have to work with [denominational] situations as they are" together with an unexpectedly complacent comment (as far as ecumenical history is concerned) that "previous generations saw structural unity as the expression of this faithfulness—an inward focus. Today we are more apt to focus outward, on the work, sharing our resources and working together." The overall impression left by these views from the top is that for the time being, the churches are felt to have done all that could be expected of them in mutual rapprochement and ways of "working together." Further steps may become clearer with time, but the inference is that for most church leaders ecumenism has been left at the bottom of the in-tray while more pressing matters arrive on the desk. This is not primarily their own fault. They are the reflection, rather than the cause, of the braking system being applied to the movement. The slow-down results from a failure of nerve going far wider and deeper than the stance of any one leading figure. John Kent's dour description of a "post-ecumenical phase" from the 1980s onwards may well now indeed be true: "a renewed series of diplomatic negotiations between separate churches, in which each was to bargain as firmly as possible for the protection of its own fundamental identity. The rhetoric of ecumenism continued, but the reality of ecclesiastical politics was much less concealed."[19]

At least symptomatic of this failure of nerve, and certainly reinforcing it, is the large-scale down-grading of the British ecumenical instruments set up in 1990. In the case of the four-nation CTBI, a virtually complete demolition job has been carried out thanks largely to withdrawal of support and funding from the Roman Catholics and the Church of England, reducing it to a small-scale agency offering its services to the churches—doing important and creative work especially in ecumenical study, but hardly any longer a body through which the churches as such work together. That is a serious reversal of the intentions of twenty years ago. There is now no longer any forum of study and public witness by all the churches at a four-nation level on matters of social and international concern. Churches Together in England (CTE) has fared better (and, some would say, at the expense of CTBI) but it is by no means clear whether CTE is "owned" by the member churches any more than was the former BCC. It would not matter greatly if the churches had felt they could now express the spirit of the Swanwick Declaration *without* such instruments and were seen to be doing so. But largely, they are not. The flesh of the instruments may have

---

19. Kent, *The Unacceptable Face*, 204.

been weak, but the spirit no longer seems willing, either. "Churches together" has become a somewhat ambiguous slogan which can mean anything or nothing, and certainly little in the way of concerted action. Indeed there is a growing isolationism. Here are some instances of current unecumenical activities:

- The Church of England in 2004 produced the report *Mission-Shaped Church* on church planting and "fresh expressions" of church appropriate for evangelism and growth in contemporary society. But, for all that the issue is one that naturally exercises Christians of all denominations, and that the working group which produced the report included a Methodist, the report is a curiously Anglican-centred document, with little recognition that other churches are in the field too and with only passing references to ecumenical action.[20]
- The Baptist Assembly in May 2010 took the theme "One World, One Mission" with a multitude of seminars and plenary events, yet without so much as a mention that missiologists and mission agency representatives from all over the world and from all Christian traditions (including the evangelical and Pentecostal) would shortly be gathering at Edinburgh (and again at Cape Town a few months later) to commemorate the centenary of the World Missionary Conference, and to plot a future for world mission.
- In the same year, the Conference of the Methodist Church resolved to close its long-established theological college in Bristol, Wesley College, without apparent regard to the effect this would have on the work of the Baptist and Anglican colleges in Bristol, and without considering the serious possibilities actually under discussion between Wesley College and the Baptist College for joint theological education.
- Relations between Roman Catholics and others have not been made easier by some recent actions of the Vatican. The institution in 2010 of the Anglican Ordinariate[21] was evidently made without any prior consultation with the Church of England. Of potentially wider ecumenical impact is the arrival of the revised English version of the Mass being issued from Rome. Not only in the eyes of many concerned Catholics

20. The Archbishops' Council, *Mission-Shaped Church: Church Planting and Fresh Expressions of Church in a Changing Context* (London: Church House Publications, 2004). For further comment on this see below, Chapter 12, The report has been criticized by some Anglicans for allegedly subverting the traditional parish system, but even more strongly by some non-Anglicans for its assumption that the "national church" can view "mission" as its special prerogative without regard to other denominations and faith communities. It is dismissive of Local Ecumenical Partnerships. For an especially trenchant critique by a United Reformed Church theologian, see John Hull, *Mission-Shaped Church: A Theological Response* (London: SCM 2006).
21. This was a scheme promulgated by the Vatican to allow Anglicans to be received into the Roman Catholic Church while continuing, if they wished, Anglican liturgical and spiritual practice.

does this represent a reversion to pre-Vatican II days, but it has been formulated without reference to the International Committee on English in the Liturgy (ICEL) and without consideration of its ecumenical implications. Over the past forty years or so, the growing use of similar prayers and responses in the liturgies of churches Catholic, Anglican, and Protestant has powerfully contributed to the sense of being "one in Christ" despite continuing differences. This now appears to be under threat.

While it would be unjust to say that such actions are typical of *all* the behaviour of these churches, they are not what one would expect from bodies which had solemnly stated that they were moving "from cooperation to clear commitment," embracing ecumenism as a dimension of all that they do.

There is no shortage of explanations or justifications (the two tend to slide into each other) of the "ecumenical winter." None of them is wholly satisfactory, nor is the sum total of them. We may consider them briefly:

Declining Churches

With most of the "mainline" churches—those that have chiefly supported ecumenical activity in the past—in steep decline in membership, leadership personnel, and financial resources, it is only to be expected that they would reduce their support for ecumenical organisations and activity. If they are not actually in survival mode, their priorities are now for their own maintenance rather than "extramural" work. This is very odd reasoning on two counts. First, the very fact that churches' resources are diminishing would logically be expected to make them more eager for pooling and sharing their rations. Indeed, we have already noted a long-standing criticism of the ecumenical movement that basically it was prompted by churches fearing their fragility in an uncertain world—safety in numbers no longer being guaranteed, it was felt necessary to draw the wagons together in a closer circle for the night. Second—and if this is so the implications are bleak indeed—it means that the British churches have forgotten completely their commitment made in 1990 that ecumenism is to be an aspect of all they do and not therefore a matter of size, resources, and financial capacity.

Growth of Evangelicalism

Evangelicalism (with or without charismatic influences) has increasingly become a dominant force in both the Church of England and the Free Churches, as it is already in many of the black-majority churches. Evangelicalism tends to sit loose to any structures, denominational or ecumenical, which do not put evangelism as the main priority, and it promotes alliances primarily between those who share its particular understanding of biblical authority. Ecumenism which aims at drawing "all churches together" is therefore regarded by evangelicals as a distraction from the "real task" of the church. Evangelical growth *ipso facto* means ecumenical decline. This argument points to a real factor on the church scene at the moment, but as a total rationale (whether in approval or disapproval) for the "death of ecumenism" it is hardly adequate. For one thing, it does not account for the ecumenical inertia in circles *outside* evangelicalism. For another, it does a disservice to those evangelicals who *do* consider themselves ecumenically committed and who demonstrate that commitment, for example by involvement at the local level.

The Priority of Interfaith Relations

In the early 1990s, Hans Küng stated the formula: "There can be no peace among the nations without peace among the religions. There can be no peace among the religions without dialogue between the religions."[22] Interreligious dialogue has now assumed huge significance, with religion being recognised as an undeniable factor in many conflicts, especially with the growth of religious fundamentalism as a motor of political struggle. The terrorist attacks of 11 September 2001 merely underlined the urgency of understanding between the religions, not least Islam and Christianity. Consequently, it has become almost axiomatic that intra-Christian ecumenism is now far surpassed in importance by interfaith relations and interreligious dialogue. One may, however, fully concede the new importance of the interreligious dimension without allowing this to supersede the search for unity between the churches, and for two reasons. First, dialogue with a partner presupposes that one is oneself an identifiable personality. If Christianity is being challenged to dialogue, it must itself become at least a more coherent entity. Second, in addition to this pragmatic consideration, there is an intrinsic theological imperative to Christian ecumenism, which is the attempt to answer how the church may more truly be the church as the body of Christ on earth. Interreligious dialogue and Christian ecumenism are complementary, not interchangeable.

Internal Church Divisions over Interchurch Differences

It is frequently stated that the most serious divisions in Christianity today are not between the different churches and traditions, but within them. In particular, issues relating to gender and sexuality and the associated questions of the authority of Bible and/or tradition form the main dividing lines. There is no point in, say, any church dialoguing with the Church of England unless and until it sorts itself out with respect to women priests and bishops and gay clergy, since these are the matters

---

22. Hans Küng, *Global Responsibility: In Search of a New World Ethic* (London: SCM, 1990), xv.

over which it is at odds with itself, and more passionately than over any theological difference with other traditions. This is indeed an intimidating challenge to ecumenism but rarely is the underlying assumption of cause-and-effect questioned. Why is it assumed that it is the intra-church arguments that have made ecumenism irrelevant? May it not equally be the case that it is the diminution of wider ecumenical interest and commitment that has *allowed* such questions to so dominate the internal life of churches? It is isolation and introspection that encourages internal power-struggles in tin-pot states—and in churches too.

The End of Institutions?

These explanations, rationalisations, or justifications for the decline in ecumenism are at least debatable. A much more formidable and wide-ranging challenge, however, stems from the total context in which the churches and ecumenical agencies, along with all social organisations, find themselves today. It is the context broadly described, almost ad nauseam, as "post-modern": a society and culture which eschews universal uniformity of belief and values in favour of the particular, even the fragmentary, perspectives which each mini-culture, each community, even each person, chooses or is content to live by. Gone is any grand narrative of history, whether political, ideological or religious, which supposedly supplies meaning to life. Instead there are specific stories, none of them claiming to supply a meaning for the whole of humanity but which shape, and are shaped by, the here-and-nowness of life. Claims to absolute or universal truths are deconstructed to reveal how they are in fact tools of particular interests, especially of power. It is not only ideas which are thereby deconstructed, but actual social structures too. It is the age of indifference to, if not disillusion with, institutions, especially in the political sphere. People no longer trust institutions, and those who operate in them, to serve their welfare, to protect their interests or to bring them fulfilment. Nor do they often feel the need of them. They prefer self-help, whether individually or in groups, ad hoc formations, whether campaigning on issues in their local community or on single issues such as climate change—or simply coming together informally for mutual support and interest. In the age of the internet, moreover, who needs to belong to a larger organisation for communication and sharing of ideas? The whole world lies readily at hand on one's laptop.

If this is the way we live now, it is clearly bad news for any inherited, overarching system of organisation or belief which claims the right and the competence to supply meaning and fulfilment to people's lives, and that includes the churches and related structures. People choose for themselves where to find their meaning and fulfilment, in matters spiritual or religious as much as anything else, and those are likely to be found in the local, the immediate and (probably) small-scale communities of shared commitments and enterprises, regardless of whether or not these are affiliated with, or owe loyalty to, larger-scale bodies. This is already affecting church life at every level. A local church, for example, may well feel called and competent to share in "world mission" by developing its own self-chosen partnership with a congregation or clinic in Kenya rather than contributing to the denominational mission agency as in the past. But, more dramatically, the mood is seen in the mushrooming of quite new, experimental forms of church life: emerging church, café church, third-place church, liquid church, fresh expressions, and so forth, to say nothing of the huge Pentecostal phenomenon. People are not just making their own choices from what is available, but are creating quite new possibilities. Obviously the question has then to be faced: if post-modernity is a solvent of inherited church structures, will it prove any less so for ecumenism? If the whole ecumenical project has been about bringing organised churches together, if not to actual union, and if those church structures are now seen to be less and less significant in the post- denominational age of fresh expressions and emerging church, then surely ecumenism as we have known it is irrelevant too. Who needs councils of churches, or even groupings of "churches together"? If the name of the game is now that of relating informally and spontaneously to one another, will not this happen naturally anyway according to our interests?

Matters are not quite so simple, however. For one thing, while it has become widely assumed that so-called mainline churches in the western world are in irreversible and terminal decline, this received wisdom is being challenged by some empirical studies which point to striking examples of renewal, both in numbers and spiritual vitality, in traditional congregations which have not opted either for popular evangelicalism or radical spontaneity.[23] Second, paradoxically there is both a loosening from and a reassertion of confessional identity going on. For one thing, a real factor in the drift of the churches into isolationist habits (or, as I termed them earlier, unecumenical activities) is that the denominations themselves are being caught up into the contemporary culture of anxiety about self-identity, hence the recent focus in just about every Christian tradition on "Who are we? What does it mean to be... Anglican... Baptist... Reformed...?" In such a climate, ecumenism is hardly likely to seem a priority, but theologically the ecumenical question becomes even more pertinent. For their part, too, far from negating ecumenism, the new expressions and developments in "church" do not remove but only call for a re-stating of the question: how may they be one? For if they do not take this question seriously, then their claim

---

23. See e.g., Diana Butler Bass, *Christianity for the Rest of Us: How the Neighborhood Church is Transforming the Faith* (HarperSanFrancisco 2006).

to be expressions of the gospel is in turn under question. Only if ecumenism is seen as primarily to do with structures rather than relationships, with organisation rather than communion, is it rendered obsolete.

Retrieving the Story and Renewing the Vision

I shall return in chapter 12 to examine more closely what has been happening in the churches, in Britain at any rate, in their search for "identity" and the dangers of this quest when identity is confused with autonomy as an end in itself. For the moment, suffice it to say that contemporary Christianity is in danger of relapsing into a collection of confessional and denominational or otherwise partisan enclaves, self-contained and autonomous in their supposed distinctive identities, touching each other only tangentially ("churches together" are not necessarily in any real relationship with each other), only fitfully engaging with the society around them and increasingly disconnected from the world church, the church of the *oikoumene*.[24] This is the situation addressed by Mary Tanner, Anglican theologian and a president of the WCC, who highlights what seems most lacking in all the churches today, "a passionate commitment to unity" as distinct from a commitment to something vague and undefined "or worse still, ourselves writ large."[25] Instead Tanner calls for an ecumenism grounded in a properly theological understanding of community and communion, which can lead us beyond maintenance of our narrow and self-sufficient denominational identities:

> It is about how we are all held in communion—when we agree and when we disagree—so that we refuse to say "I have no need of you." But, under the Spirit's guidance, stay together, learning from one another as we seek to discover the mind of Christ for the Church. It is about how local churches are held in communion with all the local churches, in the universal Church—that is the Church through the ages and around the world today.[26]

"The Church through the ages and around the world today." Mary Tanner's language prompts me to return to my own phraseology earlier in this chapter, to the effect that being "ecumenical" means being able to live in more than one place, and indeed at more than one time, at once. The main resistance to ecumenism today

---

24. See Kenneth Cragg, review of Kirsteen Kim's book *Joining in with the Spirit: Connecting World Church and Local Mission, Theology* 114, no. 2 (March/April 2011): 139.
25. Mary Tanner, "Celebrating Edinburgh 1910: Reflections on Visible Unity," *Theology* (Nov.-Dec. 2010): 403-410.
26. Ibid., 407.

comes from the mindset which assumes that one can and should only inhabit, mentally and spiritually, one's own tradition (and come to that, one particular version of the tradition) and one's own fragment of the *oikoumene* at once. This is not the same as fundamentalism, which goes one step further and insists that one's own tradition, and that alone, is to be imposed on the rest of the world. But by default this mindset can become an ingredient in fundamentalism or vicious sectarianism.[27] At any rate, to be true to their vocation the churches must have the capacity to enable their people to live in more than one place at once, that is, to envisage how the world looks from within another tradition or another context. This capacity to live in more than one place at once is fundamental to the ecumenical enterprise; indeed, it is fundamental to being Christian, to being "in Christ," for Christ is the one who stands in the place of the other even to the point of the cross. Without it, the fact of the *oikoumene* as the home of the church can never be appreciated, and correspondingly it is the incapacity to do this which vitiates the enterprise, for then ecumenism indeed becomes an "extra" to all we do, and the wider world itself is then just that—an "extra" to our own bit of world and bit of Christianity instead of that with which we vitally engage and which we allow to affect us. This is the primal heartbeat of being ecumenical, the pulse of living, daring ventures in relationships, in having eyes opened to others, to how others see the world, and to seeing how that world may be served together within the transforming possibilities of God's grace—and to venture towards a new community which is not just a rearrangement of what we have now *but is beyond anything we have at present*. It is the quest for community in Christ for the sake of the community of the world. *That* is what the ecumenical story at heart is about, and why the stories of Madeleine Barot, Herbert Jehle, David Russell, and others of that generation, are parables of it. All else, whether to be praised or castigated, is secondary. Gurs itself, a place of suffering, vulnerable, uprooted people set in a country fearful for its own future, is nothing less than a parable of the whole world, the *oikoumene*, today; and that little cell of people, incarnating through prayer and service a community transcending all divisions for the sake of the whole, is both parable and example of being ecumenical.

If the ecumenical movement is to be renewed, one of the essentials is that the current amnesia about so much of what has happened in the story must be overcome. The inner dimensions of the story need to be retrieved, recognised and affirmed—and taken forward. It is the modest intention of this book to contribute something to that retrieval. Subsequent chapters do not attempt to tell the story as a whole, but simply to uncover what was happening in some of the most creative episodes and

---

27. See below, Chapter 10, on "sectarianism" in Northern Ireland.

figures of the past and to register their pulse-beat. They are accounts of people and communities who faithfully held to their basic identity in Christ, yet who dared to test their faithfulness by reaching out to other worlds than their own, accepting new challenges both for the churches and for the wider social and international life of their time. They are stories which are inherently interesting in themselves, yet can also be resources for insights of permanent value—or perhaps still awaiting their full exploitation. They supply echoes of hope which still reverberate beyond us into our future. We shall then return to the present in the two concluding chapters.

On purpose, I do *not* begin with the 1910 Edinburgh World Missionary Conference. It has become a commonplace, indeed a virtual shibboleth in ecumenical circles (which I have myself repeated many times in lectures and sermons), to describe this event as "the birth of the modern ecumenical movement." The almost universal attribution of such significance to "Edinburgh 1910," however, betrays a misplaced regard to the formation of *structures, organisations, and ecclesiastical gatherings* as constitutive of the ecumenical movement. It is true that Edinburgh 1910 was the first in the line of large-scale, international multi-church gatherings which formed a permanent organ to further its work (in the case of Edinburgh, its Continuation Committee). But to ascribe to Edinburgh 1910 a generative influence on the movement as a whole is, as we shall see, quite another matter. Its full significance lay in other directions, and the hope it engendered rings with a specific timbre of its own. Nor was it even the first in the field in the modern ecumenical story, for before Edinburgh was conceived certain people, in Britain and Germany in particular, were awakening to the need to live in more than one place at once.

For the moment, however, we shall look further at the motif of "living there as well as here" as the dynamic of being ecumenical, first through the personal lens of my own upbringing and experience which I believe were—long before I realised—decisive in my "ecumenical formation"; second, as a feature which is fundamental in the biblical witness and therefore must be foundational for ecumenical life and thought.

Chapter 2
I Had a Dream

To Be Ecumenical

This chapter is deliberately and unashamedly personal in tone. It has to be, because it is about the commitment that lies at the heart of the ecumenical movement, and the only way I can begin to talk about commitment authentically is to reflect upon how my own came about. This, I hope, will help to make clear just what it is I feel attached to in the ecumenical story, what I think is essential and what peripheral

I noted in chapter 1 the belief, lamented by some and welcomed by others, that ecumenism as known for the past hundred years is over and done with. No less an authority than the celebrated American theologian and sociologist of religion Martin E. Marty has recently sounded the "death knell of committee ecumenism":

> For me, a central reason was illustrated in the press room at the Faith and Order (sub-WCC) meeting at Edinburgh, Scotland, in 1960, when I first got up close to ecumenical doings. The participants were defining Christian unity: "all in each place who confess Christ Jesus as Lord ... [should come to] a fully committed fellowship." The errant typist gave us in the press a draft-release that said we were "to come to a full committee fellowship." Ecumenism seemed to be the task of bureaus, task forces, commissions..[1]

Marty's works have long earned my respect and deep appreciation, and his remarks here are a neat, not to say entertaining, piece of point-scoring. But equally they do not resonate with my own experience and vision of "ecumenical doings." It is not that I have a fondness for committees and commissions. Far from it, and if I had ever thought that this was where ecumenism was centred I would never have gone near it. Such bodies are simply necessary, not as ends in themselves, but as means to

---

1. Martin E. Marty, "The Death Knell of 'Committee Ecumenism?'" *Sightings* (2 April 2012).

fulfilling certain aims. True, much energy can be spent worthlessly and precious time wasted on committees, in ecumenism as in every walk of life. But what truly important work, for human welfare or social justice for example, has ever been achieved *without* some such kind of organized cooperation and the hard graft it entails?

Ecumenical Dream

Soon after the start of the new millennium, the then general secretary of the World Council of Churches (WCC), Konrad Raiser, initiated a process of reflection on the need for a reconfiguration of the "ecumenical architecture." Given the rapidly changing Christian scene within the world as a whole and the questioning by the churches of so many different ecumenical organizations which they were being expected to support, this was widely felt to be well overdue. As always when structures are called into question, the deeper questions of their purpose and overall goal—in this case that of the ecumenical movement itself—have to be brought out and faced. Being at that time general secretary of the Conference of European Churches (CEC), I was among those invited to set down what I thought were the most important of those questions and to offer some reflections of my own. In writing my contribution to the symposium of views, I tried first to let my mind wander and collect the stray voices, stories, images, and memories that over the years had inspired and challenged my own ecumenical journeyings, ending up with a kind of dream:

> In the dream, these voices and images coalesce into something greater than the sum of the parts: a dynamic scene of churches and Christians being together, staying together and journeying together for the sake of the world as God wants it to be. It is a ballet of communities of love indwelling each other, drawing from each other, giving to each other, suffering with each other and rejoicing in each other in a way that spills over to embrace the entire world in its need and suffering and divisions. It is evangelical not so much because it deliberately "evangelises" but rather because the world actually longs to grab what is seen there, like starving people for bread. It is catholic not because it imposes an external claim to universal authority but because all people, as on the day of Pentecost, recognise their language spoken here, their deepest longings for peace, justice and reconciliation, and life in all its fullness, being met. It is orthodox, not because it defends the tradition but because the tradition speaks for itself in new, creative and empowering ways.
>
> What I think my muddled dream, both in its connections with reality and in its flights of fancy, is essentially about is a new quality of mutual relationships, focused on belonging to Jesus Christ and at the same time enabling a strange

new sense of belonging to the world. It is also about future-orientation, a hopeful expectancy born out of prayer in the Spirit which opens up to still more breathing-in from the Spirit.[2]

I am still prepared to let that stand as my vision of the hope which the ecumenical movement calls forth. For the moment, however, I wish to look at the question of how such a dream could have originated in my consciousness: what started me on a lifetime's journeying into ever-deeper ecumenical involvement or, to put it slightly differently, what made me an ecumenist. This is not just a piece of autobiography with purely private significance. For one thing, I believe there are many others of my generation with similar experiences to tell, and collectively our stories would in themselves amount to an important aspect of the modern ecumenical movement. More significantly, such stories are important for recalling what is at the heart and soul of being ecumenical. Indeed, the kind of story I have to tell is one about which I have even had to remind myself in order to remain focused on the essentials which are so apt to get lost amid all the varied tasks of the so-called professional ecumenist. The fact is that whenever one speaks about the ecumenical movement and argues its case, one is typically assumed to be promoting or at least defending the institutions and organisations—the ecumenical architecture, to recall Konrad Raiser's phrase. That assumption is to an extent justified, for there is an undoubted and continuing responsibility to give an account of those structures, to give clear descriptions of what they are doing and why, and at the very least to answer criticisms of them, both the fair and the unfair or misinformed. But in an age which is increasingly suspicious of institutions in almost every area of life, anyone who represents or works on their behalf is assumed, in whatever he or she says, to be speaking in a way that is primarily shaped by the self-interest of the institution as such. "Well, you would say that, wouldn't you, being the general secretary of CEC?" is the kind of thing I sometimes heard said when discussing greater European integration and the role of the churches. The assumption is, in effect, that one has a conviction thanks to the institution one serves. The possibility that one might have chosen to serve the institution *because of a prior conviction* about the importance of the ecumenical movement did not always register with people. Still less did it occur to them to wonder what that personal ecumenical conviction actually was and how it had arisen in one's life, any more than to ask what pioneering convictions and visions had led to the formation of the structures in the first place.

---

2. Keith Clements, "The Ecumenical Movement: My Vision," in *Reflections on Ecumenism in the 21st Century* (Geneva: WCC Publications, 2004), 24.

In fact, in the account of my "dream," immediately following the passage cited above I went into confession mode:

> I have to be honest: no ecumenical organization as such—not even CEC—appears in view in this scene. Maybe that is where self-indulgent romanticism is taking over. Or, maybe, the organization or institution is invisible because it is not itself an actor, but the self-effacing stage, the space for the drama. In which case the question is, what kind of service needs to be provided to assist or enable the scene to come on stage?[3]

That, I hope makes clear at the outset that in my perspective, the institutions are made for the ecumenical movement, not the ecumenical movement for the institutions. It is to the dynamic, the spirituality of the ecumenical movement that we must first look, that "new quality in mutual relationships" of which my dream speaks. How did I, for one, come to be caught and drawn into *this* search and commitment? I could cite, endlessly, the people, the teachers, the experiences, the reading, the engagements, which led me from one stage of ecumenical involvement to another. Or I could set out as systematically as I can the theological grounds for the ecumenical imperative as I see them. None of this would be irrelevant. But it would not touch what I now realise has always been a far more basal element in my life, a nerve which from my earliest days was sensitised to "living in more than one place at once" and which thus for me infused the ecumenical quest with a peculiarly personal impulse.

Living There as Well as Here

My early childhood was, in a strange way, rather privileged. I was brought up in an English Baptist manse. Strictly speaking that is not quite accurate. My father's first pastorate, starting in 1946, was in a village in Kent a few miles south of London. The second world war had only just ended, there was an acute housing shortage, and there was not actually a manse available. So for two years as a family of five, we had to live somewhat primitively in the church schoolroom, conditions made no easier in the bitter winter of 1947. Moving to the northern town of Darlington made for more acceptable living arrangements, but a minister's meagre stipend hardly alleviated the austerity of those post-war years. Of course, as a child one tends to accept the given, whatever it is, as normal; for a lot of my friends at school and at church, life was not much different in that uniformly grey world of draughty houses, second-hand clothes, and food rationing.

---

3. Ibid.

So where was the privilege? It lay in one great advantage over others: I was conscious of living not only in England but in China, land of my birth. My parents had been missionaries there for 14 years and I was born, their third son, in Gulin, a village in the mountains of Sichuan. I was not yet two years old when, for the sake of my oldest brother's health, they decided to leave and return to Britain—only temporarily, so they thought. Once my brother's health was restored they fully intended to return, but the Great Revolution put paid to that. In the English home, however, China was the subject of endless reminiscences and bedtime stories. Accounts of the colourful characters in Gulin and the surrounding hill country, adventures with wayside brigands, the incredible beauty of the mountains and their awesome thunderstorms, not to mention the perilous journey back to Britain across a world at war, were the stories and pictures that filled my mind. Lao-Ben-Yang, our housekeeper, who had overseen much of my infancy in Gulin and was no doubt responsible for my first recognisable speech being in Chinese, seemed no more distant than an aunt or older cousin. My mother still made Chinese food whenever she could get the right ingredients. Having been so young when we left China, did I have actual recollections? Were the pictures that filled my mind just the product of my parents' and brothers' story-telling or were there, however nebulous, some genuine memories of my own? In later life I was inclined to dismiss this latter possibility—until in 1994 I returned to Sichuan, and to Gulin itself, and became certain there were some things I was *not* seeing for the first time. Above all it was the enthusiasm with which my parents spoke of China which was infectious. I suspect that their wish to return was due as much to their simply being in love with the country and with life there as to any religiously correct desire to "preach the gospel." My father used to recall how once in Gulin some of their Chinese friends described a soldier they saw, making his way back home to neighbouring Yunnan province, as a foreigner. "Well," said my father in surprise, "what does that make me?" "Oh, *you* are not a foreigner," came the reply, "you are one of *us*." Until, nearing retirement age, my parents went to work in Sri Lanka for three years, one always had the feeling that for them life back in England was a kind of postscript to their China days. China was simply more interesting, more exciting, and more fulfilling a place in which to live. As for me, it was not just that I had been there, or even that I had been born there. It was a place that was *valued*, and moreover where I in turn had been valued. Still safely kept in a drawer were (and still are) the beautiful satin apron and baby shoes I had been given by our Chinese neighbours. My birth had caused quite a sensation in the village: a white, European woman giving birth was an unheard of phenomenon there. Queues of people came to view me. I was given the title "King of Gulin." From my earliest days therefore I too had a sense that there was another place to which I *belonged*.

So I grew up with a sense of "not only here and now, but also there and then." No doubt this consciousness of another place and another life besides the streets and playgrounds of Darlington—and far more real than the other places and lives one read about in comics or saw on film—had some drawbacks. It could encourage a sense of superiority and lead to some showing off at junior school age. But what an educational privilege it was, always to have known that the here and now was part of a larger picture and a bigger story, and was never to be assumed to be the be-all and end-all, but ever to be put in its place, both relativised and enriched by what is *other*. A good number of people I have known in later life also treading the ecumenical path have likewise had an early transnational, transcultural experience, and I do not think this is accidental. For if the root meaning of "ecumenical" is indeed the biblical Greek *oikoumene*, "the whole inhabited earth," then the generative root experience of ecumenism is the awareness of that wider world in all its exciting diversity.

There was another experience of feeling touched by "there and then" as well as "here and now." I was nearly nine years old when my mother and I went to the historic city of Durham for the day. At school we had been learning something of the history of the early middle ages, of St Cuthbert and the monks of Lindisfarne, Holy Island, a history of scholarship, adventure, and community in the face of hardship and danger, which even at that age I found utterly captivating. So to visit Durham and its great cathedral, shrine of Saints Cuthbert and Bede, was something of a pilgrimage. Having paused for a respectful glance at the great sanctuary knocker, we entered the cathedral. Nothing of what I had heard in class quite prepared me for this first impression as I stood among those great columns and arches. At that tender age I would have found it hard to put my feelings into words, but might have said something like: "It's huge, almost frightening, but at the same time somehow friendly." And although I sensed that here was a place breathing of the dim and distant past, I would also have said something like: "This is a place where something strange might also be about to happen." As well as the simplicity of a modest Baptist chapel on a municipal housing estate, there was now another kind of place and church, grand, mysterious, but accessible.

After five years of Darlington, we moved west to the Lancashire seaside town of Lytham St Anne's, famed for its golf courses and its genteel ambience that contrasted with the more raucous nearby resort of Blackpool. Life became more comfortable. Schooling was good. My father's congregation was of modestly devout middle-class believers who above all valued what Baptists call "fellowship," whether at the prayer meeting or on the bowling green. But among them I saw examples of quiet, costly kindliness and caring that still move me fifty years later. Relations between the various churches in the town were detached but polite. In our close neighbourhood, the

Baptist, Congregational, and Methodist Sunday Schools attended each other's anniversary services. Free Church ministers met in what they called a "fraternal." Anglicans, however, were regarded as a species somewhat apart, characterised by a formal "set service" in which (so I was told) one "bobbed up and down" to order; in some cases, one was warned, they were verging dangerously close to the utterly forbidden territory of Rome. Senior school was non-denominational. My closest rival for top academic prowess until our subject paths diverged at sixth-form level was a future Anglican bishop. Jewish boys trooped into morning assembly once prayers were over and announcements were to be made. On the whole, the same atmosphere prevailed in town, school, and church: religion was good in its proper place, but care must be taken lest it become an embarrassment.

Such a context could easily have become a backwater of pure here and now. It did not do so for several reasons. The first explanation may seem rather odd, and to have nothing to do with the major theme of this book, but in retrospect I have increasingly felt that what I am about to describe was very much in tune with, and reinforced, the appeal of "otherness." It was, moreover, an interest that connects with issues which in recent years have come to be seen as of vital theological concern: creation and ecology. From the age of twelve I was a passionate birdwatcher. To live by the estuary of the River Ribble, the famous winter feeding grounds for wading birds and wildfowl, was to be in an ornithological paradise. This became my place of encounter with otherness, for it was not just birds in general that excited me, but above all *migrating* birds, visitors from afar. Many of the waders that settled in their thousands to winter on the sandbanks and mudflats were from the high arctic tundra of Scandinavia and Siberia. The terns that hovered close inshore in spring had set off from southern ice floes 8000 miles away. Each autumn passage brought the chance of a real rarity showing up, blown off course from North America or Asia. Not that I was content to remain locally bound. I went in search of migrants at the bird ringing station on Skokholm Island off the coast of Wales, and even spent a month on board an ocean weather ship in the North Atlantic. But on returning home those experiences only served to emphasize even more that the familiar local scene was not *just* familiar and local. Being visited by otherness, reached from afar, it was invested with a kind of romance because now it was connected to what was so different and over the horizon.

Then, even the comfortable seaside Christianity, which was the only sort I really knew, could channel some surprises from afar. One day my father returned from the annual Baptist Assembly in London to tell the Sunday evening congregation how impressed and stirred he had been by Pastor Martin Niemöller, Hitler's special prisoner for eight years, who had addressed one of the meetings. That was the first time

I had heard anything about a Christian resistance to Nazism, or was given an inkling that Christianity might offer a political cutting edge in the modern world instead of a merely decorative addition to it. But still more striking, in the summer of 1961, was the public uproar unleashed from within Baptist circles about the atrocities being committed by Portuguese forces in Angola. The Baptist Missionary Society (BMS) had long been working in that country. First-hand accounts of recent brutalities had been brought home by missionaries and were at first kept under wraps by BMS officialdom, but the whistle was well and truly blown by a group of enterprising younger ministers. Suddenly to find the dear old BMS, hitherto regarded as one might a kindly if slightly old-fashioned maiden aunt, creating headline news in the daily press and prompting questions in Parliament was a revelation. Here was Christianity no longer a matter for mild apology or embarrassment in face of modernity. The effect on me was truly evangelistic—more so, for all its undoubted appeal, than even Billy Graham's Greater Manchester Crusade, which also took place that summer. Again, what one thought one knew close at hand took on hugely more significance when seen to be linked to dramas "over there."

It is not easy to categorize this sense of "not only here and now but also there and then" or the appeal of otherness. I am drawn towards Charles Taylor's concept of the "social imaginary," by which he means "the way that we collectively imagine, even pretheoretically, our social life in the contemporary Western world."[4] While in Taylor's scheme this is a feature of collective rather than individual mentality, as a kind of consciousness it has to reside in individual members of a society and I therefore see no reason why the term should not be used by anyone to describe a basic mindset of his or her own in relation to the world in general. Taylor amplifies what he has in mind:

> What I'm trying to get at with this term is something much broader and deeper than the intellectual schemes people may entertain when they think about social reality in a disengaged mode. I am thinking rather of the ways in which they imagine their social existence, how they fit together with others, how things go on between them and their fellows, the expectations which are normally met, and the deeper normative notions and images which underlie these expectations.[5]

I believe that my family background, upbringing, and youthful interests nurtured in me a certain "social imaginary": a sense that the bit of the world I inhabited was

---

4. Charles Taylor, *A Secular Age* (Cambridge: Bellknap, 2007), 146.
5. Ibid., 171.

not the only world; that it was part of a larger whole and only made sense as part of the larger picture; that the world over there was as significant as the world over here; and that "over there" had important things to say to "over here." This was very different from the social imaginary of the person who has never, literally or mentally, ventured beyond his or her own immediate world, which is regarded as the only, or least the "normal," world. It was also quite different from the imaginary of the person who has little or no sense of place at all, who lives in a kind of bubble of detached assumptions about the world as a whole—a kind of mentality encouraged today by the superficial surfing of the internet for global information, a cheap substitute for actual encounter and engagement with life "over there."

Cambridge: What Church Means

In 1962 I began three years' study at Cambridge University, first in natural sciences and then in theology. Christian faith truly came alive for me at Cambridge and I find it impossible to separate that flowering of faith from the discovery of a wider world than I had hitherto known. It was a new experience of community, first of all in the Baptist students' society named after Robert Hall, celebrated preacher, public lecturer, and social campaigner in Cambridge and Bristol in the early 19th century. Baptist its members may have been, but they were extraordinarily diverse in expression of belief as well as in temperament, and for the first time I came across the whole theological spectrum from radically liberal to narrowly conservative evangelical. This proved invigorating and liberating, especially as one discovered that friendship (and even romance, at least for a while) need not be tied to theological agreement, although tensions did arise during my second year when a "conservative" and a "liberal" (myself, unsuccessfully) both ran for the presidency of the society. It was in this context that I was first introduced to Dietrich Bonhoeffer. After the end of term in June 1963, a dozen of us spent a week at a kind of work camp billeted at a church in Huntingdon, painting and decorating schoolrooms during the day and reading Bonhoeffer's *Cost of Discipleship* together in the evenings. I myself was equally gripped by *Life Together*, Bonhoeffer's exposition of the theology and practice of community. Community as absolutely of the essence of Christianity—not the community we often fancifully wish for as an ideal to suit ourselves, rather the real community with others in all their awkwardness, bearing and forbearing, giving and forgiving—became axiomatic for me. I would later learn that Bonhoeffer had in his earliest works described the church as "Christ existing as community,"[6] but I think that I was believing and experiencing that already. Christ was the one who brought

---

6. See below, chapter 10.

me out of my isolated self into relationship with himself and with others, and the most vital and profound experience of Christ was to be found in the community he was creating, a community of people accepted and accepting. I cannot stress this enough: for me it was not a matter of "finding Christ" and then finding others who had also "found him"; rather it was being found by him in a community where I was accepted and enabled to accept others.

Christian relationships in Cambridge were not confined to the denominational society. There was also the life within one's own college, in my case King's. Before coming to Cambridge, I had never attended an Anglican service of any sort. At King's, world-famous for the architecture and music of its chapel, Anglicanism could hardly be avoided, and I became a devotee particularly of choral evensong. It was not only the beauty of the music and its stunning setting in stone and glass which held me; the actual content of the service proved an eye-opener too. I had an inherited Baptist belief (or more accurately, an ill-founded prejudice) that Anglican worship was not only formal but priest-dominated in contrast to that of the Free Churches, which was much more participatory and above all gave far more weight to the Bible and its exposition. I quickly learnt, however, that at Anglican evensong which included psalms, canticles, and readings from Old and New Testaments, not to mention the biblical phraseology of much of the versicles and responses, one was being treated to far more of the Bible than in a typical nonconformist service of the time. Above all it was the psalms, prayer-book of the Bible, which were opened up to me; that remains my chief spiritual debt to King's. Then, too, I discovered that the clerical leading of evensong was far more self-effacing than the virtuoso performance expected of most Free Church ministers in the pulpit from beginning to end of a service. Moreover, while there was indeed a formality about the Book of Common Prayer, it provided a structure which allowed a great deal of space for private and imaginative devotion of one's own; whereas nonconformist worship not only was all too conformist to its conventional patterns but, when subject to the singular personality of the minister, could leave little room for engaging in prayer on one's own terms. None of this led me to cease being Baptist or to become Anglican, but it immeasurably widened and deepened my understanding of worship, as did my much later encounter with Eastern Orthodoxy.

In fact, the whole Cambridge scene meant an immersion in a wider world than the immediate religious here and now of one's upbringing. There was of course the highly evangelical Cambridge Inter-Collegiate Christian Union (CICCU) a number of whose meetings I attended and in which I had friends but never actually joined: I eventually found off-putting the air of smiling self-confidence worn by so many members and which I increasingly suspected of being a façade in face of questions, doubts, and the dangerous ideas of "liberal" theology. This was, after all, the time when the tide of radical theology burst upon the English scene, especially in Cambridge with the public lectures *Objections to Christian Belief* given by four prominent university theologians in the Lent Term of 1963, quickly followed by Bishop John Robinson's sensational paperback *Honest to God*. I found more exciting and educative this atmosphere of new questions and experimental reformulations of belief, and it was a major factor in leading me to switch from studying natural sciences to theology in my final year. The Student Christian Movement (SCM), consciously more open-minded and ecumenical than CICCU, was by then becoming less conspicuous within the university, but its ethos was very much alive within the overlapping circles of friends and associates in King's and other colleges, the Baptist students' society, and those who regularly attended the Sunday evening services at the University Church of Great St Mary's, where a whole galaxy of provocative and prophetic guest preachers from near and far was on offer: George Macleod, Leslie Weatherhead, Mervyn Stockwood, James Stewart, Ambrose Reeves, John Robinson, Frank Lake, Joost de Blank, Martin Niemöller, Wim Visser 't Hooft, and Trevor Huddleston, to name but a few. What all this was disclosing was a new image of what *church* meant, a community both embodying and witnessing to true community in the world, a world riven by injustice, cold war division, and racism. It was a church being called to challenge and overcome barriers in the world and this it could hardly do unless church was likewise becoming united. I found it impossible to separate discipleship from being ecumenical; indeed, the meaning of following Christ was only becoming clear and vital to me in terms of being drawn into this movement from the immediate here and now to the wider there and then.

Nor was this ecumenism all airy-fairy student posturing. Just before my third and final year, having embarked on theology, I was invited to be the token Baptist in a party comprising Cambridge ordinands from Westcott House (Anglican), Wesley House (Methodist), and Cheshunt College (Congregational) for a week's work in the midlands industrial town of Rugby. On behalf of the Rugby Council of Churches, we were to conduct a door-stepping survey on the needs of West Indian immigrants (as they were then called) and their neighbours. It was hard work and by the end of the week we were not entirely sure how worthwhile it had all been. But the previous month, at the European Baptist Congress in Amsterdam, I had heard Martin Luther King preach on the approaching midnight hour of crisis. The church, to be church, could not but be involved in the struggles for justice and racial equality, and it could not do so unless it was itself removing its own internal barriers, whether racial or confessional. The week in Rugby also faced us with what was, to most of us, a new factor on the English church scene, when we spent a Sunday evening at worship with the New Testament Church of God. The vibrancy of black Pentecostalism seemed to come from another world—but it was very much here, and here to stay.

Still Moving

All this was part of what would now be called my ecumenical formation. As yet I had no relation, formal or otherwise, to any ecumenical organization. It was simply a commitment that one felt to the coming great church in formation, a church truly of the *oikoumene*. Time would bring a lot more experience of ecumenical life, from the informal and formal local level to the international. After ministerial training at Regent's Park College, Oxford, and ordination, I would serve as chairman of local councils of churches; be involved in ecumenical lay education; serve on boards and working groups of the British Council of Churches (BCC); become a member of the WCC Standing Commission on Faith and Order; and serve on ecumenical deputations and delegations to communist Eastern Europe, apartheid South Africa, war-torn Iraq, and other parts of the Middle East. In 1990 I would become international affairs secretary in the new Council of Churches for Britain and Ireland, successor to the British Council of Churches (BCC) and in 1997 I was appointed general secretary of the Conference of European Churches. In short, I became a professional ecumenist. But, as I hope my dream of what the ecumenical movement is all about will testify, I have throughout held to a vision of ecumenism as a movement of community-building, of relations of mutuality and participation in a shared life of service and witness, whose goal is indeed communion, *koinonia*. It is not primarily institutional. Institutions are made for the movement, not the movement for institutions.

Yes, much is heard at the present time about the end of "classic" or institutional ecumenism, as represented by the typical activities of the WCC and national and regional ecumenical bodies, theological dialogues, and attempts at organic unity. The old ecumenism is dead, one hears. We may concede and indeed welcome change, especially in view of the trends indicated in the previous chapter. There is danger, however, that in simply dismissing the architecture that was built over the past hundred years, the inner spirit and intention of which the architecture was the expression and instrumentality will be lost by default. Already there is a widespread ignorance and regrettable amnesia about much of the ecumenical story, even among (or perhaps especially among) church leaders.

Of course the ecumenical movement is open to criticism. Not only so, but part of the salvation of the ecumenical movement has always lain in its capacity for self-criticism. We cannot presume exemption from judgment: "The time has come for judgment to begin with the household (*oikos*) of God" (1 Pet. 4:17). In the course of this book we shall several times meet with the figure of J.H. Oldham, secretary of the Edinburgh 1910 World Missionary Conference and pioneer in so much of the ecumenical story that followed. But even Edinburgh 1910, not long after, had no sterner critic than Oldham himself, who felt that the conference had lacked focus and depth in many respects.[7] Thereafter he was always suspicious of the value of such large gatherings and advocated smaller, more specialist groups working at length on particular topics. But he never denied, even in later life, that Edinburgh 1910 was indeed the seed from which so much grew.[8] Equally, in old age, although he had been one of the chief architects of the WCC, he could be unsparing in his criticism of what he believed to be its centralising, bureaucratic tendencies. The late Bishop Lesslie Newbigin told how on one visit to the aged Oldham, he was greeted with: "The WCC—only the grace of God can save it!" [9] Oldham illustrates well what has always enabled the ecumenical movement to be a *movement* and not just an institution or even a single programme: the capacity for constant, honest self-appraisal; alertness to the new issues, the emerging agenda that has to be taken on board; the readiness to change tactics and methods for the new tasks that await it. That has been the case with the movement's greatest leaders. W.A. Visser 't Hooft, first general secretary of the WCC, in retirement in his mid-seventies, dared to write a short book called *Has the Ecumenical Movement a Future?*[10] Having looked at all the question marks that can be placed against ecumenism, he answers in the affirmative—not because the ecumenical movement has been a success story (for it has many failures) or because it can be guaranteed to be so in days to come (like Elijah, we are no better than our forebears[11]). It is rather, says Visser 't Hooft, because of the ever-recurring possibility of prophetic witness: "Why should this be so? Because prophecy knows of a dimension of human life which the world does not know of itself: the dimension of God's actions. Prophecy bears witness to that which God has done, to what God does and to what He will do."[12] Prophecy, we might say, keeps us open to that ultimate otherness of God and God's call.

I am glad to be in such company, to have had, and still to have, the dream.

---

7. Keith Clements, *Faith on the Frontier: A Life of J. H. Oldham* (Edinburgh: T. & T. Clark and Geneva: WCC Publications, 1999), 259.

8. Ibid., 462.

9. Ibid.

10. W.A. Visser 't Hooft, *Has the Ecumenical Movement a Future?* (Belfast: Christian Journals, 1974).

11. See 1 Kings 19:4.

12. Visser 't Hooft, 92.

Chapter 3
Where Do We Live?

The Biblical Paradigm

Living in more than one place at once, living with an awareness conditioned by the existence, worth, and claim of another and wider world, might indeed have been a vital and influential part of one's upbringing. It might, too, have supplied a decisive motivation for becoming "an ecumenical". But this by itself does not validate the ecumenical commitment as such, or at any rate this version of it: it simply demonstrates a way into that commitment and gives some psychological explanation for having it. We therefore have to ask, what are the resonances of "living in more than one place at once" with the centralities of Christian faith and especially with the core of the biblical tradition? If being ecumenical means living in more than one place at one time, then it can and should substantiate itself by exposing and laying claim to a thrust of the scriptural witness.

In this chapter I wish to argue that living in more than one place at once is a dynamic at the heart of the Abrahamic tradition of faith and most certainly a stream which flows into the gospels and the New Testament as a whole. This dynamic, however, is apt to be overlooked precisely because it is so central and fundamental, rather in the same way that we are largely unaware of our own heartbeat or breathing unless a deliberate effort is made to check them—or some sudden excitement or emergency makes them all too obvious. It is apt to be overlooked in its significance alongside all the other features of a faith wrought out of the historical experience of the people of God. We shall therefore examine, however cursorily, this element which runs through the Bible, looking mainly to the book of Genesis, the psalms, the gospels, and the apostle Paul.

Genesis: Creation, Garden, Patriarchs, and Matriarchs

A popular view of the Bible is expressed in a hymn written for children over a century ago:

> God has given us a book full of stories,
> Which was made for his people of old,
> it begins with the tale of a garden
> and ends with the city of gold.[1]

The Bible, however, does *not* begin (Gen. 1:1) with a garden (Gen. 2:8), but with the creation of the heavens and the earth and all that is in them: the immensity of the skies and the heavenly lights, land and sea and the infinite variety of living creatures rooted, fruiting, creeping, swimming, flying, walking, and in the case of humankind, mirroring the divine capacity freely to speak and to give and receive love. God indeed creates the garden of Eden when, according to the second creation account, God forms "man from the dust of the ground" (Gen. 2:7) but even then Eden is not the whole of creation. Almost immediately the narrative turns into a geography lesson about rivers, distant lands, and sources of precious minerals: "A river flows out of Eden to water the garden, and from there it divides and becomes four branches." (Gen. 2:10ff). Eden is not all there is. It has a special significance, being where both the tree of knowledge of good and evil and the tree of life are planted, but it is also in a *context*, the whole of all that God has made and which is "very good" (Gen. 1:31). The fact that this detailed description of the context, blest with a richness of its own alongside the special splendour of Eden, is given so early in the narrative indicates that the consciousness of a world outside Eden belongs to the state of obedient innocence. It is not a consequence of the "fall" and expulsion from the garden (Gen 3:24). It belongs to the original creatureliness of humankind as formed by God. Even in that state of untrammelled bliss within the garden, Adam and Eve cannot be unaware of a world beyond, whither flows the river which arises in the garden.

Immediate knowledge of that world comes with the expulsion of the man from the garden "to till the ground from which he was taken" (Gen. 3:23ff). In the succeeding generations from Adam the world becomes one of human multiplication and cultural diversification, and withal corrupt, sinful, and violent (Gen. 4:1- 6:12) An end is made on all this in the flood, but also a new beginning through Noah and his family, and the animals preserved with him in the ark. But through Noah's three

---

1. "God Has Given Us a Book Full of Stories" by Maria Penstone (1859-1910). See for example *Baptist Praise and Worship* (Oxford: Oxford University Press, 1991), no. 200.

sons, it is not only a resumption of the human story as it was before. A new structure of human society unfolds through Shem, Ham, and Japheth. Numerous "families" of peoples, "nations" emerge and are named in their astonishing diversity: "These are the families of Noah's sons, according to their genealogies, in their nations; and from these the nations spread abroad on the earth after the flood." (Gen. 10:32) The fact of distinct peopledoms is underlined in a different but telling way in the story of the Tower of Babel (Gen. 11:1-9). Human pride and ambition are checked by God "confusing the language of all the earth" and the scattering abroad of humankind over the face of all the earth (Gen. 11:9). The peoples become not only distinct, but *strangers* to each other. Yet still they inhabit the one face of all the earth. They are not consigned to different earths. Encountering one another in their strangeness is intended at the very least to induce a certain humility. There is no escape for the families of humankind from encountering each other.

At the end of the long genealogy hailing from Shem (Gen. 11:10ff) occurs the name of Terah (Gen. 11:24ff), who among his other sons and daughters fathered three sons, Abram, Nahor, and Haran (Gen. 11:26). Haran has a son, Lot. Abram and Nahor marry. Abram's wife, Sarai, "was barren; she had no child" (Gen. 11:30). The next few verses need now to be quoted in full:

> Terah took his son Abram and his grandson Lot son of Haran and his daughter-in-law Sarai, his son Abram's wife, and they went out together from Ur of the Chaldeans to go into the land of Canaan; but when they came to Haran, they settled there. The days of Terah were two hundred five years, and Terah died in Haran.
>
> Now the Lord said to Abram, "Go from your country and your kindred and your father's house to the land that I will show you. I will make of you a great nation, and I will bless you, and make your name great, so that you will be a blessing. I will bless those who bless you, and the one who curses you I will curse, and in you all the families of the world shall be blessed." So Abram went, as the Lord had told him, and Lot went with him. (Gen. 11:31—12:4)

The beginning of "salvation history," as the story of Abraham is usually recognised to be, is a migration. It does not involve first of all a nation, for Abram—as he is then known—is only one man with his wife. They will *become* a nation, but at present they do not even have any children of their own. With Terah, Abram and Sarai move from Ur, the city where they "belong," *into* the world of nations, first to Haran, where Terah, Abram's father, eventually dies. Then comes the next and decisive pulling up of roots, with God's command to leave country, kindred, and parental house for "a land that I will show you," with the promise of becoming a nation of blessing. That blessing, however, is to be not just for Abram's descendants themselves, but for all the families of the earth. The full significance of that blessing—and thus Abram's own identity—can surely be known to Abram only as he himself becomes aware of "all the families of the earth." How could that be if he remained in the safe familiarity of Ur, or even of Haran? In order to be educated into what a blessing for all the families and nations of the earth will mean, Abram must live in a way that is unreservedly open to the presence of those nations. He lives as a tented sojourner in the land of Canaan that is promised by God to his descendants but is not empty of other peoples: "At that time the Canaanites and the Perizzites lived in the land" (Gen. 13:7) Abram experiences that most ancient and oft-repeated cause of human migration, famine, which drives him with Sarai to Egypt "to reside there as an alien" (Gen. 12:10) where occurs an uncomfortably close encounter with Pharaoh's court on account of Sarah's attractiveness (a story virtually repeated later in relation to King Abimelech of Gerar (Gen. 20: 1-18). Abram comes to know about communal strife, as the competition grows between the herders of the burgeoning flocks belonging to him and his nephew Lot "so that the land could not support both of them living together" (Gen 13:6), a dispute resolved when by mutual agreement Lot chooses the fertile Jordan plain and its cities, while Abram continues his tented existence in Canaan. That proves to be no secluded pastoral idyll, however. Abram is drawn into a bloody conflict in that same Jordan plain and around the Dead Sea (Gen. 14:1-13) in order to rescue Lot after his capture in the battle of the "four kings against five" and the defeat of Sodom and Gomorrah by king Chedorlaomer of Elam and his allies. Victorious Abram receives the blessing of the mysterious King Melchizedek of Salem and gives him a tithe of all he has (Gen. 14:20)—an indication that this episode is not an irrelevant diversion from the main path of the Abram/Abraham saga, but central to it. This, then, is the context of Abram's sojourn in the land of promise, where he repeatedly receives the promise of becoming a nation—among other times, in the covenantal encounter with God in which he and Sarai receive new names, Abraham and Sarah (Gen. 17:1 ff). The promise begins to be confirmed in the birth to Sarah of a son, Isaac. But before he himself becomes a nation, Abraham the sojourner has to live out an existence in the midst of the already existing nations with no protection or security apart from the promise. That provides a unique perspective, and learning experience, on the nations.

Abraham lives mostly among the hills of Canaan, but in mind and spirit not only there. He pleads for Sodom in the Jordan plain to be spared God's judgment on account of his nephew Lot and family. The intercessory conversation with God concluded, we are told with a terse poignancy: "And the Lord went his way ... and

Abraham *returned to his place*" (Gen. 18:33). But after the fire and brimstone have fallen, and Lot has escaped,

> Abraham went early in the morning to the place where he had stood before the Lord; and he looked down toward Sodom and Gomorrah and toward all the land of the Plain and saw the smoke of the land going up like the smoke of a furnace. (Gen. 19:27ff)

Moreover, whilst committed to living in Canaan, Abraham has cause to remember Haran, which he still calls "my country" and where his kindred live (Gen. 24:4). He makes his servant take an oath to find there a bride for his son Isaac, who is on no account to marry a Canaanite woman, "only you must not take my son back there [to Haran]" (Gen. 24:8). The claims of no single place or people can be allowed to determine the family's future, which is staked solely on the promise and command of God—which require and allow a living in more than one place at once. So Isaac acquires Rebekah as a wife, and in turn Jacob (after a peculiarly entangled sojourn in Haran) marries Rachel. There is therefore no assimilation, whether into Canaanite society or back into the ancestral kindred life of Haran. But Haran is remembered, and continuity with it is maintained, while the tents remain pitched in Canaan.

There is no real home as yet except the divine promise, and thus the tents may be pitched here... or there. From Abraham onwards, the story is that of a life which is distinct but never isolated or self-contained; it is ever in interaction with the wide world. So the patriarchal saga reaches its climax in the story of the disappeared Joseph in Egypt, the extraordinary career in which Joseph saves from famine not only Egypt but in due course his father and brothers and their families, "for God sent me before you to preserve life" (Gen. 45:5). And it is in Egypt that Jacob's family, Israel, grows into a nation.

The Psalms

If it is in the psalms that we find the centre of Hebraic and Christian spirituality, then anything which they convey about belonging to and living in more than one place at once should be of special significance:

> I was glad when they said to me, "Let us go the house of the Lord."
> Our feet are standing within your gates, O Jerusalem.
> Jerusalem—built as a city that is bound firmly together.
> To it the tribes go up, the tribes of the Lord, as was decreed for Israel, to give thanks to the name of the Lord. (Ps. 122:1-4)

Jerusalem is indeed at the centre of Hebrew faith. It is Jerusalem, so the Deuter-onomists taught, that God chose "as a dwelling for his name" (Deut. 12:11). But a place can only be a centre if there is a periphery and circumference. The psalm-ist exclaims "How lovely is your dwelling place, O Lord of hosts" (Ps. 84:1) for "a day in your courts is better than a thousand elsewhere" (Ps. 84:10a) and he would rather be a doorkeeper there than live in the tents of wickedness. But relatively very few, even of the priestly tribe of Levi, could ever actually live in Jerusalem. For the many it was quite literally more like one day (or less) in a thousand. Jerusalem, for most, is at best a place *to journey to* (Ps. 84:5-7). Pilgrimage to the holy city was to became one of the most enduring, and endearing, motifs of the life of faith for both Jews and Christians (as with Muslims also). The typical Christian metaphorical use of the motif, as an image of earthly life being a waiting or striving for a fulfilment in heaven, can, however, result in a blunting of the special poignancy given by the Jewish hope of a *literal* journeying to another place on earth—or a longing to be in that place, a longing recalled most poignantly in the psalm of exile: "By the rivers of Babylon—there we sat down and there we wept, when we remembered Zion..." (Ps. 137:1, see also Ps. 137:4-6).

"Next year in Jerusalem!", the almost jocular traditional Jewish greeting at the end of the Yom Kippur service and the Passover Seder, at least preserves that literal-ism of living by faith and hope in more than one place at once. Likewise the very physical custom that evidently developed during the exile and dispersion, of facing towards Jerusalem when at prayer (see Dan. 6:10) and constructing the orientation of synagogues, everywhere in the world, accordingly.[2] Not that an unrequited pin-ing for Jerusalem marked all those deported to Babylon after the defeat of Jerusalem in 586 BCE. Indeed, such as the prophet Jeremiah encouraged the exiles to make the most of their time in Babylon until the day of return should dawn: "Build houses and live in them; plant gardens and eat what they produce. Take wives and have sons and daughters; take wives for your sons, and give your daughters in marriage, that they may bear sons and daughters; multiply there and do not decrease. But seek the welfare of the city where I have sent you into exile, and pray to the Lord on its behalf, for in its welfare you will find your welfare." (Jer. 29:5-7) Jeremiah himself, evidently, ended his days among refugees in Egypt (Jer. 43-44). It is also clear that the return to Jerusalem from Babylonian exile following the decree of Cyrus (538 BCE) was only a partial affair.[3] The life in exile was not for every Jew one of des-

---

2. We need not here enter the debate on whether the synagogue was a product of the exile, or was an already existing feature of Jewish life that became markedly more prominent during the exile and the dispersion as a whole.

3. For a recent study on the whole subject of the Jewish "exile," see John J. Ahn, *Exile and Forced*

perate hardship and misery from which escape at all costs was sought. Jeremiah's injunction to the exiles had not only been wise, but for many had evidently proved very fruitful.[4] Many chose to remain in Babylon, and found they could still be faithful Jews away from Jerusalem; presumably for such it was enough to know that the temple was being rebuilt and sacrificial worship being resumed. The payment of the half shekel temple tax would be enough to secure and signify their participation in rebuilt Zion, together with the occasional pilgrimage. Increasingly, Jewish life was one of dispersion (*diaspora*). In addition to the Babylonian exile, there been the seizure of the northern kingdom and deportation of its inhabitants by Assyria in the 8th century BCE, followed by settlement of the land of Samaria by peoples brought in from the north and east (2 Kings 17:24). But conquest and enforced exile were not the only motors of scattering. Trading and commercial interests led to more peaceful dispersions. In the 1st century CE, the historian Josephus (c. 37-100) quotes Strabo of Cappadocia in the previous century: "This people has already made its way into every city, and it is not easy to find any place in the habitable world [*oikoumene*] which has not received this nation and in which it has not made its power felt."[5] There is also the remarkable cataloguing by Philo of Alexandria (c. 20 BCE–50 CE) of the spread of the "colonies" sent by Judea into "every region of the habitable world [*oikoumene*]."[6]

"Now there were devout Jews from every nation under heaven living in Jerusalem" (Acts 2:5): the list of countries and languages represented on that day of Pentecost in Jerusalem (Acts 9-11) merely illustrates again the huge extent of the Jewish diaspora. Numbers too are telling. One estimate for the Jewish population in the 1st century CE gives 2,500,000 living in Palestine but a total of at least 3,400,000 outside (Egypt 1,000,000; Cyrenaica 100,000; Italy 100,000; Asia Minor 1,000,000; and Mesopotamia 100,000).[7]

The psalms effectively were the hymn book and prayer book of the second temple. To picture their use solely within the setting of that temple, however, and to see their meaning as determined by the temple courts and those physically present

---

Migration: A Sociological, Literary and Theological Approach on the Displacement and Resettlement of the Southern Kingdom of Judah (Berlin: De Gruyter, 2010).

4. See the "kindly" treatment in Babylon of King Jehoiachin of Judah by King Evilmerodach recorded in 2 Kings 25:27-30 and Jer. 52:31. Also note the tradition reflected in Daniel of some Jews being promoted to high office during the Exile.

5. Josephus, *Jewish Antiquities* XIV.118, in Books XII-XIV, transl. R. Marus (London: W. Heinemann, 1943), 509.

6. "On the Embassy to Gaius," *The Works of Philo*, trans. C.D. Yongue, ed. D.M. Scholer (Peabody: Hendricksen, 1993), 783ff.

7. "Dispersion," *Interpreter's Dictionary of the Bible* (New York: Abingdon, 1962).

there, would be to miss out on a great deal of their significance. To imagine them, rather, as being recited or sung with a consciousness of the diaspora, for the whole of which—not just Jerusalem and Palestine—the temple was the centre, is to see a quite new dimension to them. Thus:

> Ascribe to the Lord, O families of the peoples, ascribe to the Lord glory and strength.
> Ascribe to the Lord the glory due his name, bring an offering and come into his courts.
> Worship the Lord in holy splendor; tremble before him, all the earth.
> Say among the nations, "The Lord is king!
> The world is firmly established, it shall never be moved.
> He will judge the peoples with equity." (Ps. 96:7-10)

> Make a joyful noise to the Lord, all the earth.
> Worship the Lord with gladness; come into his presence with singing.
> (Ps. 100:1)

It was by no means a flight of fancy that called on "all the earth" to praise the Lord from that small location in Jerusalem. That was being said by, as well as on behalf of, Jews throughout the known world. The name of the Lord was indeed being invoked "from the rising of the sun to its setting" (Ps. 50:1), for "God is the king of all the earth" (Ps. 47:7). In sum:

> By awesome deeds you answer us with deliverance, O God of our salvation; you are the hope of all the ends of the earth, and of the farthest seas...
> Those who live at earth's farthest bounds are awed by your signs; you make the gateways of the morning and the evening shout for joy. (Ps. 65:5, 8)

Through the fact of the diaspora, the world beyond Jerusalem and Palestine was not incidental to the temple worship as expressed in the Psalms, but formed its ever-present and pressing context. Those who worshiped in the temple—itself ordained to be a "house of prayer for all peoples" (Is. 56:7)—whether as regular attenders or as pilgrims, could not help being aware of worship also being offered in synagogues far and near. In mind they dwelt also in the diaspora, and therefore in that whole world being called through the witness of Israel to glorify God. No less, those who lived in the diaspora also lived inwardly in Jerusalem. As they prayed facing the beloved city they were already glad "when they said unto me, 'let us go to the house of the Lord!'"

and in spirit their feet were "already standing within your gates, O Jerusalem" as they prayed for its peace. (Ps. 122:6ff)

The psalms in yet another way situate the worshippers in a place other than where they are immediately, physically present. For all the sense of possession and fulfilment given by living in the land of Canaan, the Hebrews were never allowed to forget the tradition that they had once been wanderers in the desert, and this consciousness was brought into the heart of the temple worship as expressed in the psalms no less than in the history recounted in the Pentateuch. Psalm 95 opens with the call to worship the Lord, "the rock of our salvation" in joy and thanksgiving, for the heights and depths, sea and dry land, are in his hand. The ground for the call to worship stresses the immediate, personal relationship between the community and their God: "For he is our God, and we are the people of his pasture, and the sheep of his hand" (Ps. 95:7). If that encouraged in the worshippers a sense of privilege and security, what immediately follows must have come as a rude awakening:

O that today you would listen to his voice!

Do not harden your hearts, as at Meribah, as on the day at Massah in the wilderness, when your ancestors tested me, and put me to the proof, though they had seen my work.

For forty years I loathed that generation, and said, "They are a people whose hearts go astray, and they do not regard my ways."

Therefore in my anger I swore, "They shall not enter my rest." (Ps. 95:7b-11)

The worshippers are, in effect, pushed in imagination back into the desert in order to be tested in comparison with the faithlessness of their ancestors. The wilderness experience is not over and done with, a mere memory whose pastness is—if it is recalled at all—a matter for unreflective gratitude. The desert is always there, and very near even for those who have never journeyed to the Negev or across the Jordan to see it for themselves. Only by continually in heart and mind re-entering the desert, re-living the Exodus experience, do the Hebrews retain and renew their identity. That is the necessary corrective to the complacent assumptions that grow with too settled an existence in the land of promise. There is another world than the here and now of "fine, large cities that you did not build, houses filled with all sorts of goods that you did not fill, hewn cisterns that you did not hew, vineyards and olive groves that you did not plant" (Deut. 6:10-11). There is a harsher world, where springs have to be sought in the desert, and manna awaited from heaven. There is another world, moreover, than that of cultic sacrifices, as the prophets repeatedly pointed out:

Did you bring to me sacrifices and offerings the forty years in the wilderness, O
house of Israel? (Amos 5:25)

Add your burnt offerings to your sacrifices, and eat the flesh. For in the day that
I brought your ancestors out of the land of Egypt, I did not speak to them or
command them concerning burnt offerings and sacrifices. But this command I
gave them, "Obey my voice, and I will be your God, and you shall be my people;
and walk only in the way that I command you, so that it may be well with you."
(Jer. 7:21-23)

The psalms at a number of points resonate with those warnings from the prophets. It is the broken spirit and contrite heart which God most desires (Ps. 51:17). It is
no surprise, therefore, to find continual references in the psalms to the wilderness as
the place in which the empowering care and promise of God—"who led his people
through the wilderness" (Ps. 136:16)—to his people were revealed. There, Israel's
faithfulness to him repeatedly was tested (and found wanting), and the core of their
identity as God's people was forged. It is Psalm 78 which narrates this contest of faith
and faithlessness at greatest length and in finest detail: "Mortals ate of the bread of
angels" (Ps. 78:25), "He led them in safety, so that they were not afraid" (Ps. 78:53),
yet "they tested the Most High God, and rebelled against him" (Ps. 78:56).[8] In effect,
the temple worshippers, in order to understand what their worship is all about, have
to be prepared mentally to leave that place, re-enter the desert, and re-live the wilderness experience. What is more, for all the emphasis in the psalms that Zion is
the place where the Lord has caused his name to dwell, the holy mount where stand
his courts to be entered with praise and thanksgiving, there is no losing sight of the
belief that the Lord *came* to Zion *from elsewhere,* his original holy mountain in the
Sinai desert:

O God, when you went out before your people, when you marched through the
wilderness, the earth quaked, the heavens poured down rain, at the presence of
God, the God of Sinai... (Ps. 68:7ff)

With mighty chariotry, twice ten thousand, thousands upon thousands, the Lord
came from Sinai into the holy place.
You ascended the high mount, leading captives in your train... (Ps. 68:18)

---

8. See also, e.g., Ps. 68:7-10; 74:12ff, 81:5b-7; 105:37-41: 106.

The Lord himself, in short, is a migrant God, able to live in more than one place.[9] That capacity is a key manifestation of his transcendence, his holy freedom. If the glory of the Lord chose to descend upon the temple, it could also choose to depart from it (Ezek. 10:18ff). The Hebraic faith therefore has to be prepared to be as migratory as the divine self-disclosure. (Num. 9:15-23). How ironic therefore is the lamentation over Judah's plight following the defeat and destruction of Jerusalem: "she lives now among the nations, and finds no resting place" (Lam. 1:3). To live among the nations, where her God is to be found, is indeed her calling.

The Gospels

History is reaching its climax and the reign of God is breaking in: so Jesus announces the good news (Mark 1:14ff et al.). This means a radical break with any fixed attachment to any one particular place. No one context is specially privileged to be a recipient of God's coming reign. In view of the astounding effects of his preaching and healing on the Sabbath, the population of Capernaum may assume to have rights on Jesus continuing his ministry there. But next morning before daybreak he has left to pray in a deserted place. The disciples hunt for him:

> When they found him they said to him, "Everyone is searching for you." He answered, "Let us go on to the neighbouring towns, so that I may proclaim the message there also, for that is what I came out to do." And he went throughout Galilee, proclaiming the message in their synagogues and casting out demons. (Mark 1:37-39)

"Home" acquires an uncertain meaning for the Son of Man who, unlike the foxes and birds—but like lamented and exiled Judah "among the nations"—has nowhere to lay his head (Matt. 8:20). Indeed, Jesus' very notion of family is by conventional standards distinctly unstable, as when word is passed to Jesus through the surrounding crowd that his mother and brothers are looking for him:

> And he replied, "Who are my mother and my brothers?" And looking at those who sat around him, he said, "Here are my mother and my brothers! Whoever does the will of God is my brother and sister and mother." (Mark 3:33-35)

Luke's account of Jesus' return to the place that was literally home for him, Nazareth, sees him presenting a no less radical claim as to where he would regard himself as

---

9. Cf. Elijah's visit to Horeb, "the mountain of the Lord," in 1 Kings 19:8-18.

being at home. Foreseeing the Nazarenes' cynical demands that he repeat for them the wonders he has done in Capernaum, he says:

> The truth is, there were many widows in Israel in the time of Elijah, when the heaven was shut up three years and six months, and there was a severe famine over all the land; yet Elijah was sent to none of them except to a widow at Zarephath in Sidon. There were also many lepers in Israel in the time of the prophet Elijah, and none of them were cleansed except Naaman the Syrian. (Luke 4:25-27)

The result is an enraged physical rejection of Jesus, who has dared to suggest that God's reign of justice, mercy and, healing will find for itself *more* of a home beyond the assumed borders of Israel than within his hometown. There will be a universality about God's reign which, while it will not extinguish local identities and loyalties, will certainly relativise them. For "people will come from east and west, from north and south, and will eat in the kingdom of God" (Luke 13:29). But Jesus does not locate the kingdom in any one particular place. This is closely paralleled in the Johannine gospel in the conversation between the Samaritan woman and Jesus:

> "Sir, I see that you are a prophet. Our ancestors worshiped on this mountain, but you say that the place where people must worship is in Jerusalem." Jesus said to her, "Woman, believe me, the hour is coming, and is now here, when the true worshipers will worship the Father neither on this mountain nor in Jerusalem." (John 4:19-21)

If God's reign and the faith which receives it can occur anywhere in the world, by the same token this means that foreigners, non-Jews away from home, can also be at home in Israel. The Roman centurion, a representative of the oppressive occupying force, who "loves our people" even to the point of funding the building of a synagogue, impresses Jesus as demonstrating a personal faith unmatched in Israel itself (Luke 7:1-10). The Syro-Phoenician woman, desperate for her daughter's healing, is goaded by Jesus' apparent dismissal of her right as a gentile to have "the children's food" and points out to him that even "the dogs under the table" eat the children's crumbs. Her impudent faith, in contrast to the complacent religiosity of so many of "the children," is rewarded: "For saying this you may go—the demon has left your daughter" (Mark 7:24-30). For this reason, Jesus' sending of the apostles on a ministry of proclaiming and demonstrating the reign of God not to the Samaritans or gentiles but only to "the lost sheep of the house of Israel" (Matt. 10:5ff) is not as exclusivist as it may sound. It is Israel that is most in need of hearing the kingdom. In its lostness it thinks it is at home when in fact it is homeless. By contrast, it is the outsiders, the foreigners, who are capable of showing to Israel what its faith should be, and Jesus is content simply to make such outsiders visible, and therewith the coming of God's reign visible too. Hence Jesus' provocative attack on the very heart of Israel's current religious practice in his cleansing of the temple, justified by him in his appeal to the words from Isaiah:

> Is it not written, "My house shall be called a house of prayer for all the nations?" But you have made it a den of robbers. (Mark 11:17, cf. Is. 56:7)

By denying its vocation to provide a "house"—home (*oikos*)—for the nations, Israel has itself become lost, homeless. It is the Samaritan, not the priest and the Levite, professional religious experts, who on the Jericho road knows instinctively what the Torah means by loving one's neighbour (Luke 10:25-37) and in so doing, as Charles Taylor puts it, "cuts across the boundaries of the permitted 'we's' in his world."[10] It is a Samaritan, alone of a group of people healed of leprosy, who shows true gratitude to God (Luke 17:11-19). These are the people who are truly at home in Israel, who really do *live* there as well as in their native territory, as distinct from simply "travelling through" as tourists or as natives residing within walls of indifference. The true and final separation between righteous and unrighteous will be between those have, and who have not, helped the Son of Man in the stranger and have welcomed him—been *home* to him—with the sick, the hungry and thirsty, the naked and imprisoned (Matt. 25:31-46). Jesus does not preach an abstract internationalism. He simply uncovers and highlights the presence of the strangers within the borders of Israel who are signs of the reign of God—both those who are literally foreigners and those who are outsiders for other reasons such as sin or uncleanness or demon-possession. The gospels thus radically subvert all conventional assumptions about *where* "home" is and *who* is at home under the reign of God.

---

10. Charles Taylor, *A Secular Age* (Cambridge Mass and London: Bellknap Press of Harvard University Press, 2007), 738. Taylor is drawing on Ivan Illich's comment on the Good Samaritan as one who subverts the assumption that moral "oughts" derive from pre-determined norms and social conventions, and thus radically recasts the notion of "we": "The Samaritan has the possibility of establishing a proportion, a relatedness to the other man which is entirely free and conditioned solely by his hope that the beaten-up Jew will respond to it by accepting this relationship. No doubt ... the Samaritan parable was scandalous for the Pharisees ... because the Master told them who your neighbour is is not determined by your birth, by your condition, by the language which you speak, but by you. You can recognize the other man who is out of bounds, culturally, who is foreign linguistically ... and create the supreme form of relatedness which is not given by creation but created by you." See Ivan Illich, *The Rivers North of the Future: The Testament of Ivan Illich; As Told to David Cayley*, ed. David Cayley (Toronto: Anansi, 2005), 206ff.

Paul

Early Christianity, having arisen as a movement within Judaism, both in Palestine and in the dispersion, and now moving beyond the geographical bounds of Palestine and the cultural limits of Judaism, readily saw itself as likewise a "dispersion": the people of God in exile—not from a homeland of the past but from the promised realm of the future commonwealth of God (see James 1:1, 1 Pet. 1:1). It is the apostle Paul who states this future orientation most strongly against the claims of this present world: "But our citizenship is from heaven, and it is from there that we are expecting a Savior, the Lord Jesus Christ." (Phil. 3:20).

This orientation towards the future consummation of God's reign might be expected to produce a sense of detachment from any local loyalty, or from any commitment to living in even just one place, let alone two or more. Strikingly, however, it is in Paul above all that we see most clearly set out, both theologically and—especially—*practically*, the vocation to be at one with people in a situation very different from one's own.

> We want you to know, brothers and sisters, about the grace of God that has been granted to the churches of Macedonia; for during a severe ordeal of affliction, their abundant joy and their extreme poverty have overflowed in a wealth of generosity on their part. (2 Cor. 8:1-2)

Paul is organising a collection from among the churches of his gentile mission, to aid "the saints" in the mother church of Jerusalem, evidently beset by famine. He is unashamedly goading the community at Corinth by the example of the Macedonian Christians over a hundred miles to the north—just as he has been likewise "boasting" to the Macedonians about the zeal of the Corinthians (2 Cor. 9:1-5) for the same project. He admits to "testing the genuineness of your love against the earnestness of others" (2 Cor. 8:8), but the primary nerve he wishes to touch is that of membership in Jesus Christ, Christ who as saviour is the main motivator and example: "For you know the generous act of our Lord Jesus Christ, that though he was rich, yet for your sakes he became poor, so that by his poverty you might become rich" (2 Cor. 8:9). Paul is arguing that Christ's great and unique saving act took the form of an *exchange* of his richness as Son of God with the poverty of the human state; as he says earlier in this letter: "For our sake [God] made him to be sin who knew no sin, so that in him we might become the righteousness of God" (2 Cor. 5:21). This exchange lies at the heart of the *reconciliation* of humanity with himself wrought by God in Christ (2 Cor. 5:16-20), a reconciliation to be embodied, communicated and thus furthered by the "ambassadors for Christ" in the world. In fact, Paul's Greek verb *katalasso*, translated as "reconcile," is closely related to *halasso,* "exchange." It is a relational action summed up by Irenaeus, the great theologian of the second century: "He who was the Son of God became the Son of man, that man ... might become the son of God."[11] Or, as Irenaeus's saying is sometimes rendered, "He became what we are that we might become what he is."

But Paul is now doing more than using "exchange" as a metaphor. He is enfleshing it in a very concrete action—financial aid—by the Christian communities. What is more, Corinth and Macedonia are not merely to be aware of each other as doing the same or similar charitable thing. They are in a living mutual relationship, each in some way dependent on the other for fulfilling their calling to embody the generosity of Jesus Christ. Both, equally, are caught up into relation with the saints in Jerusalem even farther away—some 800 miles to the east—whose needs they are meeting. As gentile Christians they are fulfilling a debt they owe to the mother church—and the reciprocity will continue in unexpected, boundless ways of mutual enrichment and thanksgiving to God: "Through the testing of this ministry you glorify God by your obedience to the confession of the gospel of Christ and by the generosity of your sharing with them and with all others, while they long for you and pray for you because of the surpassing grace of God that he has given you" (2 Cor. 9:13-14).

In short, to be a Christian in Corinth means to live in imagination and spirit also in Macedonia and in Jerusalem, while in turn to be a Christian in Jerusalem will mean to live also in... and so on. The relational possibilities are endless. That is the consequence of being, on the wider as well as the local level, "the body of Christ and individually members of it" (1 Cor. 12:27). Shortly after writing to the Corinthians, Paul was able to write to yet another church, just coming into being, nearly as far west of Corinth as Jerusalem was to the east, and destined to become the most famous of all churches in the empire. He sums up the reciprocity of love manifest in the giving and reception of the aid to Jerusalem and builds on it his hopes for the future, for he is casting his missionary gaze even further westward over the *oikoumene,* to Spain:

> At present, however, I am going to Jerusalem in a ministry to the saints; for Macedonia and Achaia have been pleased to share their resources with the poor among the saints at Jerusalem. They were pleased to do this, and indeed they owe it to them; for if the Gentiles have come to share in their spiritual blessings, they ought also to be of service to them in material things. So, when I have completed this, and have delivered to them what has been collected, I will set out by way of you

11. Irenaeus, *Against Heresies* XIX.1, *Writings of the Ante-Nicene Fathers,* vol. I, ed. A. Cleveland Coxe (Grand Rapids: Eerdmans, 1885), 448.

to Spain; and I know that when I come to you, I will come in the fullness of the blessing of Christ. (Rom. 15:25-29)

Paul goes on confidently to ask for prayers from Rome to accompany him in whatever he might face in Judea. Rome, too, is being asked to live in Jerusalem. And when eventually Paul did arrive in Rome under rather different circumstances from those he originally envisaged, Macedonia was invited, and indeed already found, to be living there with Paul, if indeed it was from that imprisonment that the apostle wrote his Letter to the Philippians. It is that letter which above all others is saturated with the Greek prefix *sun-*, "with," and the motifs of sharing and participation, with overflowing gratitude for a life in grace and love. By and through this life the Philippians are where Paul is, although hundreds of miles apart, and he with them: "It is right for me to think this way about you all, because you hold me in your heart, for all of you share in God's grace with me, both in my imprisonment and in the defence and confirmation of the gospel." (Phil. 1:7) Karl Barth places over the verses 1:3-11 the title "Copartners in grace!" and states of Paul's phrase "sharing in the gospel" (Phil. 1:): "he will surely also have been thinking not only of gifts of money and suchlike, but of the active collaboration of the Philippians in the *proclaiming* of the Gospel, of their earnestness in letting it *be* Gospel in their own midst, of their *prayers* for its progress through the world and *to that extent* their company on his own high, hard apostolic way."[12] Further, according to the account in the Acts of the Apostles, even under house arrest in Rome Paul was welcoming "all who came to him" and still proclaiming[13] the reign of God even in the heart of the Roman *imperium* which held him captive (Acts 28:30). Barred from walking abroad, he is still inhabiting the *oikoumene*. Under the reign of God which embraces the whole of the inhabited world, it ultimately matters little where one is physically, for there is always somewhere else to live in spirit (see1 Pet. 5:9). The community of the reconciled thus already manifests now, in the present world of division, enmity and fragmentation, the new creation (2 Cor. 5:17) in Christ.

In the End

If it is not true that the Bible begins with the tale of a garden, neither is it the case that it ends just with the city of gold. Just as the opening tale is of the creation of heavens and earth in their entirety, so too the final two chapters tell of "a new heaven, and a new earth" (Rev. 21:1). The holy city, the new Jerusalem, "prepared as a bride

---

12. Karl Barth, *The Epistle to the Philippians* (London: SCM, 1962), 16.
13. See likewise Phil. 1:12-18.

adorned for her husband," is indeed the centrepiece of this new creation (Rev. 21:2). But it is not the whole new creation as such. It is set within the new creation as its context. Shimmering and translucent with the endless light of God Almighty and the Lamb, the holy city is not self-enclosed. In each of its jewel-encrusted walls are gates "which will never be shut by day—and there will be no night there" (Rev. 21:25). It is a city where people will come and go. Its light is not for itself, but is shed abroad for the nations to walk by; and the kings of the earth, no longer holding in their own wealth and glory for themselves and their own nations, will gladly bring into it the glory and honour of the nations (Rev. 21:24). It is neither a prison for those inside nor a fortress barred against those outside, for in the new creation there is not really an inside and outside any more as far as belonging to it is concerned. If one lives outside, one nevertheless belongs inside and is welcome to come. Those who dwell inside live for those outside, ensuring the free flow of the river of the water of life to the earth beyond the walls, and the harvesting of the leaves of the tree of life "for the healing of the nations" (22:2). It is the ultimate vision of living in and for more than one place at once. It is the social imaginary of the kingdom of God.

People Look East!

From very early times the Christian church sought to image in a very physical way its vocation of living in expectation of the end and the life of the world to come. It could not help noting that in its parent Judaism (as we have noted above) synagogues were constructed so that the praying community, anywhere on earth, faced towards Jerusalem. What would be the corresponding orientation for Christians? The mother church in Jerusalem, even by Paul's time, was losing out in significance to centres such as Antioch in Syria. According to the Book of Revelation (chapters 2-3), by the late first century the churches in seven major cities of Asia Minor—Ephesus, Smyrna, Pergamum, Thyatira, Sardis, Philadelphia, and Laodicea—were receiving prophetic messages direct from the risen Christ without any reference to an earthly Jerusalem as their conduit. Meanwhile Rome, sanctified particularly by the tradition that both Peter and Paul had been martyred there, was clearly in the ascendant as first among equals in the Christian dispersion. But the ultimate orientation of Christian faith and hope towards the "new Jerusalem" could not be confounded with a gaze or posture directed to any one earthly city, however precious to the affections, since "here we have no lasting city, but we are looking for the city that is to come" (Heb. 13:14). What is remarkable is that the oldest known Syrian church is found facing not towards Jerusalem but *the East*, and it is this feature which has become so continually and widely followed down the ages, certainly in traditions that claim to be catholic in practice. "The East, as the place of the rising sun for early Christians, was the only fitting symbol of the last appearance of Christ in His parousia, as that Sun of justice sung already in the canticle of Zechariah... Already Tertullian, in his treatise on prayer, supposes that it is an apostolic tradition to pray either publicly or privately always facing East."[14]

Ex oriente lux.[15] It is hard to exaggerate the importance, potential or actual, for the Christian consciousness that in looking to the future it looks away from wherever it happens to be here and now, to the East. It is the most emphatic statement that there is another world than where we happen to be just now. In one sense of course it means looking beyond this world and this secular age. The posture however is not vertically upwards, a gaze into the heavens beyond the stars; note the angelic warning to the disciples witnessing Jesus' ascension (Acts 1:11). It is a horizontal orientation towards the point where the sun just lifts above the horizon. As such, in imagination it is a low-level flight over the contours of the earth, keeping in view all that upon which the rising sun sheds its light, the whole *oikoumene* which the risen and coming Christ illuminates in judgment and grace. Elsewhere inescapably impinges on us, as it did upon the patriarchs and psalmists, upon those who encountered Jesus, and upon the great apostle to the gentiles. Living in more than one place at once does indeed resonate with the central biblical witness and its embodiment in the church as the body of Christ on earth.

---

14. Louis Bouyer, *Liturgy and Architecture* (University of Notre Dame Press, 1967), 28ff.
15. "The light comes from the East."

Part Two

The Dynamic Illustrated

Chapter 4

First to See the Future

The Anglo-German Churches' Peace Exchanges 1908–1909

If the dynamic of the modern ecumenical movement is learning to live in more than one place at once, then it can be said to have begun on 27 May 1908, when the German steamship *Kronprinzessin Cäcilie* docked in the southern English port of Southampton. The passenger list was unusual, comprising 131 representatives of the German churches—Protestant, Roman Catholic, and Free Church. The ship was in fact several hours late, since on leaving Bremen the previous day it had run aground on a sandbank. Those with an eye for irony will no doubt see in this misfortune a parable of ecumenical voyaging as a whole. But the setback proved only temporary, and as they walked down the gangway to set foot on English soil, many of them for the first time, these pastors, priests and professors, court chaplains and prominent laypeople, were conscious of a warm and hearty welcome from their English hosts. They could have little idea, however, that they were starting to write the first significant chapter in the modern ecumenical story. Their week's stay in England, followed for some of them by an extension to Scotland, was matched the next year by a reciprocal visit from the British churches to Germany. From these exchange visits, designed to foster friendlier relations between the British and German peoples as a whole, there was formed a joint British-German organisation aimed at peace-building through the churches, which in turn was pivotal for the formation in 1914 of the World Alliance for Promoting International Friendship through the Churches.[1]

---

1. The primary source material for this chapter comprises material in the WCC archives, Geneva, Boxes 212.020 and 212.021 (World Alliance for Promoting International Friendship through the Churches) and the two souvenir volumes of the visits, *Der Friede und die Kirche. Peace and the Churches. Souvenir Volume of the visit to England of representatives of the German Christian Churches May 26th to June 3rd, 1908. Including the visit to Scotland June 3rd to 7th, 1908* (London: Cassell, 1908); and *Friendly Relations between Great Britain and Germany. Souvenir Volume of the visit to Germany by representatives of the British Christian Churches June 7th–20th 1909*, ed. Friedrich Siegmund-Schultze on behalf of the Kirchliches Komitee zur Freundschaftlicher Beziehungen zwischen Grossbritannien und Deutschland (Berlin: H.S. Hermann).

The Background

The exchanges took place at just the time when the diplomatic tensions and military rivalries between Germany and Britain were growing alarmingly. These tensions originated in the imperialistic and colonial rivalries of the two powers (especially in Africa) and in the anxiety of each country not to be outweighed by the other in the balance of power in Europe. In British eyes, Germany, especially as embodied in the person of its *Kaiser* (Emperor) Wilhelm II, was arrogantly strutting beyond its status as an imperial power. For many Germans, any such assertiveness was more than justified as a reaction to the centuries-old British assumption of the right to rule the waves, and they were demanding parity as of right. By 1906 the naval competition had itself become a serious diplomatic issue between the two countries. In 1908 Britain launched the *Dreadnought*, a revolutionary type of battleship that gave its name to a whole new generation of ships, unprecedented in speed and fire-power, which were now launched on both sides. The arms race seemed unstoppable, and there was growing mutual public hostility, especially in sections of the press, on both sides of the North Sea.

At the turn of the century there had in fact been British-German negotiations on Far East interests, but these proved abortive. Even by then any formal alliance would have proved difficult in the face of public opinion on both sides. As one historian comments:

> Indeed, an important factor in Anglo-German relations before 1914 was the lukewarmness or antagonism of British popular feelings towards Germany and the positive and increasing hostility of the great mass of German opinion towards Britain. This mutual antipathy, which dates mainly from the Boer [South African 1899-1902] War, was all the more widespread since the development of a cheap popular press in both countries in the 'nineties, for neither country properly understood the workings of the press in the other and neither government was fully able to restrain the hostile outpourings of its own newspapers.

At the same time, in both countries there were groups concerned for better relations, and some exchange visits took place including newspaper editors, mayors and other civic leaders.

Nor had a concern for peace been absent from the churches. As early as 1889 Brook Foss Westcott (1825-1901), noted New Testament scholar, professor of divinity at Cambridge and from 1890 bishop of Durham, convened an interconfessional conference of church representatives to consider the excessive armaments in Europe. One outcome was the formation of a "Provisional Committee of the Christian Union for Promoting International Concord," a title foreshadowing that of the World Alliance 25 years later, but of which little was heard subsequently. Speeches and resolutions deploring warmongering and armaments were to be heard regularly at national and international church assemblies throughout the early 1900s, certainly in the English-speaking world. Even the German Peace Society included some Protestant clergy.[2] Moreover, some church voices were heard at the second Hague Peace Conference of 1907, which focused especially on the settlement of disputes by arbitration and at which a number of "memorials" from churches around the world were presented. That conference—no more successful than its predecessor in halting the arms race—might have seen no more than yet another stage in churchly pronouncements. That it did not wholly do so, but instead prompted the beginnings of a modest yet more concrete witness by the churches, was largely due to two Christian laypeople, one British and one German, who were present there.

The English Quaker and the German Aristocrat

Joseph Allen Baker[3] was born in Canada in 1852 and moved to London in 1876 in order to advance his family's manufacturing business in Britain and on the continent. This he did very successfully but his interests were not limited to trade. He was a Quaker, a convinced pacifist, and fired by a strong social conscience, In his London neighbourhood he became deeply involved in local issues and for twelve years from 1895 served on the London County Council as a member for the Progressive Party and proved a doughty campaigner on housing, education and temperance. But his Quaker pacifism, together with a widening overseas experience resulting from his travels and business contacts, led him increasingly to address the international scene and the rising threats to peace. Baker was not the kind of doctrinaire pacifist who dismisses any deviance from the non-violent line as moral dereliction, or who refuses to work with any who do not share exactly the same commitment. Rather, he believed in seeking the widest and most effective co-operation possible among those who sincerely wanted peaceful relationships between nations, who were repelled by the jingoistic outpourings from much of the popular press and who wished to create a better understanding between peoples. In due course he had a national platform for his views, for in 1905 he was elected Liberal member of parliament for East Finsbury in London. Already known as a "pro-Boer" on account of his anti-imperialist stance during the South African war of 1899-1902, he was firmly on the left wing of the party. At the same time, he was coming to prominence in interchurch circles. In

---

2. See R.P. Chickering, "The Peace Movement and the Religious Community in Germany, 1900-1914," *Church History: Studies in Christianity and Culture*, Booklet 3 (Red Bank: American Society of Church History, 1969), 300-311.

3. E.B. Baker and P. J. Noel Baker, *J. Allen Baker, MP: A Memoir* (London: Swarthmore, 1927).

1907 he became president of the Metropolitan Free Church Federation (MFCF). He rhetorically asked in his presidential speech: "Have we, as representing Christian Churches, as professed followers of the Prince of Peace, done our full duty on the great subject of the brotherhood of nations? Have we spoken out boldly in favour of peace, and denounced war and all that makes it possible as utterly opposed to the spirit and teaching of Jesus Christ?"[4] Baker clearly answered his own question in the negative, and there were many in the MFCF who agreed with him. He was a natural choice to present the memorial of the MFCF at the Hague Conference in 1907, but at the same time he was increasingly anxious that the churches should put living flesh on their skeletal statements.

It is evident that Baker went to the Hague already with the idea of fostering friendlier contacts between Britain and Germany through exchange visits of the churches, and that he had backing from the MFCF for this. He also wanted to explore the possibility of some kind of international body being set up to enable a united witness of the churches for peace. The Hague conference sparked that wish further, for when he presented the British churches' memorial the president of the conference, Count A.I. Nelidoff, remarked: "Too much should not be expected from this Conference; it has taken nineteen hundred years of Christianity to give us the first International Peace Conference, and this is only the second that has been held."[5] It was apparently this remark that further stirred Baker's vision, and it is a fair surmise that his thoughts on that occasion are expressed by what he was to write a year later:

> The first Conference of the Churches in Christendom in the interests of international peace has yet to be convened. That such a conference is not only desirable, but even imperative must be admitted by all who, in sincerity, pray "Our Father ... Thy Kingdom come, Thy Will be done on earth," and who earnestly desire to fulfil the Angel-song at Bethlehem—"Glory to God in the Highest, and on earth peace, goodwill toward men."
>
> Surely the time is now fully come when the professed followers of the Prince of Peace, the religious leaders of every land, should unite to form themselves into a Universal League of Peace, and to make impossible for the future the crime and wickedness of war.[6]

How and where even to begin to implement such a grand vision, was of course the question. There was not even a ready-made point of contact with the Germans,

4. Ibid., 169.
5. *Der Friede und die Kirche* (see note 1), 9.
6. Ibid., 9ff.

whose churches were not represented in any visible way at the Hague Conference. The answer, as appropriate as it was modest, lay in a simple conversation. During the Hague Conference, Baker encountered an aristocratic German and Protestant layperson, Baron Eduard de Neufville from Frankfurt-on-Main, who himself was acutely embarrassed by the absence and silence of the German churches at the Hague. De Neufville had been closely involved in the exchange visits of British and German editors, and his name was already known to Baker as that of an enthusiastic and tireless worker in the peace cause. At this their first actual meeting, their differences in background notwithstanding they found an instant rapport. They quickly agreed that the British and German churches must be mobilised no less than the editors, civic leaders and working men's groups had been and that similar exchanges should be organised. In this, both men were thinking pragmatically. They were less concerned with a theological understanding of the church as peacemaker than with the potential which the churches—especially their leaders—offered for challenging and changing public opinion in each country so as to "remove suspicions." But there could be no doubting the faith that underlay their motivation, summed up in de Neufville's simple credo: "Whenever the hand of brotherly love is seeking to grasp your own, then do not be slow, but take it with thanks. For therein is God's love manifested."[7] Baker proposed that the exchanges begin with a German visit to Britain. De Neufville told him that the German church leaders would be sympathetic to an invitation, and undertook to make definite enquires and inform Baker of the results. It now remained for Baker, on returning to London, to engender the invitation, to seek adequate support and funding, and to see to the organisation of all that such a visit would entail.

Preparation

Allen Baker's ideas on what the Germans' visit to Britain entailed, if it was to have any significance, were both precise and far-reaching. In his own words:

> The leaders of every section of the Churches in both countries, Protestant and Catholic alike, must take part;
>
> The Governments of both countries must give the movement their recognition, and if possible their active co-operation;
>
> The King of England and the German Emperor must, if possible, be induced to give their practical support;
>
> The German visitors to England must represent all parts of Germany, must be

---

7. Ibid., 11.

the personal guests of English friends during their stay in London, and must, if it could be arranged, preach from London pulpits on the Sunday of their stay. They must also be our guests from the moment they left Germany till they reached home again.[8]

For the breadth of its ecumenical vision and the basic practicality of its design this conception was remarkable. Equally remarkable was the way in which every part of it came to be implemented, thanks largely to Baker's industry and imagination. The challenges were huge. There could, at the outset, be no guarantee that the whole range of churches, in either country, would be persuaded to join together on the enterprise. In both Britain and Germany relationships between the Roman Catholic and other churches were, if they existed at all, cool, suspicious or reserved to the point of frigid hostility. In England the main nonconformist or Free Churches (Baptist, Congregational and Methodist) were still in rivalry with the established Church of England for public influence, the Free Churches smarting over what they saw as continuing Anglican privileges, and since 1902 there had been a particularly bitter dispute over public funding for church schools. In his efforts at bringing the often fractious churches together, it perhaps helped that, being a Quaker, Baker was identified with the Free Church constituency, but did not wear the aggressively anti-Anglican mantle more typical of the larger nonconformist communities. He was also politically shrewd, and as his very first move made a personal approach to the prime minister Sir Henry Campbell-Bannerman, who gave his warm approval. Next, with wisdom equally worthy of the serpent, he secured the necessary funding, largely from his fellow-Quaker Joseph Rowntree of York, the chocolate magnate, but also from several other philanthropically-minded industrialists. Only then, with the innocence of the dove, did he approach the church leaders. The archbishop of Canterbury, Randall Davidson, was, typically, initially cautious and reserved: Lambeth Palace habitually glanced over its shoulder at Westminster across the river. But Baker was able to assure the archbishop of the government's endorsement. And it was equally typical of Davidson that, once having been convinced, he gave his whole-hearted and unswerving support to the project throughout. Baker's next most decisive call was on the Roman Catholic leader, the cardinal archbishop of Westminster, Francis Bourne, whom Baker found to be "frank and friendly from the start." It also has to be said that for both archbishops what counted heavily was the assurance that "the sole object of the visit was to promote closer friendship with Germany, and that it had no sectarian or ecclesiastical character," and on that basis they were quite

---

8. Baker and Baker, *J. Allen Baker*, 175.

prepared to join with the Free Churches. The latter hardly needed persuading: as we have seen, much of the initial impetus had in fact come from the Free Churches in London. Their chief spokesperson, both in the capital and nationally, was the veteran Baptist John Clifford, "the uncrowned king of militant nonconformity" and long-standing anti-war preacher. Two younger ministers who had grown up in Clifford's congregation were to be especially important in relations with Germany, for both had studied in Berlin: Newton H. Marshall and J.H. Rushbrooke, of whom (especially the latter) more will be heard. This broad and diverse support now had to be welded into an organising committee. It comprised some 60 personalities including the archbishops of Canterbury and Westminster and the (Anglican) bishops of London and Southwark, the main Free Church leaders, prominent Anglican clergy, and a variety of lay notables and benefactors from politics, industry and commerce. Allen Baker himself was president, and William Thomas (a Baptist minister) general secretary. Most of the actual work of course had to be done by Baker himself, his officers and an executive committee. Very time-consuming and meticulous it had to be, planning in detail a crowded programme of visits, public meetings, excursions, worship services, banquets and hospitality, all to be fitted into little more than a week in May 1908.

Meanwhile, in Germany, Eduard de Neufville was also busy, preparing the ground for a visit by Allen Baker in late 1908. Baker arrived in Berlin with the official invitation, from the British committee, and with de Neufville (and British diplomatic help) secured the support of the leading Protestant and Catholic personalities.

The German Visit

Baker thus returned to London fully assured that the visit would take place. It was fixed for 26 May–3 June 1908, and the next few months were for Baker and his executive "a strenuous and sometimes anxious time."[9] But it was time well spent, and on 25 May 1908, Allen Baker and H. Russell Wakefield (later bishop of Birmingham) were in Bremen to greet the 131 German guests assembling there prior to embarking on the *Kronprinzessin Cäcilie*. By far the largest contingent, as would be expected, was from the Evangelical (Protestant) *Landeskirchen*. Among the clergy were Court Chaplain Ernst von Dryander, the *Probst* of Berlin General Superintendent Faber, several other general superintendents and presidents of church consistories including Julius Kaftan of Kiel, together with notables such as the missiologist Julius Richter. There does not seem to have been an officially designated leader, but Dryander certainly was regarded as chief spokesperson once the party arrived in England.

---

9. Ibid., 179.

Academics were well represented; among the 13 professors being Paul Althaus of Göttingen, Martin Rade of Marburg, and Hans von Soden of Berlin. There was a handful of laypersons, including Eduard de Neufville. There were no women, either in the Protestant contingent or in the party as a whole. Among the youngest pastors (and probably the youngest) was 23-year-old Friedrich Siegmund-Schultze from Marburg, who had previously visited England to study social work methods there, and who was to play a leading role in nurturing the fruits of the exchange visits— and much else in German church life. The Roman Catholics numbered 15, the most senior being the *Probst* of St Hedwig's Cathedral in Berlin, C. Kleineidam, representing the archbishop of Cologne (no actual bishops were in the group). The free churches—Baptist, Methodist, Evangelical Association (*Evangelische Gemeinschaft*), and Independent Congregational (*Freie Gemeinden*)—made 20 in all.[10]

On disembarking from the *Kronprinzessin Cäcilie* on 27 May, the visitors were entertained at a reception given by the mayor and all the churches of Southampton and then conveyed by train to London. Here they were received formally by the English committee, and each was then introduced to his hosts: "For it had seemed well to the organisers of the visit, and consistent with their aim and ideal, that the larger part of it, or, if practicable, all of the guests should stay in some English family, where in the closer intimacy of home-life they might learn to know and appreciate the English nation at its best."[11]

So began a hectic week of sight-seeing, public meetings, lunches, banquets, receptions with church and political leaders all over London, and a reception held by King Edward VII. A day was spent with academics and civic leaders in Cambridge during which there was a spontaneous addition to the programme:

> In the magnificent chapel of King's College an unrehearsed but beautiful incident occurred. Deeply moved by the sublime solemnity of the architecture and of the occasion, all with one accord burst into the singing of that great Christian hymn, "We praise Thee, O Lord Almighty"[*Grosser Gott, wir loben dich*]. It was a striking testimony to the unity of spirit and purpose which throughout the visit animated the representatives of every section of the Churches, and formed the keynote of the sympathy and comradeship that everywhere characterized its proceedings.[12]

It was the age of the platform and the pulpit, and it is hardly necessary to rehearse all that was being said by both hosts and guests. The great and close ties between

---

10. A full list of the German participants is found in *Der Friede und die Kirche*, 22ff.
11. *Der Friede und die Kirche*, 71.
12. Ibid., 82.

England and Germany in history, common Christianity, and royal blood provided a constant refrain. English voices were raised in praise of Kant and Goethe, the Germans eulogised Shakespeare and Dickens. Speaker after speaker declared the unthinkability of war between two such great and closely related nations endowed with a common destiny to bring the benefits of Christian civilisation to the rest of the world. All such sentiments were brought to a grand climax on Monday, 1 June, at a lunch followed by a formal conference in the King's Hall, Holborn, presided over by Allen Baker. A resolution was submitted expressing the warm welcome to the German delegates, the need for more brotherhood between nations and the duty of Christians to make their best efforts in the furtherance of international peace. The German responses were warm and grateful, and the whole meeting concluded in powerful unanimity. In terms of the purpose of the whole visit, the evening saw the grand finale in the form of a great public meeting in the Albert Hall, chaired by the Marquis of Northampton. A letter of cordial greeting from Prime Minister Asquith was read out. The resolution agreed earlier at the King's Hall conference was presented, and speeches followed. On the English side, John Clifford and the bishop of London, Winnington Ingram, for once were not only on the same platform but on the same side. Every speech that evening, a according to the official report, "breathed out the conviction that what the German guests had seen and heard was but one example of what relations between England and Germany, between English and Germans, ought to be and might be."[13] A concluding resolution, greeted with unanimous acclaim throughout the Albert Hall, summed up these sentiments and declared that "frank co-operation between [the churches and peoples of Britain and Germany] us will do much to promote the coming of the Kingdom of Peace on earth and good-will among men."[14]

The visit, in terms of its aim of promoting greater mutual understanding and appreciation, was, as far as the actual hosts and participants were concerned, regarded as a great success. On the German side General Superintendent Faber declared: "The immediate aim ... was to bring the *British* and the *German* character nearer to one another; and that appears to me to have been in a high degree successful. We have learned to understand and to honour the *peculiarities* of our two nations, as well as what we have *in common* as a great uniting force. And we have come to see more clearly that these have to supplement ad mutually help one another."[15] Allen Baker deservedly felt much encouraged. The immediate follow-up was the production of

13. Ibid., 92.
14. Ibid., 190ff.
15. Ibid., 12.

the official souvenir volume *Der Friede und die Kirche. Peace and the Churches*,[16] superbly produced with the German and English text in parallel and lavishly illustrated with photographs of nearly all the participants and many of the key events and the places visited. Enough funds were raised for it to be sent as a present at Christmas 1908 to every participant, to members of both governments, to every member of the Reichstag and to peace campaigners in many other countries. Letters from peace activists in France, expressing a desire to do the same, showed that the visit was starting have a wider catalytic effect. But for Baker all this was just the beginning. Clearly there would have to be a reciprocal visit to Germany—and still wider possibilities beckoned him.

The British Visit to Germany 1909

In the winter of 1908-09 Baker set his sights on a personal meeting with Kaiser Wilhelm II, which took place at Postdam on 20 February 1909. The Kaiser was fulsome, even emotional, in his approval of a return British visit to Germany that year. Meanwhile, the German churches issued their invitation for a return visit from their British counterparts to take place in June 1909. There had for a time been hesitations on the German side due to the "naval scare" during the winter of 1908-09 (Britain suspected a new acceleration of German shipbuilding). But Baker insisted to de Neufville that it was precisely such renewed tension which made the visit essential. The British group recruited in response totalled 109, slightly less than the German party the previous year but the seniority of many of those involved left no doubt of the seriousness with which the visit was being taken. Among the 42 Anglicans there were no fewer than six bishops, (including Hereford, Salisbury, Southwark and Manchester) and three deans (Westminster, Worcester and Waterford), together with several other names already or soon to become prominent in church, ecumenical or academic life, such as W.R. Inge (later dean of St Paul's Cathedral) (at that time Lady Margaret Professor of Divinity at Cambridge), A.S. Duncan Jones (also of Cambridge) and the Old Testament scholar W.O.E. Oesterley. The Free Churches (Baptist, Congregational, Presbyterian, three forms of Methodist, Quakers and Unitarians) made 45. They included the president of the National Council of Evangelical Free Churches, the Welsh Presbyterian Evan Jones, but their most publicly well known figure was probably the Congregationalist Charles Silvester Horne. There were 13 Roman Catholics of impressive standing, including two bishops (P. Collins, bishop of Selinus, Newcastle-on-Tyne, and Mgr Moyes of London). A further group, mainly of Presbyterian clergy, are listed as "Representatives from Scotland and Ireland." Except

---

16. See note 1 above.

for the small group of English Presbyterians, Nearly all the denominational groups included one or more laymen, a total of twelve being members of parliament.[17]

If anything, the visit to Germany was even more elaborately planned and generously hospitable than the visit to Britain the previous year, the programme even more full of encounters with religious leaders, academics, politicians and royalty. The speeches and dining began at Dover on the evening of 7 June, as the guests were welcomed on board the *Meteor*—"a Noah's ark for all kinds of men and denominations," in the words of Silvester Horne—by the chairman of the German committee, the layman and industrialist F.A. Spiecker. Next day they sailed to Cuxhaven, whence they arrived by train in Hamburg and were received in the homes of their hosts: as in London, there was a conscious policy for all the visitors to stay with families. Hamburg, Berlin, and finally Bremen, were the main venues. In the capital, Berlin, on the evening of 11 June there took place one of the most memorable events of either visit: a great welcome meeting in the Philharmonie Hall attended by over 2,000 Berliners. The aptness of the name of the hall was not lost on the speakers who reiterated the duty to foster peace and goodwill between the two nations. For the British, Silvester Horne spoke eloquently on the mutual dependence of nations, Germany and Britain no less than others, as the law of life for the modern age. Three days later the party was received by the Kaiser at Potsdam. But in terms of substance for the main purposes of the visit, more than all the toasts and speeches, the meeting next morning, 15 June, in the chapel of the Domkandidatenstift, the Berlin Preachers' Seminary, was paramount. For here the main resolution was presented and unanimously adopted. It first reiterated the resolution adopted the previous year in London and continued:

> That this Assembly of representatives of the Christian Churches of Germany and England is of opinion that the resolution of June 1st 1908 and that which has just been passed together with an account of the circumstances under which they were arrived at, should be communicated to the Churches in both countries with an expression of hope that each church will formally endorse the sentiments therein expressed.[18]

To this were added two further paragraphs which ensured that the visits, however rewarding in themselves, were not be ephemeral but would see the start of a continuing and appropriately structured relationship:

---

17. In addition to information in the souvenir volume, *Friendly Relations etc* (see note 1), the full list of participants is found in a booklet published by the Provisional Afterwork Committee, *An Account of the Visit of Members of the Christian Churches of the United Kingdom to Germany in June, 1909.*
18. Ibid., *Friendly Relations*, 140.

And this Assembly further expresses its desire that some permanent means of communication should be established between the Christian communities of England and Germany with the object of promoting goodwill between the two nations.

It also requests D. Spiecker, Generalsuperintendent D. Faber, Mr J. Allen Baker and Revd. H. Russell Wakefield to take steps to form a provisional committee to consider as to the best method whereby to accomplish this purpose.[19]

With such sentiments, the party sailed back to England on the *Bremen.* In Germany, the young Friedrich Siegmund-Schultze set to work editing the souvenir volume of the visit,[20] produced bilingually in similar impressive fashion to the first volume.

Follow-up to the Visits: Formation of the Associated Councils

In long retrospect, and in light of the catastrophe of 1914, it is easy to dismiss the exchanges of 1908-09 as mere ecclesiastical tourism, weighted with speeches, wining and dining. In all the many words uttered deploring "misunderstandings" between the two nations there is scarcely a question asked about how those misunderstandings might actually have arisen, or indeed whether underlying them there might be some uncomfortable but very real issues making for conflict. No specific point of disagreement between Britain and Germany is ever mentioned—whether of the naval arms race, or colonial interests in Africa, or the threat of encircling alliances within Europe. All the attention was devoted to lowering the public emotional temperature without enquiring as to any actual systemic causes of the fever. The approval of monarchy and government had been obtained, but had this been at the cost of being co-opted by the powers only too pleased to have some credence given to their "peaceful" aspirations?

This, however, was not the whole story. As has been noted earlier, public feeling *was* itself a real factor in British-German relations and it *is* the case that direct and personal encounter with the other can be an important factor in changing attitudes. The exchanges were pathfinding exercises in what would later be called ecumenical encounter and exposure visits. A number of new friendships began with the visits, to become important in the coming years. Further, given the relative significance of the pulpit as a means of public communication at that time, the conception of Allen Baker and de Neufville was serious and responsible. What is more, through Baker

---

19. Ibid.
20. See note 1.

and de Neufville these were in origin *lay* initiatives and remarkably inclusive (Protestant, Anglican, Free Church, and Roman Catholic) in their confessional embrace, to a degree that "official" ecumenism for a long time to come found very difficult.[21] Above all, as has been made clear, Allen Baker never saw the visits as goals in themselves but stages to something both firmer and more widely established. And if the platform and table speeches of the 1908-09 visits tended to repetitive platitudes it was precisely in order to move beyond these to more serious reflection and engagement that Baker and his colleagues now wished to create a more permanent structure. The key decision on this was taken with the resolution of 14 June 1909 in Berlin which, for its longer term ecumenical significance, stands well alongside that which was taken a year later in Edinburgh, to form a continuation committee of the World Missionary Conference.

Very quickly, a Provisional Afterwork Committee was formed in England, with Allen Baker as chairman and W.H. Dickinson MP as secretary, and 20 Anglican, nonconformist, and Roman Catholic members. A corresponding group was set up in Germany. Among the first actions of the British group was to launch an appeal to all the churches, commending the resolutions passed during the visits in 1908 and 1909, and seeking their endorsement. Over 2,000 positive responses were received, from individual bishops, Free Church leaders, Anglican deaneries and Free Church congregations. On the basis of this support the committee resolved to form, in concert with their partners in Germany, *The Associated Councils of Churches of the British and German Empires for fostering Friendly Relations between the Two Peoples.* The stated objectives were:

- The associating of the Christian Churches in the British and German Empires in the cause of international friendship.
- The maintenance of brotherly relations between the British and German peoples and the inculcation in both countries of the Christian precept of goodwill amongst men.
- The exchange of thought and information for the purpose of preventing international misunderstanding and distrust.
- The furtherance of all efforts calculated to promote and preserve permanent peace between the two nations.[22]

---

21. This inclusivity was of course possible only because of the assurance that doctrinal issues would not be on the agenda but that does derogate from its "ecumenical" standing. Edinburgh 1910 was likewise organised with the understanding that it was about "cooperation" rather than "doctrinal agreement"—yet had no official Roman Catholic (and very little Orthodox) participation in response to its invitation.
22. "Objects and Constitution" in *The Associated Councils of Churches in the British and German Empires for Fostering Friendly Relations between the Two Peoples,* preliminary announcement and

In both countries a council and an executive were set up. In Britain the archbishop of Canterbury was president. Allen Baker as would be expected was chair of the executive, with W.H. Dickinson as secretary. In Germany, F.A. Spiecker was president of the executive, with Friedrich Siegmund-Schultze secretary, although in due course he had to relinquish much of the secretarial responsibility due to pressure of other work. As well as membership by churches, people were invited to join the Associated Councils as individual members and the British Council soon had 6,000 on its list, rising to nearly 11,000 by 1912 (including, within the "Empire" category, supporters from Canada, Australia, and New Zealand).

The inaugural meeting of the British Council took place in the Queen's Hall, London, on 6 February 1911.[23] Archbishop Randall Davidson presided. F.A. Spiecker, as President of the German Council, and Adolf von Harnack, an active member of that council, were guest speakers alongside the usual British church celebrities. Annual reports were issued by the councils, reviewing the situation and the activities of the churches. Support was also given to the "Anglo-German Understanding Conference" that took place in London 30 October–1 November 1912. But not least in importance for the Associated Councils were the quarterly journals published in both countries as their official organs. The British Council's *The Peacemaker* first appeared in July 1911. Its editor was the Baptist J.H. Rushbrooke, fluent in German from the time he had studied in Berlin (where he and his friend N.H. Marshall had attended Harnack's famous lectures in 1900-01, *Das Wesen Christentums*, published in 1901 in English as *What is Christianity?*) and was married to a German. The opening editorial stated its function as being "to impress upon its readers such considerations as to bring the British and German peoples together as friends and lead them to realise the real duties and interest they have in common," through articles and correspondence from both British and German writers, comments upon relevant books, newspaper articles and other publications in both countries. This it proceeded to do, including also pieces by political commentators and articles on international law, excerpts from government policy papers, and speeches from politicians. By 1913 *The Peacemaker* had a circulation of 67,000, and was proving a valuable educational tool for the council's approach to schools, colleges and theological seminaries. In January 1913 appeared the first issue of the German *Die Eiche*—the title taken from the oak tree which was regarded as the German national symbol and also had strong character associations in England, and which provided the

---

information leaflet in World Alliance files Box 212.020.

23. The meeting had been scheduled for autumn 1910, but was postponed due to the constitutional crisis on reform of the House of Lords and the consequent general election in December. Information on this meeting and other activities of the Associated Councils in the form of reports and memoranda is held in the World Alliance material, WCC Archive, Geneva (see note 1).

emblem on the front cover of both the British and German journals. *Die Eiche* also carried the heraldic coats of arms of both the Prussian and British royal houses. Its editor was Friedrich Siegmund-Schultze. Through the reciprocity of much of the contents of these journals the British-German conversation was continuing at a deeper level than on the platform.[24] Further exchange visits were also being planned by the Associated Councils on a city-to-city basis. All this was taking place amid an international atmosphere of continual anxiety and occasional real alarms, as with the Agadir crisis of 1911 when the German gunboat *Panther* appeared off the Moroccan port in what was seen by France and Britain as a dangerously provocative gesture. In his capacity as a member of parliament, Allen Baker was frequently in close contact with the British foreign office and Lambeth Palace in trying to clarify and communicate what was, or was not, actually happening. By 1914, however, Anglo-German relations seemed better than for several years. As late as June 1914, *The Peacemaker* was speaking glowingly of "the new atmosphere" in both diplomatic relations and public opinion.[25] Of the dreadful events that would unfold on Europe within weeks, there was no hint.

The Formation of the World Alliance

Meanwhile, much interest in the Anglo-German movement and the creation of the Associated Councils was developing elsewhere in the world, not least in the United States where among some in the Protestant churches there had been long-standing concern for peace issues.[26] In the summer of 1910, the British Council, still technically in process of formation, was invited to send two representatives across the Atlantic to give an account of what was happening. The occasion was the regular summer conference convened each year at Lake Mohonk, the lakeside resort upriver from New York City, by the hotel proprietor, A.K. Smiley, for academics, clergy, judges, military personnel, industrialists, and others. A special interest at these conferences was international arbitration. The two British delegates were the dean of Worcester, W. Moore Ede, and William Thomas, secretary of the Metropolitan Free Church Federation. They went with the full support of the Archbishop of Canterbury, and moreover intended not only to share what was happening with the Associated Councils but also,

---

24. Files of *The Peacemaker* and *Die Eiche* are found in the World Alliance material, WCC Archive, Geneva (see note 1).

25. Editorial, "British-German Unity," *The Peacemaker* 2, no. 1 (June 1914): 1ff.

26. See C. S. Macfarland, *International Christian Movements* (New York and Chicago: Fleming H. Revell, 1924); C.S. Macfarland, *Steps Toward the World Council: Origins of the Ecumenical Movement as Expressed in the Universal Christian Council for Life and Work* (New York: Fleming H. Revell, 1938), 27-37; and Rouse and Neill, *A History of the Ecumenical Movement*, 511-515.

to appeal to the representatives of the American Churches to take up the work and carry it forward by convening a World Conference of representatives of all Churches in every nation, if possible before the next Hague Conference, since such an Oecumenical Conference in support of friendly relations between the nations could not fail powerfully to influence public opinion and strengthen the hands of diplomatists in their endeavours to solve the difficulties in the way of the establishment of courts of international justice and righteousness rather than armed force.[27]

The American churches, stated the British delegates, were in a unique position to lead on this as their country stood outside the jealousies and antagonisms of Europe. So great was the interest aroused by this at Lake Mohonk that the organisers decided to devote a whole session of the next year's conference to the idea, and that both the British and German Councils be invited to send representatives. The Americans themselves went into action to mobilise church interest and support, especially through the recently-formed Federal Council of the Churches of Christ in America. Accordingly, the 1911 Lake Mohonk conference was attended by Allen Baker, Dean Moore Ede and John Clifford for the British Council and Friedrich Siegmund-Schultze for the German. Both at Lake Mohonk and at a 1,000-strong meeting of clergy in New York City there was great enthusiasm for action along the lines of the 1910 British proposals, with appropriate resolutions passed. No concrete public action followed immediately but the idea of a world conference was not lost. An undeniable momentum had been created. The secretary of the Federal Council, Frederick Lynch, in turn visited London and Berlin later in 1911—a time of renewed tensions between Britain and Germany.

Among Lynch's significant contacts was Andrew Carnegie, who was already deeply impressed by the work of the Anglo-German Associated Councils, the more so as he visited Berlin in 1913 for the Kaiser's jubilee. At Lynch's suggestion, Carnegie endowed the Church Peace Union which was to work in close partnership with the Federal Council (with Lynch as its secretary as well). It was the Church Peace Union that now took up the conference idea, strong impetus being added by a gathering in Switzerland in May 1914 of Swiss, British and German leaders (and following an "Appeal to the Christian Churches of Europe" made by Swiss church leaders in January of that year). Here it was resolved to convene the main conference at Constance, at the beginning of August that year.

On 28 June the Austrian Archduke Ferdinand was assassinated in Sarajevo, and there was set rolling the catastrophic chain of events and mistakes that led to war. At

---

27. *The Churches and International Friendship. Movements leading up to the Conferences at Constance and Liege, August 1914*, booklet in World Alliance material, WCC Archive, Geneva (see note 1), 9.

the end of July Europe was already mobilising as the 153 delegates tried to make their way to Constance. Only 85 actually arrived, from Britain, France, Germany, Switzerland, Netherlands, Denmark, Norway, Sweden, Bulgaria and the United States. It opened on 1 August, the very day war was declared between Germany, France and Russia, with Britain to follow three days later. The conference barely had time to address a statement to all rulers and statesmen, before delegates had to leave and make their ways home as best they could. A group that reached London nominated an international committee and named the continuing body the World Alliance for Promoting International Friendship through the Churches.

Against the Odds: Survival, Persistence and the Ecumenical Future

The World Alliance was thus was created in circumstances as tragic as could be imagined, save for the finger-nails of faith and hope clinging on amid the maelstrom of conflict. Such as Allen Baker and Eduard de Neufville must have been tempted to feel that the outbreak of war between Britain and Germany made a mockery of all the hopes and idealism that had motivated the exchange visits of 1908-09, and had proved right the cynics who had dismissed the goal of "friendlier relations" as hopelessly naïve. *Realpolitik* and armaments had triumphed. Indeed, even within the churches, in both countries, patriotic fervour and the sacralisation of the national cause in a holy war seemed largely to carry the day. Within weeks leading German church figures and theologians addressed a letter to their counterparts in Britain protesting at the wilfully unjust "web of lies" in which Germany had been caught and declaring support for the Kaiser's war. Among the signatories were several such as Harnack who had been involved in the exchanges of 1908-09 and others who had been at the 1910 Edinburgh World Missionary Conference. Led by the archbishop of Canterbury, British church figures replied with a corresponding sense of justice in the righteousness of their cause. On both sides, as the war proceeded ever more brutally there were accusations of unchristian betrayal. Remarkably, however, the British and German journals continued. *The Peacemaker* was modestly re-named *Goodwill* in a new series beginning January 1915, edited as before by J.H. Rushbrooke.[28] Under the courageous guiding hand of Friedrich Siegmund-Schultze, *Die Eiche* continued as before—except that on the front cover the British royal crest was replaced by the black, red and gold shield that, dating from 1848, represented German national unity. Several issues of *Die Eiche* carried blank spaces, witnessing to the censor's displeasure.[29]

---

28. Files in World Alliance material, WCC Archive, Geneva.
29. Siegmund-Schultze, in addition to his manifold work as pastor, social ethics teacher, ecumenist, and co-founder of the World Alliance and the Fellowship of Reconciliation, continued

There was, moreover, always still the World Alliance itself, newborn, frail but undeniably existing, and providentially with enough support—especially in neutral countries—to ensure its continuance and indeed to begin constructive international activity. Further, in Britain and Germany, the Associated Councils placed themselves under the World Alliance's aegis while continuing their particular activities; the British Council, for example, regarded itself as the British manifestation of the World Alliance.[30] The World Alliance was even able to hold a conference in Bern, Switzerland, in August 1915, attended by delegates not only from neutral countries but from three of the belligerents—Britain, Germany, and Italy. It was the only Protestant conference held during the war attended by delegates from both sides of the conflict.[31] Relief for war victims and the development of international law after the war were topics high on the agenda. After the war, it was the World Alliance that convened the first Christian conference to enable a large-scale meeting of figures from the belligerent as well as neutral countries to meet and face the challenges of reconciliation and a new beginning. This took place at Oud Wassenaar, near the Hague in the Netherlands, 30 September–3 October 1919.[32] Sadly, Allen Baker did not live to see this, having died in 1918 before the war ended. Among the participants however were two figures who were soon to play crucial roles in the leadership of the new ecumenical generation: Nathan Söderblom, archbishop of Uppsala, and George Bell, at that time chaplain to the archbishop of Canterbury.

The World Alliance grew in strength and breadth of membership in the post-war years and, while overwhelmingly European and North American in its constituency, was joined by supporters from China, India and Japan. It undoubtedly did foster reconciliation and cooperation among the churches, if not more widely *through* them. The treatment of religious minorities within the new borders of Europe and, later, disarmament, became key topics at its series of international conferences. In 1925 there took place the first conference on "Life and Work" at Stockholm, called by Archbishop Nathan Söderblom. This was the first major international ecumenical

---

to edit *Die Eiche* until its suppression under the Nazi advent to power in 1933. He was deported by the Gestapo to Switzerland on account of his aid to Jews, returning to Germany in 1948. See also, on his ecumenical role in the German Church Struggle, Chapter 5 below. He died in 1969.

30. See "World Alliance of Churches for Promoting International Friendship: British group: Preliminary Notice," memorandum, World Alliance files, Box 212.021, WCC Archive, Geneva.

31. Rouse and Neill, *A History of the Ecumenical Movement*, 517.

32. Ibid., 530-534. The role of J.H. Oldham, secretary of the Continuation Committee of the Edinburgh World Missionary Conference, in reconciliation with the German churches and mission bodies and in securing their participation in the new International Missionary Council (1921), should also be noted. See chapter 5 below and Keith Clements, *Faith on the Frontier: A Life of J.H. Oldham* (Geneva: WCC Publications,1999), chapters 7 and 8.

conference for 15 years. Its ancestry, however, was not Edinburgh 1910, but rather Oud Wassenaar 1919, which Söderblom had attended and found inspirational and encouraging in his long-standing work for peace and reconciliation. Out of Stockholm 1925 was created the Universal Christian Council for Life and Work. This now became the major ecumenical body addressing social and international issues—and indeed relations between the churches themselves—and moreover comprised official representatives of churches, whereas the World Alliance, while attracting the involvement of many senior church figures, remained a more loose-knit and voluntary organisation. In fact, not only had the World Alliance contributed towards the setting up of the Stockholm conference, but there continued a very close, if at times frictional, co-operation between the World Alliance and Life and Work. There was some overlapping of membership of the executives of the two bodies and accordingly for convenience they often met at the same time and place. Indeed from 1933 to 1938 there was a joint secretaryship in Geneva in the person of Henry-Louis Henriod. It was only with the official inauguration of the WCC in 1948 that the World Alliance felt the time had come to dissolve itself. This was entirely appropriate given that its founding visions had been an inclusive, worldwide assembly of all the churches.

Undoubtedly the close relationship benefited Life and Work, for the World Alliance precisely by its less official nature and more open, flexible style of working was able to recruit a wider constituency into ecumenical activity, especially youth and women. It was is worth noting, for example, that it was at the World Alliance's eighth international conference at Cambridge, England, in 1931 that Dietrich Bonhoeffer made his entrance into the ecumenical movement as a German youth delegate and was appointed one of the European youth secretaries of the Alliance.[33] Through it and the joint meetings with Life and Work, he was brought close to such as George Bell, bishop of Chichester, and was able in due course to play a vital role in bringing the ecumenical movement and the German Confessing Church into mutual engagement.

It was, moreover, at the joint conference of Life and Work and the World Alliance at Fanø, Denmark, in August 1934, that Bonhoeffer issued his famous call for an ecumenical peace conference of the churches.[34] Recent generations have seen in that call an inspiration for the churches' continuing ecumenical witness for peace, and a key stimulus for the covenantal process on Justice, Peace and the Integrity of Creation (JPIC) that was so prominent after the seventh assembly of the WCC at Vancouver,

---

33. Eberhard Bethge, *Dietrich Bonhoeffer: A Biography*, rev. ed. (Minneapolis: Fortress, 2000), 189-202; Keith Clements, *Bonhoeffer and Britain* (London: Churches Together in Britain and Ireland, 2006), chapter 2, "Cambridge 1931."
34. Bethge, *Dietrich Bonhoeffer*, 372-391; Bonhoeffer, "The Church and the Peoples of the World," in *Dietrich Bonhoeffer Works*, vol. 13, *London 1933-35* (Minneapolis: Fortress, 2007), 307-309.

1983. But, as will be clear from this chapter study, in making that call Bonhoeffer was reiterating what had been said much earlier by J. Allen Baker and his collaborators of 1908-09. They were the real pioneers who were prepared to take steps which, however questionable and even jejune in some respects they may appear today, were nevertheless concrete and led towards the creation of one of the most important strands of the modern ecumenical movement. They were prepared to act and, when much to seemed to speak of failure, to persist. There is a clear line—much clearer than from Edinburgh 1910—from the 1908-09 Anglo-German visits, through the formation of the Associated Councils and the World Alliance, to Life and Work and thence to the WCC. But quite apart from ecumenical genealogy, the significance of those visits lies in their manifesting the first impulses towards discovering what it means to live elsewhere than in one's own narrow national and religious tradition, and this for the sake not just of the church but the wider world as a whole. For all the apparent naivety that was so rudely shaken by war, this was the dynamic set in motion All in the ecumenical movement owe gratitude to that first conversation at the Hague in 1907 when a British hand and a German hand reached to each other in friendship. All in the ecumenical movement owe gratitude to that first conversation at the Hague in 1907—and it should be noted that the fully ecumenical council still awaits us.

Chapter 5
Creative Disempowerment
The Real Legacy of Edinburgh 1910

The *Real* Legacy of Edinburgh 1910": the subtitle has a polemical ring, implying that the actual historic significance of that World Missionary Conference is a contested one.[1] As indeed it is. Many of us were taught in church history classes that Edinburgh 1910 "was the birthplace of the modern ecumenical movement"[2] and we have grown used to describing it as such ever since. Further, "the ecumenical movement" has usually denoted that series of international gatherings which followed on from Edinburgh, and the organisations generated by them, leading to the formation of the World Council of Churches (WCC) and its subsequent development, and of course to corresponding developments at national levels. This has been given graphic expression with the so-called "river chart" produced by the WCC to celebrate the Edinburgh centennial, "Highlights of the Ecumenical Movement 1910-2010."[3] In it, Edinburgh 1910 is depicted as the wellspring from which have flowed the three organisational streams of the International Missionary Council, Life and Work, and Faith and Order, which later flowed together into the WCC.[4] Meanwhile along the banks of the river are located the formative events like the first Life and Work conference at Stockholm 1925, the first Faith and Order conference at Lausanne in 1927, the Oxford conference on "Church, Community and State" in 1937, the inaugural assembly of the WCC itself at Amsterdam in 1948, and subsequent meetings and assemblies right down to the most recent WCC assembly, the ninth, in Porto Alegre, Brazil in 2006; and so to the centenary celebrations of Edinburgh in 2010. The usual justification given for this understanding of the importance of

---

1. For the most recent full study of Edinburgh 1910 and discussion of its significance see Brian Stanley, *The World Missionary Conference, Edinburgh 1910* (Grand Rapids: Eerdmans, 2009).
2. K. S. Latourette, in *A History of the Ecumenical Movement 1517-1948*, ed. Ruth Rouse and Stephen C. Neill (London: SPCK, 1967), 362.
3. See above in Chapter 1, n. 6.
4. On this general history, see Rouse and Neill, *A History of the Ecumenical Movement 1517-1948*.

Edinburgh is the fact that, unlike any previous gathering of enthusiasts for world mission (and there had been several), Edinburgh 1910 did not just meet and go away again, but set up a Continuation Committee to ensure concrete and long-term cooperation. This continuation committee proved to be the first enduring international body of interchurch cooperation, eventually giving birth in the 1920s to the International Missionary Council, several of whose key players, like John R. Mott and J.H. Oldham, were also to become important in the Life and Work and Faith and Order movements that emerged in that decade. As I have suggested in the preceding chapter, however, such a claim for Edinburgh and its continuation committee cannot ignore the near-contemporary formation of the World Alliance for Promoting International Friendship Through the Churches, which owed much to the Anglo-German church exchanges of 1908-09 and was much more directly a parent of the Life and Work movement than was Edinburgh 1910.

Quite apart from these particular historical questions, the standard view of the legacy of Edinburgh 1910 in terms of ecumenical organisations is challenged by some in Protestant evangelical circles. They point out that the more than one thousand delegates of missionary organisations and churches who met at Edinburgh in July 1910 had no thought or intention of "starting the ecumenical movement." The organisers had even studiously avoided labelling the conference "ecumenical." They were inspired by the watchword of the Student Missionary Volunteer movement, "the evangelisation of the world in this generation"; and even though one of the eight commissions whose reports fed the conference discussions was on "Co-operation and the Promotion of Unity," the main thrust was on practical co-operation as the only kind of unity that really mattered in the evangelistic task. Therefore, it is argued, the real legatees of Edinburgh 1910 today are those who still see *this*, the evangelisation of the world, as the paramount Christian task, a task from which much ecumenical organisation and activity has side-tracked the churches.

What Kind of Perspective on Edinburgh? Consciousness and Relationships

Trying to adjudicate between such rival claimants to the Edinburgh legacy might be an interesting but not necessarily the most useful exercise. The trench between "evangelicals" and "ecumenicals" is not always as deep as assumed, certainly not in the global South. The centennial conference of missiologists which met in Edinburgh in June 2010 was sponsored jointly by the WCC and the World Evangelical

Alliance,[5] while the gathering later that year in Cape Town, South Africa, organised by the evangelical Lausanne Movement, also attracted a broad spectrum of participation and was addressed by the general secretary of the WCC, Olav Fyske Tveit. There is, however, yet another point of view that wishes to be heard in the discussion, arguing that organisational ecumenism is indeed the genuine inheritance from Edinburgh 1910, but has proved a fateful result in the dead hand of institutions, bureaucracy and clericalism.[6] The "river chart" might be held up triumphalistically by professional Geneva ecumenists as depicting the glorious story of a hundred years' endeavour; or denigrated by ardent evangelicals as a betrayal of the real vision of Edinburgh 1910; or simply regarded as a dangerous irrelevance, especially by many in the younger generation who are suspicious of all attempts to channel spiritual energy within institutional conduits. I would rather, however, suggest a quite different perspective from all these, from which to view Edinburgh and what followed. We need not focus only on the precisely stated intentions of the conference, nor exhaust ourselves either justifying or criticising the organisations which ensued. We should rather look at the kind of *consciousness* which grew from Edinburgh onwards and the kinds of *relationships* that developed among the churches and persons participating in the movement. Edinburgh 1910 was a classic case of people meeting with a definite agenda, with clearly defined hopes and intentions, of decisions taken which set them on a new course into the future, but a future which proved to be rather different from the one they had expected and which set an agenda which they had not foreseen. In other words, what is really interesting and significant is not just what happened *at* Edinburgh (important though that was) but what happened *to* Edinburgh in its subsequent engagement with the world. And what happened was the development of an unforeseen agenda, and the start of a transformation of relationships within the members of the body of Christ across the world. In both cases, this involved the felt loss of total control by those who had previously been in charge.

Hence the title of this chapter, "Creative Disempowerment." I know that In terms of much of our contemporary theological and political discourse this sounds like a contradiction: surely it is empowerment that leads to liberation and creativity, but I cannot help speaking as a white, European male Protestant—that class of people overwhelmingly represented at Edinburgh 1910. Edinburgh 1910 marked the beginning of the end of that white, EuroAmerican (and male) hegemony within world Christianity. It was the beginning of western Christian disempowerment, which was

---

5. "Edinburgh 2010—Witnessing to Christ Today." See www.edinburgh2010.org.
6. See John Kent, *The Unacceptable Face: The Modern Church in the Eyes of the Historian* (London: SCM, 1987).

to mean its liberation from being tied to the seat of worldly imperial power, and freedom to enter into the space where true community is born. That is the story to which we should pay heed. If our ecumenical energy and imagination are to be renewed, we need to re-read the story and with some fresh perspectives.

Post-Edinburgh: New Agendas

The Edinburgh conference was quite clear about its agenda, as indicated by the titles of its eight commissions and their reports: Carrying the Gospel to the Non-Christian World; The Church in the Mission Field; Education in relation to the Christianisation of National Life; the Missionary Message in relation to Non-Christian Religions; the Preparation of Missionaries; the Home Base of Missions; Relation of Missions to Governments; and eighth, as mentioned earlier, Cooperation and the Promotion of Unity. Thus was set the basic agenda to be followed up by the continuation committee, chaired by that formidable human dynamo, the American Methodist layman John R. Mott,[7] and served by its indefatigable and ingenious secretary, the Scotsman J.H. ("Joe") Oldham.[8]

But another agenda had started to write itself almost as soon as the delegates assembled in Edinburgh. It is a beautiful irony that Edinburgh was only allowed to take place because a number of the missionary bodies—and some church voices like High Church Anglicans—insisted that it should not deal with doctrinal and other divisive issues but only "practical matters of cooperation." Unity as such was therefore taboo. But once at Edinburgh, people began talking about the need for closer structural unity and thus implicitly acknowledging the need to address doctrinal questions, as a natural and necessary adjunct to cooperation "on the mission field."[9] Lord Balfour, president of the conference, put his foot in it even in his opening speech of welcome. Even that most cautious archbishop of Canterbury, Randall Davidson, concluded his opening address with a dramatic hint that if missions became central in the life of the church, the final issue might be one akin to the kingdom of God coming with power in the lifetime of some of those present—and everyone knew what he was implying. From the floor, during debates on the various commission reports, delegate after delegate expressed hopes that there might ensue a greater degree of unity than even the formation of the continuation committee

7. See C. H. Hopkins, *John R. Mott 1865-1955* (Geneva: WCC Publications, 1979).
8. See Keith Clements, *Faith on the Frontier: A Life of J.H. Oldham* (Edinburgh: T. & T. Clark and Geneva: WCC Publications, 1999).
9. This, as other aspects of Edinburgh 1910, is graphically if sometimes over-dramatically recounted in the earliest full-length account of the conference by W.H.T. ("Temple") Gairdner, *"Edinburgh 1910": An Account and Interpretation of the World Missionary Conference* (Edinburgh and London: Oliphant, Anderson & Ferrier 1910).

might facilitate. It was one delegate in particular, the American Episcopal missionary bishop Charles Brent, who, encouraged by the Edinburgh experience, was to be
instrumental in igniting the Faith and Order movement.

The continuation committee appointed at Edinburgh met twice, in 1911 and
1912, and vigorously set about the cooperative tasks remitted by the conference.
There was no doubt that a new strategy of international missionary cooperation
was being developed and implemented, especially as regards Asia, if somewhat
unevenly. Under Oldham's influence especially, there was emphasis also upon
study and research, as evidenced by the most enduring tangible legacy of the
Edinburgh enterprise, the *International Review of Missions* which he founded and
began to edit in 1912 and which continues[10] to this day. But in August 1914 all this
apparent progress, like so much else, was thrown into mayhem by the outbreak of
war in Europe. Conflict between the warring parties of Germany and Austria on
the one hand, and France, Britain and Russia on the other, later joined by the USA,
did not just bring obvious physical disruption to the post-Edinburgh enterprise.
It called into question much of the actual theological basis and the strategy of that
enterprise and of the Edinburgh Conference itself. The German Kaiser, Wilhelm
II, rallied his country to the defence of Christian civilisation, and his call was soon
followed by a manifesto signed by leading Protestant church figures and theologians who, protesting against the "systematic network of lies" being spun abroad
against Germany, declared that Germany had a right to defend herself and seek
the aid of God to defend her Protestant faith from being ravaged by "Asiatic [i.e.
Russian] barbarism" and heathenism.[11] As is well known, it was this and like dec-
larations which roused the young Swiss pastor Karl Barth to anger by its demon-
stration that Protestantism, seen especially in its liberal theology, had lost its soul.
Prominent among the signatories were leading figures in the German missions
including Julius Richter, actually a vice-chairman of the Edinburgh Continuation
Committee,[12] and the manifesto expressed especial bitterness that the ideals of
Edinburgh were being shattered: "The mission fields which the World Missionary
Conference in Edinburgh indicated as the most important in the present day—
mid-Africa with its rivalry between Christendom and Islam for the black races,
and eastern Asia remoulding its life—are now becoming the scenes of embittered
struggles between peoples who bore in a special degree the responsibility for the
fulfilment of the Great Commission in these lands." It was indeed soon the case

---

10. Slightly differently titled now as *International Review of Mission*.
11. "Appeal to Evangelical Christians Abroad." It appeared in the London *Times* on 30 September
1914. See Clements, *Faith on the Frontier*, 126.
12. Richter had also been on the German church delegation to Britain in 1908. See above, chapter 4..

that British and German gunboats were attacking each other on Lake Victoria and in the Zanzibar Channel, and German colonies from Togoland to East Africa and South West Africa fell prey to British military conquest. The German Protestants in their manifesto were justified in their protest that such conflict was hardly an advertisement for the Christian gospel which was supposedly the supreme spiritual inspiration of the British and German nations, but equally they were ingenuous in their blind support for their own country's cause. It took the shock of war and its aftermath—humiliating defeat for the Germans, and a perilously costly victory for the allies—to make the churches on all sides begin to realise their own complicity in the nationalism which had led to it.

But above all the war had shattered the basic paradigm of Edinburgh: a distinction between the "Christian" and "non-Christian" worlds.[13] What business had now those European nations which had gone to war so brutally to call themselves "Christian"? Was barbarism only a prerogative of the so-called "non-Christian" world? On the British side, such as J.H. Oldham regarded the war as a judgment upon the acquisitive, materialistic culture and its values which had infected the whole of the west. Oldham was foremost in calling for a distinction between the church of Christ and so-called Christian civilisation.[14] The theme of Commission III at Edinburgh— education in relation to the Christianization of national life—had been presumed to refer to the Christianisation of the national life of the lands of the "mission fields." Oldham argued that the process needed to begin at home. In a remarkable book written in 1916, *The World and the Gospel*, he stated:

> The Christian protest against the unchristian forces in social and national life must be clearer, sharper and more patent than it has been in the past. It may be that the Church as it was before the war could never have evangelized the world; that its witness had not the penetrating force necessary for so gigantic an undertaking; that before God could answer the prayers of his people some deep-seated evil had to be removed, however terrible the cost.[15]

In a telling footnote, Oldham remarked on the alarming statistics of child poverty in England, and questions whether a church that tolerated such a state of things in its own society "possessed the moral passion that would enable it to evangelise the

---

13. Note the theme of Commission I at Edinburgh, over which Mott himself presided: "Carrying the Gospel to the Non-Christian World."
14. See Clements, *Faith on the Frontier*, 140.
15. J.H. Oldham, *The World and the Gospel* (London: United Council for Missionary Education, 1916), 21ff.

world." The agenda thus remained evangelism, but the understanding of what that entailed was being deepened and widened, at both national and international levels. When the IMC was eventually established in 1921, Oldham insisted that as well as what had been regarded as the normal "missionary agenda," its brief had to include "to help unite Christian forces in the world in seeking justice in international and inter-racial questions,"[16] and it was in 1924 that his own pioneering work appeared, *Christianity and the Race Problem*.[17] It was not however the IMC but rather the Stockholm conference of 1924, under the leadership of Archbishop Nathan Söderblom, which took up this wider agenda and set up the Universal Christian Council for Life and Work. Until the formation of the WCC, this was the most comprehensive ecumenical body capable of addressing social and international issues, and indeed fundamental theological concerns too, on behalf of the churches. For his part, Oldham became increasingly frustrated with the IMC, and although he remained secretary of the IMC until 1938, by 1934 most of his energies were going into the Life and Work programme.[18]

Clearly, the mission agenda had been enlarged following Edinburgh, not because those responsible for the continuation of Edinburgh had diverted from the evangelism agenda, but precisely because they had allowed that agenda and the reality of the world to confront each other. Edinburgh had rightly sought to obey the call to make disciples of all nations. But the world was now forcing the churches to ask, "What is discipleship? What does following Christ mean in the actualities of conflict, war, economic depression, racial injustice, and the struggles of colonised countries for independence?" Half a century later, during the 1960s, "Let the world write the agenda" became a popular slogan in ecumenical circles. Oldham, still just alive, would have smiled had he heard that. If Edinburgh (and its implementation) should be seen as foundational for the ecumenical movement, it is not just because it stands at the start of the linear process of that movement, but because like a musical theme announced at the start of a symphony, it sets a pattern that in different ways is to recur again and again as the movement goes on.

Changing Relationships: Towards Community

Among the stewards at Edinburgh in 1910 was a young Oxford scholar and teacher called William Temple. Thirty-two years later, in 1942, Temple was enthroned as archbishop of Canterbury, and in his enthronement sermon referred to "the great new fact of our time," by which he meant "the worldwide fellowship of Christians."

16. See Clements, *Faith on the Frontier*, 178.
17. J.H. Oldham, *Christianity and the Race Problem* (London: SCM, 1924).
18. See Clements, *Faith on the Frontier*, Chapter 12.

Temple himself had contributed greatly to the growing ecumenical consciousness throughout the 1920s and 1930s, and was deeply involved in all the three main streams, the IMC, Life and Work, and Faith and Order. But the great new fact of *our* time is still more remarkable than anything that even Temple could have envisaged, in that Christianity is today not only a worldwide fellowship, but a growing phenomenon with its main centre of gravity and its missionary momentum in the global South. It is now a commonplace to state that Christianity has become a growing movement of the non-western world and that Europe, either wringing its hands or rejoicing over the apparently inexorable advance of secularism, is the exceptional case.[19] It is remarkable, moreover, that it is often in the postcolonial contexts that Christian communities are growing fastest, as in parts of Africa, or in contexts where western missionaries for one reason or another have long been banned or virtually absent, as in China. Missiologists such as Gambian-born Lamin Sanneh point out that a new paradigm of mission is required to understand this phenomenon: it is no longer the missionaries who are the agents of mission, but the indigenous recipients of the message who are apprehending it and inculturating it for themselves.[20] They moreover will eventually be writing a new version of the story as a whole out of their experiences and perspective, which will include their own appraisal of the west. Sanneh himself writes pointedly about the Christian countries of Europe leading the rest of the world into their wars, which brought tragedy to his own family, and Christianity's failure to prevent the cold war and nuclear proliferation: "I don't know what conclusion we should draw from this except to say that the story of Christianity is still unfolding, *is still cutting for itself fresh channels in Africa.* We do not yet know how that story will end. All we know is that many more are yet to join that story."[21]

All this might seem at farthest remove from Edinburgh 1910, where the overwhelming majority of delegates were white, western—and male—representatives of their churches and missionary organisations; where there were very few indigenous Asians; and no black African was invited.[22] The evangelisation of the world was assumedly in the hands of the west. This however was not quite the whole story, and Edinburgh 1910 can be seen as both marking the zenith of western mission-

---

19. See Grace Davie, *Europe: The Exceptional Case. Parameters of Faith in the Modern World* (London: Darton, Longman and Todd, 2002).

20. See Lamin Sanneh, *Whose Religion Is Christianity? The Gospel Beyond the West* (Grand Rapids: Eerdmans, 2003).

21. Ibid., 38ff. (Emphasis mine.)

22. A single African figure did appear, however, in the person of M.C. Hayward, secretary of the Native Baptist Union of West Africa, though in what capacity is not clear. See Stanley, *The World Missionary Conference*, 97ff.

ary strength and confidence, and heralding—albeit with a somewhat hesitant note on the trumpet—the advent of a different understanding of mission. There was a dawning recognition of the reality of initiatives for mission and unity independent of the western enterprise, and with voices demanding to be heard. During the debate on the proposal to form a Continuation Committee the Chinese delegate Cheng Ching-yi, reinforcing earlier remarks from the Anglican bishop of Hankow, warned that if the western missionary agencies did not get their act together then a new, indigenous leadership in China might take matters into their own hands, so important was unity to the Chinese mind and culture. "Speaking plainly we hope to see, in the near future, a united Christian Church without any denominational distinctions. This may seem somewhat peculiar to you, but, friends, do not forget to view us from *our* standpoint, and if you fail to do that, the Chinese will remain always as a mysterious people to you!"[23] The only obstacle to such a church was "our western friends and not ourselves." Here the East was speaking with its own voice, on its own terms, and for its own aspirations. *Do not forget to view us from OUR standpoint*: that could well have served as an instruction for every subsequent ecumenical gathering.

Yet more dramatic in its impact was the address given at one of the informal evening sessions of the conference by a young Indian Anglican priest, Samuel Azariah, on "The Problem of Cooperation between Foreign and Native Workers." He dwelt, among other things, on the financial dependency of the indigenous staff on their foreign paymasters, a dependency which created a barrier and encouraged paternalism. But it is his concluding words which have acquired almost legendary status in the Edinburgh annals:

> Through all the ages to come the Indian Church would rise up in gratitude to attest the heroism and self-denying labour of the missionary body. You have given your goods to feed the poor. You have given your bodies to be burned. We also ask for *love*. Give us FRIENDS.[24]

Many in the audience applauded. From others there was a disconcerted, even offended, silence. While it is these final comments of Azariah that are typically quoted, his even more provocative statement did not appear in the official report: "Too often you promise us thrones in heaven, but will not offer us chairs in your

---

23. *World Missionary Conference, 1910. Report of Commission VIII: Co-operation and the Promotion of Unity* (London: Oliphant, Anderson & Ferrier and New York: Fleming H. Revell, n.d., 196.
24. See Stanley, *The World Missionary Conference*, 125 and Clements, *Faith on the Frontier*, 44, 89ff.

living rooms."[25] But that final peroration was just the climax of a lengthy exploration of the significance of racial relationships[26] and the heart of his presentation was
an exposition of the Pauline teaching on community found in Ephesians 3:18ff and
1 Corinthians 13. Not by any one language or racial group acting alone, but by all
working and worshipping and learning together to reflect the perfect image of our
Lord Jesus Christ—"with all the saints"—could the kingdom come. This was prophecy in the fullest sense: prophecy in delivering a word that spoke truth both to cut
and to heal in the present situation; and prophecy in pointing the way that, at its
best, the ecumenical journey was to take in the succeeding decades, a journey which
Azariah himself was to lead in India when he became a bishop and an advocate of the
movement that led to the formation of the Church of South India.[27]

The ecumenical movement means the creation of a community in which people
and churches move from inequality to equality; from relations of dominance and
subservience towards partnership; from patterns of assumed authority and defer-
ence to mutual respect, appreciation, and accountability in line with the Pauline
social imagery of the body of Christ stretched across the world; from independence
and dependency to interdependence; and as such, in this unity to become a sign
and instrument of the unity of humankind under God. That is a continual, perhaps unending journey. Being ecumenical means the creation of space for a genuine meeting of parts of the *oikoumene*, of listening and learning from the other, the
other's experience, the other's insights, the other's pain, the other's anger, the other's
strengths and gifts. That means a disempowerment of the those who were previously dominant in worldly terms as they give space and place to let the others be
themselves, in terms of confession, culture, gender, age. But this disempowerment of
the previously powerful means in fact their liberation: liberation from the inherited
roles they had been unwittingly forced into, roles which progressively burden and
dehumanise them with pride, arrogance, and self-justifying defensiveness; liberation

---

25. Stanley, *The World Missionary Conference*, 125.

26. Ibid., 124.

27. Recently the story has come to light of how condescendingly Azariah was treated by Mrs Isa-
bel Whitehead, the wife of an Anglican bishop, with whom he travelled from India to Edinburgh,
and this may partly account for his speaking so frankly. It is also possible to use such a story to
reinforce the impression of the Edinburgh conference itself as embodying Western paternalism.
But not to be overlooked is that on his arrival in Britain Azariah was invited to the select pre-
conference retreat organised by Oldham and Mott for themselves and other leaders in Yorkshire,
and there it was no doubt there that he was asked and encouraged to make his presentation (see
Clements, *Faith on the Frontier*, 90, and Stanley, *The World Missionary Conference*, 123). No less
significantly, Azariah's remarks closely resemble Oldham's own comments on Western missionaries' superior attitudes, made while working for the YMCA in India 1897-1909 (see Clements,
Faith on the Frontier, 49-51).

to be their human selves alongside other brothers and sisters in the body of Christ. Edinburgh was just the starting point for this trajectory of ecumenical learning, as people began to realise that "the mysterious East" had its own reality and could take its own initiatives; that India had its hurts to be recognised and its need for love to be received and its desire to give love in return to be appreciated. This learning is still going on today. Edinburgh is significant because, more than it realised, it launched the churches on this trajectory which was to mean liberation for mission, in the west as much as elsewhere. It meant a process of liberation of the church, in the west above all, from collusion with the imperial syndrome.

Dynamic Relationships and Reconciliation

We certainly should not try to claim *too* much for Edinburgh. Some of its material from Edinburgh 1910 sounds embarrassingly innocent, not least in the discussion of the report of Commission VII, "The Relation of Missions to Governments," which spoke warmly of the "mutual helpfulness" of missions and colonial governments, or even—as one ex-Governor of Bombay put it—of missions as "auxiliaries" of government.[28] There was some discussion of the iniquitous responsibility of western countries for the opium trade in China and forced labour in Africa, but rather inconclusive. Much of what was said about race and culture did reflect the prevailing imperial, paternalistic assumptions of the time, bolstered by essentialist views of race and eugenics, and it would be anachronistic to pretend otherwise. It is not Edinburgh as such that is finally significant, but the trajectory on which it lies and whose future direction it indicates. Moreover, one of the most important early fruits of Edinburgh lay not in any organisational development, or any stated programme laid down in 1910, but in generous and courageous actions which embodied the spirit of Christian unity and readiness for reconciliation even during 1914-18. Many of the German Protestant missions in Africa and Asia suffered tremendously right from the start of the war, either because they were working in British territories and therefore were subject to internment and expulsion of their staff, and confiscation of their property; or were in territories invaded and occupied by British forces and therefore subject to a like fate. It was largely due to J.H. Oldham, working as secretary for the Edinburgh Continuation Committee and therefore seeing himself as *servant of the German missions as much as of the British or any other bodies*, who saved the day for the German work. First, through the Conference of British Missionary Societies he sought to create a fund to help bring relief to German missionaries. This had very limited success at a time when "German frightfulness" was shocking British public

28. See Gairdner, "*Edinburgh 1910*," 157.

opinion even in the churches. Next, he and colleagues sought to make arrangements for British, American and Scandinavian missions staff to carry on the work on behalf of their German partners—a move which was unfortunately seen in Germany as tantamount to annexation of the missions. Undeterred by German misunderstandings and accusations of betraying the transnational nature of Christian mission, in 1917 Oldham most decisively of all organised a delegation to the Colonial Office led by the archbishop of Canterbury, which resulted in blocking the confiscation of German mission property as part of any reparations policy, and secured the right of German missionaries to return and resume their work after the war. In 1919 Oldham even achieved the insertion in to the Versailles Treaty of a clause guaranteeing freedom of religion and missionary work in all colonial territories, which eventually enabled German missionary work to be resumed unhindered.[29] This was one of the finest hours in the ecumenical movement: at the very moment when all the nationalistic pressures were mounting to think of oneself as *only* British, Oldham was in imagination and spirit living also in Germany and viewing the *oikoumene* as still the place where British and Germans had a shared responsibility. It placed reconciliation at the heart of ecumenical life. When after the war, in 1921, the International Missionary Council (IMC) was formed with Oldham as secretary the full picture of what he had achieved emerged. The German missions were not only deeply grateful, they never forgot it and when in 1933 a new and sinister peril threatened them from within their own country it was to Oldham and the IMC that they turned for help.[30]

Towards a New Community: Dynamic and Holistic

The real legacy of Edinburgh is not any one institution, nor any one programme, nor any single activity which can simply be repeated as if it was still 1910. It is a movement, a trajectory aiming towards a new community. Like all trajectories, it is determined by not one but several forces in combination. There is the forward thrust of mission, the witness to God's coming reign and the call for people to hear that gospel and respond. Although the full cost of what *confessing* Christ might mean in the modern age may not yet have been realised in 1910, the missionary calling is what was most overt at Edinburgh. But there is also the gravitational pull of the need for visible unity of the churches without which the message of reconciliation is empty and disappears into the stratosphere. That clearly began to stir at Edinburgh, as we have seen. Then there are the less predictable currents of air, the winds pulling

29. For the whole story of Oldham and the German missions see Clements, *Faith on the Frontier* chapters 7 and 8; and W.R. Hogg, *Ecumenical Foundations: A History of the International Missionary Council and Its Nineteenth Century Background*, (New York: Harper 1952).
30. See below, chapter 6.

the churches sideways, whether they like it or not, into engagement with the critical social and political challenges of the day. These may not have been highlighted at Edinburgh itself but they very soon became part of the post-Edinburgh agenda and certainly from August 1914 onwards. World Mission and Evangelism; Faith and Order; Life and Work: start with any one of these vocations, and we quickly have to connect with the others as well. The ecumenical vocation is holistic, like the *oikoumene* itself. What we have to leave *out* of the whole is our desire to dominate, to control, to exercise power at others' expense, which is the greatest retarding force. We can be glad that from Edinburgh onwards there have been pioneers and faithful followers who have been prepared to be disempowered in worldly terms in order that all might be freed to grow together in a new community of witness and service, so that the world might believe. Bearing in mind these reflections, we can surely still make our own, yet also inject added meaning into, one of the most evocative statements submitted to the Edinburgh 1910 Conference:

Unity when it comes must be something richer, grander, more comprehensive than anything which we can see at present. It is something into which and up to which we must grow, something of which and for which we must become worthy. We need to have sufficient faith in God to believe that he can bring us to something higher and more Christlike than anything to which at present we can see a way.[31]

---

31. *Report of Commission VIII* (see n. 23 above), 138ff.

Chapter 6
Beginning All Over Again

Barmen 1934 and the Ecumenical Movement Questioned

There could be no greater contrast, in many ways, between the meeting that took place in Barmen, in the Ruhr district of Germany, at the end of May 1934, and the Edinburgh Missionary Conference of 24 years earlier. Edinburgh 1910 was an international gathering of missionary organisations and churches of many denominations and from many countries concerned for evangelising the whole world. The Free Synod of Barmen was a wholly German Protestant affair, and occupied itself only with the theological basis of the German Evangelical Church. Yet no less than Edinburgh 1910, Barmen 1934 was to prove of huge ecumenical interest and significance. Edinburgh 1910 focused attention on evangelising the whole world. Barmen 1934 called for the churches of the whole world to focus attention on what was happening in just one country, Germany, and therewith in turn to view afresh their own responsibility in their own contexts. The dynamic of living in more than one place became peculiarly intense—and worked in both directions between Germany and the wider world. If Edinburgh 1910 may be claimed to lie at the start of the modern ecumenical movement (let us for the moment not again argue in quite what respect), Barmen 1934 may equally claim to have faced the movement—as never before—with the question of its true identity and purpose.

The advent of Adolf Hitler to power at the end of January 1933 had ushered in the Nazi revolution with its attempt to exploit and control every aspect of German life for its ideological ends. That attempt embraced the churches, Protestant and Catholic. Protestantism in particular proved vulnerable to the blandishments of nationalism and the ideology of *Volk*, race, and nation under strong political leadership. The so-called "German Christians" (*Deutsche Christen*), effectively a Protestant wing of the National Socialist Party, made an outright bid to nazify the Protestant churches. They campaigned to impose on the church the "Aryan" laws which would ban pastors of Jewish descent holding office, and replace the biblically-based faith of the Reformation by a neo-pagan amalgam of belief in Germanic racial superiority and the cult of the *Führer* as the divinely appointed messiah and saviour of the German people. The fifteen months following Hitler's accession were therefore a turbulent time for the churches. Opposition to the "German Christians" and their state-appointed patron "Reich bishop" (*Reichsbischof*) Josef Müller, and the use of heavy-handed police tactics to intimidate and muzzle all protests (many pastors found themselves in prison), grew and crystallised into the Pastors' Emergency League led by Martin Niemöller, pastor of Dahlem in Berlin. It presently became clear, however, that the "Church Struggle" was not just about who should control the church, but about what the bedrock basis of belief of the church should be. Many Protestants—and not just the "German Christians"—were being swept along in the tide of excitement at what appeared so obviously to be a national revival with a strong religious element. Had not Hitler promised a place for "positive Christianity" in his vision of the new Germany?

To a number of theologically-minded pastors, strongly influenced by the Swiss Karl Barth, professor at Bonn University, it was evident that the German Evangelical Church—effectively an umbrella term for the various Lutheran, Reformed, and United regional (*Land*) churches taken together—needed to make a clear statement on what was, and what was not, to be regarded as Christian truth as distinct from political ideology and nationalistic fervour. The churches which had emerged from the Reformation had clear confessions of belief, based on interpretation of scripture, which defined the doctrinal basis of their life, worship, ministry and unity with each other. How did these now stand in the new context of the Nazi revolution? Were they being superseded by racial theories? Had revelation been replaced by ideology and the speeches of the *Führer*? Had a *status confessionis* now been reached, where a question about church polity was in fact a question of obedience or disobedience to the gospel itself? These questions eventually drew together 139 delegates as a "Free Synod" of the various churches at Barmen, close to Wuppertal in the Ruhr, from 29 to 31 May 1934. The synod culminated in agreement to a "Theological Declaration," its essential points set out by Karl Barth, which in effect became the charter of the Confessing Church, that is, that section of Protestantism which resisted the nazification of the church and indeed claimed that it alone was the true Evangelical Church of Germany.

The declaration, after noting the present turmoil and the divisive influence of the "German Christians," reaffirmed that the only creedal basis of the German Evangelical Church was the holy scriptures and the confessions which had interpreted the biblical faith at the Reformation. It then set out six theses, each comprising scriptural citations, a positive affirmation of belief reflecting those texts, and then a statement of what equally had to be rejected as false belief and practice. The first thesis runs:

"I am the way, and the truth, and the life; no one comes to the Father but by me" (John 14:6); "Truly, truly, I say to you, he who does not enter the sheepfold by the door, but climbs in by another way, that man is a thief and a robber... I am the door; if anyone enters by me, he will be saved" (John 10:1, 9).

Jesus Christ, as he is attested for us in Holy Scripture, is the one Word of God which we have to hear and which we have to trust and obey in life and in death. We reject the false doctrine, as though the church could and would have to acknowledge as a source of its proclamation, apart from and besides this one Word of God, still other events and powers, figures and truths, as God's revelation.[1]

The following five theses deal equally succinctly with: the claim of God in Christ over the whole of life; the church as the community of forgiven sinners under the sole lordship of Christ; the pastoral ministry as one of service, not domination; denial of the claim of the state to be the sole and totalitarian order of life; refusal to let the Word of God's free grace to all be put at the service of arbitrarily chosen desires, purposes and plans. Whatever else may be said about the Barmen Declaration (and much was, and still is), here was a remarkably clear and courageous voice amid the nationalist and pseudo-religious clamour in which altars were being draped with the swastika and children baptized into the three-fold name of nation, race, and *Führer*.

An Ecumenical Event

The Free Synod of Barmen and its Theological Declaration, though focused on the German church situation, constituted from the beginning an ecumenical event. This was even the case on the German level, bringing together as it did so many from the regional and confessional diversity of the German Evangelical Church (and not without severe misgivings on the part of some Lutherans who felt they were being enticed into a Reformed plot by Karl Barth). But this intra-German and intra-Protestant ecumenism manifest at Barmen immediately exploded onto the wider ecumenical scene. Indeed, the events leading up to Barmen for the past year and more had already been sending sparks of excitement around the Christian world, first of all at popular and public levels. Still today, to read the contemporary accounts of what was happening, in for example the London *Times,* has almost cinematographic effect, witnessing to the extraordinary excitement aroused in both church and public opinion on the international level. So, on Monday 4 June 1934 under the headline THE BARMEN SYNOD we read:

---

1. This citation is drawn from the English translation by A.C. Cochrane in his *The Church's Confession Under Hitler* (Philadelphia: Westminster, 1962), 237-242. The full text may also be found in F. Schlingensiepen, *Dietrich Bonhoeffer 1906-1945* (London: T & T Clark, 2010), 407-411.

The first session of the Free Reich ("Confessional[2] Synod of the German Evangelical Church") Synod ended at Barmen on Friday and there is no doubt that the gathering gave evidence of a new psychological, as well as practical, phase in the development of the so-called Oppositional movement.

The furtive atmosphere which prevailed before the revival at Ulm in April has given way to a cheerful indifference to such possibility of persecution as may remain. The leaders seem conscious that the movement has got into a swinging stride behind them.

After some further account of the procedure at the synod, there appeared the theological declaration itself—a summary of the preamble and then the famous six theses in full. There is no doubt that such a rapid translation and transmission of the declaration outside Germany had an electrifying effect and made Barmen synonymous with a decisive "no" to the totalitarian claims of the Nazi regime, even though, as the *Times* report made clear, at the synod there was no expression of political opposition to the regime as such. If this and other reports were not enough, throughout the period of the Church Struggle there were also the letters from Bishop George Bell[3] and others commenting critically upon developments. And what happened in the secular press was of course echoed in much of the church press throughout the English-speaking world and beyond. What is more, it soon became clear that such reportage and comment was not just *about* the Church Struggle but was a vital part of the conflict itself, as the Nazi state and the "Reich church"[4] authorities sought to counter not just pro-Confessing Church views but any mention of church turmoil, as such, as malicious propaganda. Therefore even on this immediate popular level, Barmen became a phenomenon in much of the *oikoumene*.

The View from Outside: A Matter of Freedom?

To speak of Barmen and the ecumenical movement is, however, to invite complexity to the table. The "ecumenical movement" at that time, as at other times, comprised no single affair but several distinct if related currents within the overall stream, and they did not all react to Barmen in the same way. Today we would perhaps call the

2. I retain "Confessional" as the title of *Bekennende* Church or Synod when used in English citations from the time, and the more accurate and generally used later rendering "Confessing" in my own usage.
3. On Bell, see below, Chapter 7.
4. The "Reich church" under "Reich bishop" Müller was the state-approved body that attempted to unite all the Protestant churches and was heavily influenced by the "German Christians." On the basis of Barmen, the Confessing Church claimed that it alone, not the Reich church, was the "Evangelical Church of Germany."

wider impact of Barmen its "reception process." It is important to note, however, that a process of ecumenical *receptivity* was already well under way before the Free Synod met and arguably this significantly encouraged what happened there. Ever since the Church Struggle opened in the spring of 1933, churches, ecumenical bodies, and public opinion in many parts of the *oikoumene* had taken intense interest in what was happening in Germany, and this interest was overwhelmingly sympathetic to the various manifestations of the "church opposition." Moreover, it found notable public expression just days before the Barmen Synod, when on Ascension Day 1934, Bishop George Bell, as president of the Universal Christian Council of Life and Work, issued a special message to members of Life and Work regarding the German Evangelical Church. This received wide international publicity (published in the *Times* 12 May 1934). It voiced alarm at the autocratic methods being foisted on church government, the measures taken against oppositional pastors and "the introduction of racial distinctions in the universal fellowship of the Christian Church," and drew attention to other problems "which are the concern of the whole of Christendom"— regarding the nature of the church, its witness, freedom and relation to the secular power. A major factor in prompting Bell to issue this statement was the increasingly desperate appeal being made from within Germany by a number of pastors for a word of solidarity from the ecumenical fellowship, an appeal cogently conveyed to Bell by Dietrich Bonhoeffer, who by then had been in London for six months as pastor of two German congregations there. Bonhoeffer personally thanked Bell for his letter "which has made a very great impression on me and all my friends here who have read it ... I am absolutely sure that this letter of yours will have the greatest effect in Germany and will indebt the opposition very much to you" and "which is a living document of ecumenic and mutual responsibility."[5] Those who met at Barmen knew the ecumenical world was watching, listening and praying with them—and waiting for the decisive word.

In qualification of what has been stated thus far, it has to be said that churches outside Germany, in all their sympathy with the German church opposition, were more excited by the *fact* of the Barmen Declaration than its actual content in detail. The basic issue was clear enough: the Christian church had to declare its allegiance and its identity in terms of the gospel and not the dictates of the state or nationalistic impulses. This was very evident barely a week after Barmen, and only three days after the publication of the declaration in English, when on 7 June 1934 the house of bishops in the Convocation of the Church of England took the unusual step of debating and passing a resolution on a "foreign" event, declaring that there could be

---

5. Dietrich Bonhoeffer, *Dietrich Bonhoeffer Works*, vol. 13, *London 1933-35* (Minneapolis: Fortress, 2007), 147ff. The full text of Bell's message is in ibid., 144-146.

"no compromise on the principle that the primary spiritual allegiance of a Christian is to Christ and not to the State, and that no earthly leader can be a new Messiah." It was moved by the archbishop of Canterbury, Cosmo Gordon Lang, and its major advocate was naturally George Bell, who "insisted that the issue was one which could not possibly regarded as relating exclusively to Germany but the actual substance of the Christian faith."[6]

But outsiders are naturally prone to view situations abroad through the lenses of their own interests and concerns, and reactions to the German drama, especially in the English-speaking world, tended to focus on the threat to "freedom of conscience" posed by the state and the brutal methods of the nazified church leadership, rather than the positive witness of confessing the faith. Even Bell, in preparing his Ascension Day message, had needed some warning and correction from Bonhoeffer in this regard.[7] Generally in the English-speaking world the German Church Struggle was persistently seen as one about "religious liberty" or "freedom of conscience" and Barmen as a stand for such freedoms. During the Baptist World Alliance Congress, which ten weeks after Barmen actually took place in Berlin in August 1934, M.E. Aubrey, general secretary of the British Baptist Union, stated: "We stand for liberty of conscience in all matters of faith, liberty to speak, and worship as the Spirit of God directs us, and we stand for a free, unfettered Church ... We stand by the noble declaration of the Synod of Barmen which ended on June 1."[8] Such sentiments were typical, and not only among the Free Churches for which, due to deeply embedded historical factors, "religious freedom" was the supreme touchstone by which all priorities of the churches in the public sphere had to be assessed. Karl Barth inveighed heavily against what he saw as the typically Anglo-Saxon misjudgement about the significance of Barmen, as when visiting Britain in 1937 he declared the fight being "not about the freedom, but about the necessary bondage, of the conscience; and not about the freedom, but the substance, of the Church" and continued:

> Dear brothers and friends in the Church of Great Britain and of all other countries, the only real help, apart from your prayers, which you can render the German Church, would consist in this: in your declaring with as much publicity and solemnity as was done in Barmen itself that in your conviction also, a conviction arising from Holy Scripture, this statement with its positive and negative content

---

6. See *The Times* of London, 8 June 1934, and R.C. D. Jasper, *George Bell. Bishop of Chichester* (London: Oxford University Press, 1967), 113.
7. See below, Chapter 7.
8. See K. Clements, *What Freedom? The Persistent Challenge of Dietrich Bonhoeffer* (Bristol: Bristol Baptist College, 1990), 84.

is the right and necessary expression of the Christian faith for our day and therefore also your confession of faith.[9]

Barth referred to how the reforming churches of the 16th century helped each other by reciprocally recognising their confessions, and in a like way the churches abroad should today make known to the Confessing Church that they are one with it—not in political disapprobation of Hitler or in concern about "freedom" but rather "in the theological presuppositions of the conflict it is waging." Barth's challenge does not seem to have been significantly taken up by any of the churches abroad and one can only speculate on what might have happened if it had. (How, for example, would Anglicanism with its triple love of revelation, reason, and tradition, have espoused the first thesis of Barmen?) Dietrich Bonhoeffer, for his part, was similarly to complain that as the Church Struggle wore on, the ecumenical interest abroad always flared up in response to dramatic police activity against the church, but tended to flag during the ongoing, more mundane campaign for the confession itself. Nevertheless, such sympathy and solidarity as was shown by churches outside Germany, and their admiration for Barmen—however partial their understanding of it—as a symbol of opposition to the totalitarian regime, did matter to the Confessing Church. If there was at some points a misunderstanding from the outside world, at least it was a creative one.

A Diversity of Ecumenical Responses

As far as the main ecumenical organisations of the time are concerned, their perspectives on the Barmen Synod and its declaration reflected their particular self-understandings, interests and relations with the German scene, and the impact of Barmen varied accordingly. We may look briefly at the International Missionary Council (IMC); the Universal Christian Council for Life and Work (together with the closely associated World Alliance for Promoting International Friendship through the Churches); the Faith and Order movement; and the World Student Christian Federation.

The IMC, child of the Continuation Committee of the 1910 Edinburgh World Missionary Conference, and its agenda still largely that of the work of European and North American missionary societies in Africa, Asia, and Latin America, might have been expected to afford little attention to an intra-national church dispute in Europe. But the case was far otherwise. For one thing, the Nazi revolution had immediate and savage consequences for the German Protestant missions, and on two levels.

---

9. *The British Weekly*, 22 April 1937.

First, in parallel with the attempts to impose *Gleichshaltung* (coordination) on the churches themselves, there was an attempt inspired by the so-called German Christians to force all the mission bodies into one organisation under central control. Second, the regime's severe restrictions on the export of Reichsmarks meant that virtually overnight German work on the mission fields faced destitution and closure. Both these issues landed on the London desk of the IMC secretary, the British ecumenical pioneer J.H. Oldham and his assistant William (Bill) Paton, as the German mission leaders appealed for solidarity and help—and within their means the IMC leadership did respond.[10] This in itself impelled the IMC leaders to an innate sympathy with the church opposition in Germany. In its survey of developments in the "sending countries" for 1934, the year of Barmen, the IMC journal could report on the difficulties being faced by the German missions, but that they were allied with the Confessing Synod and the "German Christian movement" was "disintegrating."[11] Similarly, the following year it was reported that the growth of "neo-paganism" in Germany was being met by the uncompromising attitude of the Confessional Synod to "this new menace to Christ."[12] It is, admittedly, of some surprise that the IMC does not appear to have convened or published any reflections on the Barmen Declaration as such, given the central concern of the IMC at that time for a renewed contemporary understanding of the Christian message.[13] What is difficult to assess, however, is the extent to which a knowledge of the contents and significance of the Declaration may be *assumed* to have been part of the consciousness of those speaking and writing at the time. Even Hans Ehrenberg, philosopher and Confessing Church pastor and for a time imprisoned in concentration camp, as a refugee in London in 1941 could write a cogent article for the IMC on "The Nazi Religion and the Christian Man"[14] without a word about Barmen—yet it is hard to imagine its absence from his mind. Perhaps there is no more telling clue as to the pervasive effect of Barmen than the way in which J.H. Oldham himself—admittedly already becoming attuned to the theological notes being sounded by Karl Barth—could speak at an international student gathering in 1935 on "The Christian World Community," and with unmistakable echoes of the first Barmen thesis could ask what more momentous question

---

10. See Clements, *Faith on the Frontier*, 290-296.

11. *International Review of Missions [IRM]* 24 (1935): 101.

12. *IRM* 25 (1936): 91.

13. It would for example have been very apposite, in view of Samuel Azariah's forthright protest at the Edinburgh Missionary Conference in 1910 against Western missionary attitudes of superiority to Asians (see above, chapter 5), to have had an IMC comment on the third Barmen thesis which on the basis of Matthew 20:25ff points to service as the motif of office in the church and rejects "a dominion of some over the others."

14. *IRM* 30 (1941): 363-373.

there can be for a person than "whether there is a living Word which he may hear, which he may trust, which he can and must obey?"[15]

The respective responses of Life and Work and Faith and Order to Barmen and to the Church Struggle as a whole make for one of the most controversial chapters in the ecumenical story,[16] and still pose pertinent questions for today. The Universal Christian Council for Life and Work, set up in 1930 out of the continuation committee of the 1925 Stockholm Conference, according to its constitution had as its principal aim "to perpetuate and strengthen the fellowship between the churches in the application of Christian ethics to the social problems of modern life."[17] Faith and Order, emanating from the Lausanne conference of 1927, understood itself as primarily "to draw churches out of isolation into *conference*" on the major doctrinal issues in order to discuss obstacles to reunion and create better mutual understanding. Put over simply perhaps, Life and Work concerned itself with the responsibility of churches in the socio-political field, and Faith and Order with fundamental doctrines of the churches and the basis of the unity they sought. There is, therefore, immediate irony in that while what was produced at Barmen was a *Theological* Declaration, and that while Barth and other framers of the declaration stressed its "theological" nature in order to distinguish it from any political or socio-ethical statement, it was not Faith and Order but Life and Work which engaged most closely with it and with the ensuing career of the Confessing Church. Certain of the reasons for this are quite clear. Given its agenda of ethical concern, Life and Work could not help already being seriously exercised by the overall German situation since the Nazi revolution of January 1933, as seen by the resolutions on the persecution of Jewish and other minorities passed by the executive committee of Life and Work at its meeting in Novi Sad in September 1933 (and the still more outspoken statements made by the World Alliance in Sofia a few days later). As the Church Struggle unfolded during the winter of 1933-34, the harassment and persecution of the church opposition could hardly be ignored. Sympathy with the Pastors' Emergency League was a natural concomitant, culminating, as we have seen, in the solidarity expressed in Bell's Ascension Day Message to the Life and Work membership just days before Barmen.

Then, barely three months after Barmen, came the scheduled biennial meeting of the council of Life and Work on the Danish island of Fanø, 22-28 August 1934, in conjunction with the management committee of the World Alliance and concurrently with a youth conference sponsored jointly by Life and Work and the World

---

15. See Clements, *Faith on the Frontier*, 290.
16. The "official" accounts, e.g. in R. Rouse and S. Neill, eds., *A History of the Ecumenical Movement 1517-1948* (London: SPCK, 1967), do not bring the tensions into relief.
17. Ibid., 553.

Alliance. Fanø was the first major international ecumenical gathering since Barmen and it was obvious that the German situation was going to dominate the agenda, bound up as this was with the final decisions to set the theme of the 1937 Oxford conference "Church, Community and State." The tensions and dramas of those six days are well documented.[18] They included Dietrich Bonhoeffer's call for a universal church council to declare against war. But as far as the immediate future of the ecumenical movement went, the crucial step was taken by Life and Work to identify with the Confessing Church as its German Protestant partner. A resolution was passed confirming Bell's Ascension Day message and condemning the autocratic methods of government and the attempts to ban free discussion in the church. This was a blunt "no" both to the "German Christians" and to the Reich church as led by bishop Ludwig Müller—and as represented at Fanø by bishop Theodor Heckel, director of the church foreign office, who had made strenuous but counter-productive appeals to the gathering to mind its own business as far as German church affairs were concerned. The resolution declared unequivocally: "The Council desires to assure its brethren in the Confessional Synod of the German Evangelical Church of its prayers and heartfelt sympathy in their witness to the principles of the Gospel and of its resolve to maintain close fellowship with them."[19] Bell, in his Ascension Day message, had been able to refer only in an undefined way to pastors suffering for loyalty to the gospel. Now, a quite specific identification had been made: the Confessing Synod. Without Barmen, and by unmistakable implication its Theological Declaration, the ecumenical movement as represented by Life and Work would have had no clear marker for relating to the German scene. Not that Fanø was a complete victory for the Confessing cause, for Heckel managed to get inserted into the final resolution an additional clause stating that the Council wished "to remain in friendly contact with all groups in the German Evangelical Church." This sounded innocent enough at the time, but it was to have troublesome consequences.

Faith and Order, on the other hand, never saw itself as called to "take sides" in the German Church Struggle, and regarded Barmen merely as representing one "party" within the German church. Certain human elements came in here: it did not help, for example, that the chair of Faith and Order's theological committee was A.C. Headlam, Anglican bishop of Gloucester, who for years was strongly sympathetic to the Nazi regime and contemptuous of the church opposition. The same could not be said of the secretary of Faith and Order, Leonard Hodgson, another Anglican and one of the ablest English theologians of the day. Hodgson was no friend of

---

18. See especially K. Scholder, *The Churches and the Third Reich*, vol. 2 (London: SCM, 1988).
19. Minutes of the Fanø Conference cited in Eberhard Bethge, *Dietrich Bonhoeffer*, rev. ed. (Minneapolis: Fortress Press, 2000), 383; cf. Rouse and Neill, op. cit.,583

Nazism, but saw Faith and Order as essentially a conference round-table at which all sincere Christian convictions could sit in mutual converse. As far as Germany went, this would mean both the Confessing Synod and the "Reich church"—and whoever else "accepts Jesus Christ as God and Saviour." Just how far this could be from the self-understanding of the Barmen Synod and its adherents was seen in the correspondence in 1935 between Hodgson and Dietrich Bonhoeffer. Bonhoeffer, by now director of the Confessing Church's illegal seminary at Finkenwalde, had been invited by Hodgson to attend a forthcoming meeting of the Faith and Order continuation committee in Denmark. On learning that Bishop Heckel would also be attending, Bonhoeffer protested. The eminently fair-minded Hodgson explained the wish of Faith and Order to be guided "by all sections of Christian thought" and that Germany "should not be represented exclusively by the Reichskirche." Bonhoeffer was incensed, in his reply declaring that the Reich church did *not* "accept the Lord Jesus Christ as God and Saviour" but subjected itself to worldly masters and powers and the Antichrist. In the light of Barmen, the Reich church government could no longer claim to represent the Church of Christ in Germany or any part of it. This was too much for Hodgson or the leadership of Faith and Order as a whole to cope with, and the matter was dropped.[20]

The Ecumenical Movement Exposed

Barmen, clearly, had exposed very different self-understandings of the ecumenical movement as well as differing perceptions of what was happening in Germany. No-one saw this more sharply than Dietrich Bonhoeffer in his 1935 essay "The Confessing Church and the Ecumenical Movement," which can be read as a follow-up to his exchanges with Hodgson:

> The Confessing Church represents a genuine question for the ecumenical movement insofar as it confronts the latter in all its totality with the question of the confession. ... It is fundamentally impossible to enter into conversation with this church at any point without immediately raising the question of the confession... Here the Confessing Church seals herself off hermetically against political, social or humanitarian inroads. The confession occupies her whole sphere.

---

20. See the Hodgson-Bonhoeffer correspondence in Dietrich Bonhoeffer, *Gesammelte Shriften* vol. 2 (Munich: Kaiser Verlag, 1965). This correspondence will also appear in the forthcoming vol. 14 of the *Dietrich Bonhoeffer Works* English series (Minneapolis: Fortress).

To this confession as it has been *authoritatively* expounded in the decisions if of the Synods of Barmen and Dahlem, there is only a Yes or a No. Thus here too neutrality is impossible.[21]

If Barth's wish that the churches at large should affirm the Barmen Declaration as their own confession was not fulfilled, so also was Bonhoeffer disappointed that the ecumenical bodies did not as a whole relate exclusively to the Confessing Church as the sole legitimate expression of the German Evangelical Church and refuse all contacts with the Reich church. Faith and Order, as we have seen, felt that this would contradict its own purpose and methodology as a "conference." Even Life and Work felt it had to compromise here, despite the undoubted recognition by such as George Bell, J.H. Oldham, and Marc Boegner that the Confessing Church's claim was right and just. That last-minute clause about "friendly contacts" inserted into the Fanø resolution allowed Theodor Heckel and the Reich church to keep a foot inside the door at the Life and Work meetings up till 1936 (aided, it has to be said, by the "open-minded" attitude of the Research Department in Geneva led by the German Lutheran pastor and economist Hans Schönfeld). But at least Bonhoeffer and the Confessing Church leaders knew that Bell and his colleagues were doing their best to support the Confessing Church within their legal constraints, whereas Faith and Order was doing its best to keep its distance by appeal to its constitution. Due to travel restrictions imposed by the German authorities in 1937, there was no effective German representation at either the Oxford Life and Work conference (July) nor the Edinburgh Faith and Order conference (August), at each of which crucial steps were taken towards forming the World Council of Churches. Therefore at neither event could the implications of Barmen, or the German Church Struggle generally, for the ecumenical movement and its future be discussed in any depth. But at least Oxford delivered a substantial message of concern on the German situation and explicitly affirmed: "We are greatly moved by the afflictions of many pastors and laymen who have stood firm from the first in the Confessional Church for the sovereignty of Christ, and for the freedom of the Church of Christ to preach His Gospel."[22] The brief message to Germany from Edinburgh which got as far as saying "we are one in heart with all suffering Christians in your land" was diffuse to the point of vacuity.[23]

---

21. "The Confessing Church and the Ecumenical Movement," in Dietrich Bonhoeffer, *No Rusty Swords: Lectures and Notes 1935-39* (London: Collins, 1965), 329. A new English translation will appear in the forthcoming vol. 14 of the Dietrich Bonhoeffer Works series (Minneapolis: Fortress).
22. *The Churches Survey Their Task: Report of the Conference at Oxford, July 1937, on Church, Community and State* (London: George Allen & Unwin, 1937), 275.
23. L. Hodgson, ed., *The Second World Conference on Faith and Order, Edinburgh, August 3-18, 1937* (London: SCM, 1938), 39.

Receiving the Legacy: Recipe for Disturbance

To summarise the story told thus far, in the years immediately following Barmen, even by those in the ecumenical movement who identified with the Confessing Church, relatively little attention was paid to the specific *contents* of the theological declaration, and much more attention to what the Confessing Church was suffering than to what it was actually *confessing*. In more recent ecumenical history however, there has been no lack of interest in "confession." It has especially become an emphasis to describe Christian witness in the socio-ethical sphere. From nuclear warfare to apartheid to the global market economy, the issues have been examined as to whether they constitute a *status confessionis*. This renewed attention to what *confession* means is the long-term ecumenical legacy of Barmen. But how did it come about that this legacy with its essentially theological concerns was transmitted to the ecumenical world following the second world war, given that Faith and Order had been so nervous or bemused about "taking sides" in the German Church Struggle, while even Life and Work was not always clear as to just why it identified with the Confessing Church, nor had it studied especially closely the Barmen theological declaration?

In answering this question, another vital player in the 1930s ecumenical scene should not be overlooked: the World Student Christian Federation (WSCF). Among the ecumenical bodies, none was more definite on where its sympathies lay in Germany, not least because so many (though not all) of its present and former German leaders (such as Hans Lilje, general secretary of the German SCM 1924-34) identified with the Confessing Church. Throughout the 1930s, W.A. Visser't Hooft, secretary of the WSCF and close theological ally of Karl Barth, was able to report at first hand on his visits to Germany in the journal *Student World* and in 1935 wrote: "The German Church stands at the cross-roads, one road leading to new life, the other one leading to death" and commented that like St Paul that church was learning that to suffer for Christ's sake was a gift. But crucially and prophetically, he continued, "Whether it will prove to be worthy of that gift is a matter which concerns the whole of ecumenical Christendom"[24]—a remark that Bonhoeffer himself could have made. It was in fact in the WSCF, which published articles including by such as Karl Barth and Paul Maury as well as by Visser 't Hooft himself, that the most intensive studies of the theological issues of the German Church Struggle and their implications for ecumenism took place, not to mention also the *Evangelische Wochen* conferences organised by the SCM in Germany, which gave much-needed platforms for the Confessing leaders like Martin Niemöller to encourage their communities.[25] If a long-term route is to be traced from

24. L. Hodgson, ed., *The Second World Conference on Faith and Order, Edinburgh, August 3-18, 1937* (London: SCM, 1938), 39.
25. See W.A. Visser 't Hooft, *Memoirs* (Geneva: WCC Publications, 1973), chapter 13, "The Church Struggle in Germany."

Barmen to the ecumenical movement as it developed through the WCC after the second world war, much of it will lie through the WSCF circles and the ecumenical leadership that emerged from it as exemplified by Visser 't Hooft himself (he became general secretary of the WCC-in-formation in 1938) and others such as Hans Lilje.

Much debate has surrounded Barmen and the question whether for all its protest against the nazification of the church it was too silent about the Nazi state itself. Even in its statements about the church, nothing is said about the exclusion of Jewish pastors under "Aryanisation."[26] At the time, Barth and others were relieved that at least a clear *theological* word had been spoken, marking where the church must stand in sharp contradiction to the surrounding political and cultural—and indeed "religious"—pressures and from where a political witness *could* be mounted. Nor can there be any doubt that Barmen, as a free voice in the context of a totalitarian state, was nothing if not a challenge to that totalitarianism. That is what alarmed the regime and excited and inspired observers all over the world. Did Barmen, however, alarm as well as excite the ecumenical family as Barth and Bonhoeffer hoped it would? For what Barmen did was to shake and uproot German Protestantism out of its assumed identification with its national cultural home by challenging it to recover its true identity, its true *belonging* as church in belonging to Christ, not first to the nation. In the first Barmen thesis, there is in fact almost a word-play in the German original, for to say that Jesus Christ is the one Word of God whom we are to "hear" (*hören*) is very close to saying "to whom we 'belong' (*gehören*)." But such a challenge to the church in Germany was a challenge to churches everywhere on where they stood and to whom they really belonged. That remains the fundamental question as put to the ecumenical movement itself by Bonhoeffer. It is not enough for churches to "be together" unless they ask on what basis they are together. Is it just on the basis of generalised goodwill? Or is it actually on the confessing of Christ as Lord above all other, and being with Christ where *he* is in the world today. That at times means taking sides rather than seeking the comfort of total inclusivity. By the same token, it is attachment to Christ the suffering Lord which liberates us to live in more than one place at once and to see the world through the eyes of those with whom *he* identifies. Those who, post-Barmen, took the step of identifying with Christ and, in his footsteps, with the plight of the Jews and other victims of the regime, found themselves opened up to other situations also. There is no more eloquent testimony to this than that of Otto Dudzus, one of Bonhoeffer's students in his illegal seminary at Finkenwalde, who tells of how surprising and strange it was for the ordinands to

---

26. Nine months before Barmen, in August 1933, several theologians including Dietrich Bonhoeffer had drafted the "Bethel Confession," which included specific references to the Jews. This, however, was watered down by senior church figures and was never formally presented.

hear Bonhoeffer's gramophone records of the spirituals he had brought back from the black ghetto in Harlem, and then of the gradual realisation that there, too, was a community under oppression and calling for solidarity.[27]

Barmen thus bequeaths an ecumenical legacy and example. Of course, as with all legacies there arises the possibility of misuse. In calling for a "confessing" stance on a particular issue, are we doing any more than saying "This is a *very* serious issue on which the church's voice must be heard"? What is really to be gained, other than rhetorical effect, by using the language of "confessing"? Or might it even be, as one recent careful examiner of the whole issue of "confessing" puts it, "self-dramatizing paranoia"?[28] Notwithstanding its ambiguities and unclarities, what Barmen—both the synod and the theological declaration—stood for were the supremacy of God's word in Christ and the universal embrace of the gospel without qualification, over against the divisive powers and claims of this world. Wherever it is these which are at stake, and where a quite specific and concrete measure is required by the church in its own life and ordering, and where this consequently asks for a decision from the whole ecumenical family, the echoes of Barmen are truly heard and the ecumenical movement can expect to be both disturbed and renewed. In measured retrospect, one could wish that the Barmen declaration itself could have been examined and discussed more thoroughly in ecumenical circles at the time. The ecumenical family might thereby have been more severely and healthily challenged. Equally, for all that it was a "misunderstanding," the concern by many ecumenical friends for the issues of "religious freedom" might in turn have prompted the Confessing movement to see that notwithstanding its insistence that Barmen was a purely "theological" statement, it was at least implicitly political and, whether acknowledged or not, in taking its stand the "Free Synod" was also taking a stand for aspects of the whole *humanum* as well as for the Evangelical Church of Germany. Therewith, Dietrich Bonhoeffer's complaint written from prison in 1944, that the Confessing Church had largely lapsed into a defence of its own cause rather than "existing for others" might have been mitigated. All this, however, is a way of saying that for its own good the ecumenical movement needs continually to attempt to re-live how it would have faced up to the challenges presented by Barmen, and how much has really been learned and applied since then in its own life in order to recover its challenging and invigorating dynamic.

---

27. In documentary film *Bonhoeffer,* Journey Films, Alexandria, VA, USA. See www.journey-films.com.

28. R.W. Bertram, *A Time for Confessing* (Grand Rapids: Eerdmans, 2008), 3. This posthumously published work offers many important insights both into Barmen and subsequent situations of "confessing."

Chapter 7

Apostle for Unity

Why George Bell Is Important

Christ is the King! O friends rejoice;
brothers and sisters, with one voice
make each one know he is your choice.
Alleluia![1]

It is probably in the singing of this great hymn that people of the present generation will feel most directly connected with George Bell (1883–1958), and it is an especially precious link for the increasing numbers of us who have no personal memory of him. In addition, those who attend meetings in the Ecumenical Centre in Geneva may well find themselves sitting in the "George Bell Room" named in his honour. One can also take a short walk from there to the archive of the World Council of Churches and quickly lose all sense of time amid the files of Bell's correspondence with the ecumenical leaders and organisations during the 1930s. There are the typewritten letters, some long, some short, always carefully and diplomatically phrased and, even when addressing protests to the Nazi-dominated church authorities in Germany, courteous to a fault. But there are also a number of postcards—and perhaps the essence of a person is often conveyed in what they scribble on a card at least as much by what they write at length in a letter. One card is from the end of June 1933, five months into the Nazi era, written to Henry-Louis Henriod, who was one of the early ecumenical officials in Geneva. It is written from Lambeth Palace, where Bell had been to see Archbishop Lang and (with or without permission) he has used the archbishop's stationery. Marked "Private," the card has obviously been penned in a great hurry, in barely decipherable scrawl diagonally across the card, with many abbreviations:

---

1. G. K. A. Bell. First verse of hymn in version in *Baptist Praise and Worship* (Oxford University Press 1991).

My dear Henriod.

Siegmund-Schultze's[2] private secretary has been in London, gone to Holland today and is in touch with German churchmen. Things are very bad.

She is going to inquire whether a protest wd be a help <u>now</u>: and I tell you privately that the Archbishop of Canterbury is disposed (if she reports that it might help) to sign a protest to Hitler, with the other British church leaders, on the lines of the enclosed.

I am thinking how and whether something similar might be said by Life and Work and the World Alliance jointly; and am writing to Cadman and Germanos... Will you give me your views?

Yours ever,

George Cicster

Will you be in England for July at all? Very anxious to see you, if so.

I will refer back to that card later, but actually to hold that urgent little missive in one's hand is to feel some of the tension of those days and to sense the personal commitment to action of the writer

"An *Apostle* for Unity": an apt title. George Bell was far from being the only British ecumenical mover and shaker of his time, but to call him an apostle does capture something distinctive about him. J.H. (Joe) Oldham is often described as the ecumenical *architect* who crafted so much of the new institutions that emerged in mid-century especially the World Council of Churches. Archbishop William Temple was the *engineer* who by his magisterial presence and diplomatic skills got those new structures into being and accepted by the churches. But for George Bell the quest for unity was a divine calling and *mission*, imbuing him with a truly evangelistic zeal for the cause, caught up a by a vision whose fulfilment was far more important than anything that might happen to himself. To quote Bell's hymn again, it meant recapturing the spirit of "Christ's brave saints of ancient days,"

Who with a faith for ever new
followed the King, and round him drew
thousands of faithful servants true.

It is a mighty challenge to try to do justice to George Bell as an apostle for unity in a short space. I will first sketch *what* he did in the cause of Christian unity; second, because it is at least as important, highlight the *why and how* of his ecumenical work;

---

2. On Siegmund-Schultze, see above, chapter4, and below in this chapter.

then, in conclusion, suggest why he remains significant for us and the ecumenical situation today. This is not to suggest that Bell is beyond criticism or was without limitations in his perception on matters ecclesiastical or political, as is recognized by a number of recent historians and commentators.[3] Notwithstanding these he exemplifies as few others of his or later generations have done what it means to live in another place than his home. He, the epitome of Englishness who officially resided nearly all his working life in the confines of Lambeth Palace and the cathedral precincts of Canterbury and then Chichester, nevertheless inhabited and identified with very different worlds of suffering and conflict beyond British shores, and in order to fulfil the law of Christ (Gal. 6:2) took on the burdens of churches other than his own.

Bell and Unity: What He Did

Saint Paul asserted to the Galatians (Gal. 1:1) that his apostleship was by no human commission or from human authorities. George Bell, likewise, began his apostolic work for unity well before he had any official ecclesiastical position in that regard. From 1914 he was chaplain to Archbishop Randall Davidson and served as assistant secretary to the Lambeth Conference of 1920. That relatively junior role, however, he used to the full in servicing the small group of bishops who drafted the Lambeth "Appeal for Reunion to All Christian People." In fact, the drafting was largely Bell's work. The appeal, with its invitation to all Christians and denominations to consider the conditions they would regard as essential to reunion, was an ecumenical landmark. Bell himself was deeply involved in the follow-up work on the British scene, being the Anglican secretary of the committee of Anglican and Free Church representatives that produced an eventual joint report.

Even before this, however, Bell had shown himself concerned with the wider possibilities beyond his own communion, in society at large and beyond his own British shores. In particular, in 1919 Bell was sent by Archbishop Davidson to the first postwar meeting of the World Alliance for Promoting International Friendship through the Churches in Oud Wassenaar, Holland.[4] This first taste of ecumenical reconciliation and peace-building proved decisive for Bell in a number of ways, not least because there he met for the first time Nathan Söderblom, archbishop of Uppsala (Sweden) and the continental pioneer of ecumenism on the grand scale. It must be remembered that at this time ecumenical life was a still a very young and frail plant. Apart from the youth and student movements out of which it had emerged in the late 19th century, there had been nothing permanent at the international level until

---

3. See for example the essays in A. Chandler, ed., *The Church and Humanity: The Life and Work of George Bell, 1883-1958* (Farnham: Ashgate 2012).
4. See above, Chapter 4.

the Edinburgh Missionary Conference of 1910, which had formed a continuation committee, and the World Alliance, which had been constituted with tragic irony only on the very eve of war in 1914. Not only so, but much of this early growth had been all but blasted away by the war and there was much mutual suspicion, and indeed bitterness, between both peoples and churches of the belligerent nations. It was Söderblom who led the churches, on the widest possible scale, to find each other again that they might grow into a fellowship, a fellowship of serving the world in its social and international brokenness. Accordingly, under his leadership the first Life and Work conference met at Stockholm in 1925. George Bell, by now dean of Canterbury, was on the Anglican delegation and not only played a full part on one of the conference committees and in drafting the conference message but, crucially, persuaded the conference to set up, as had Edinburgh 1910 in the sphere of missions, a permanent organ for cooperation by the churches. What followed was a continuation committee, with Bell as a member, and therefrom the "Universal Christian Council for Life and Work" with its principal aim "to perpetuate and strengthen the fellowship between the churches in the application of Christian ethics to the social problems of modern life." This council was among the first of the ecumenical bodies to set up an office in Geneva with a secretariat and research staff.

As dean of Canterbury (1924-29) Bell used his new-found senior status, and the scope for independent action now given him, for decidedly ecumenical purposes. He was instrumental in the getting the Assembly of the Church of England to set up its own council on foreign relations. He initiated the conferences between British and German theologians at Canterbury (1927) and Eisenach (1928). It might have been expected that after he became bishop of Chichester in 1929 the rigours of episcopal responsibility would have somewhat diverted his energies from ecumenism, but such was not to be the case. In 1932, Bishop Theodore Woods of Winchester, president of the Council of Life and Work, died. Bell was appointed in his place and so began the definitive chapter of his ecumenical career. He was now at the helm of the most widely representative body of the churches then in existence—mostly western Protestant but also including a number of Orthodox—designed to enable the churches' joint action and speaking. (The Faith and Order Commission, following on the Lausanne conference of 1927, was a rather different kind of body furthering theological consultation and dialogue.) Moreover, Bell's appointment came at a most critical time for the ecumenical movement. Nathan Söderblom, founding father of Life and Work, had died the previous year. A new leader—indeed a new apostle—was needed. The following year, 1933, another kind of leader emerged on the political scene as Adolf Hitler came to power, and with the onset of the German Church Struggle, the ecumenical witness of the churches would be tested as never before.

Bell steered the Council of Life and Work through the treacherous waters of the 1930s with a diplomatic skill combined with clear theological perception of the threat both to the churches and to Europe posed by totalitarianism. He ensured that at the meeting of Life and Work at Novi Sad in 1933, the Council faced up to the challenge of antisemitism and state criminality in Germany. Crucially at the famous council meeting at Fanø, Denmark in 1934, the Council threw its weight behind the Confessing Church in its struggle to maintain the gospel in face of the nationalism and racism masquerading as "German Christianity."[5] Vital to Bell's perception of the issues in Germany, his public advocacy of the Confessing Church in sermons, speeches, and letters to the *Times*, and his unswerving loyalty to the Confessing leaders, was the close friendship that developed between him and the young pastor and theologian Dietrich Bonhoeffer, who arrived in London in the autumn of 1933 to spend 18 months in charge of two of the German congregations there. Part of the importance of this friendship lay in the fact that Bonhoeffer was fluent in English, while Bell knew hardly any German.

Under Bell, Life and Work's stance during the German Church Struggle had significance well beyond that particular period of time. It meant that when ecumenical life was fully constituted after the second world war, and the World Council of Churches was inaugurated in 1948, there was a vital strand of proven integrity within the ecumenical movement. But that is to anticipate slightly. The Fanø meeting of 1934 also took the decision to hold the first world Life and Work conference since Stockholm 1925, at Oxford in 1937 on the theme "Church, Community and State." The study process and programme of Oxford 1937 was largely of Joe Oldham's devising, but with Bell in close support. Oxford 1937 enabled the churches of the world, as another dreaded world war approached, to face together the threats of totalitarianism and the challenges of nationalism, peace and war, economic chaos, and social questions at every level. It meant that the churches were far better prepared to face war in 1939 than they had been in 1914. There was still further significance, for following this conference, and the World Faith and Order conference that took place in Edinburgh shortly after, the crucial steps were taken towards forming the World Council of Churches. The constitution for the World Council was agreed upon at a meeting in Utrecht in 1938, and a general secretary appointed in Geneva in the person of the young Dutchman W.A. ("Wim") Visser 't Hooft. So the "WCC in formation" was in existence just in time before war broke out, and enough was in place to maintain an ecumenical witness during the war years. George Bell was not as immediately concerned with the mechanics of this process as were, for example, Joe

---

5. See above, Chapter 6.

Oldham and William Temple, but he was appointed to the Provisional Committee of the WCC. Above all he was a chief spokesperson for the new body, as seen in his short book *Christianity and World Order*, which appeared in 1940 and which is essentially a survey of the ecumenical story thus far and an affirmation of the calling of the church to give answers to the crisis facing the world. Bell speaks hopefully: "In spite of the divisions of the nations, there is this community of Christians. Wherever they are, or whatever their race or nation or class, Christian disciples are bound to one another, because they are disciples of Christ. He is above the battle. He does unite men and women. In His Church a real world unity is to be found, despite the variety of confessions and communions."[6] These differences must not prevent standing together on common ground, "from giving a common witness, from striving for peace and justice and love and from the responsibilities of the nations. I believe in the Holy Catholic Church, the Communion of Saints!"[7]

During the war years Bell lived out his apostleship for unity both at home and further afield and in many different ways: in his support of Pope Pius XII's "Peace Points" issued at Christmas 1939; in his collaboration with leading Roman Catholics in Britain in the promising but short-lived "Sword of the Spirit" movement; in his maintaining contacts through Geneva with the beleaguered Confessing Christians in Germany and most notably, through secretly meeting Dietrich Bonhoeffer in Sweden in 1942, with the actual German resistance to Hitler and his pleading the claims of that resistance with the British government; with his courageous speeches in the House of Lords against the area bombing of German cities; and in his ongoing, tireless labours for refugees and exiles from Nazi Germany—work which was a direct inspiration for what became known after the war as Christian Aid.

Long before the surrender of Nazi Germany in May 1945, Bell, with other British Christians, was giving thought and speech to the post-war reconstruction of Europe and its church life, not least in Germany itself. He wrote on this for Joe Oldham's *Christian News-Letter*, and speaking in the House of Lords in December 1944, he stated: "Not only has Europe never attained political organization as a real society of peoples, but something deeper than a political impulse is required to secure lasting unity now... [W]e are more likely to achieve the goal of European unity if we build on the culture which all European peoples have in common."[8] Bell recognised that that "culture" comprises the diverse traditions of humanism, science, law, and government as well as the Christian religion, although not surprisingly he considered

---

6. George Bell, *Christianity and World Order* (London: Penguin, 1940), 128.
7. Ibid.
8. See J. A. Zeilstra, *European Unity in Ecumenical Thinking* (Zoetermeer: Uitgeverij Boekcentrum, 1995), 179.

this last "to be the most important and potentially unifying of them all." Note, however, that slight qualification—"most potentially" unifying. In other words, European unity would be an ecumenical challenge for the churches as well as a political one for governments. European unity and Christian unity would require each other.

After the war, Bell was the senior figure in that group of ecumenical representatives who in October 1945 met with leaders of the German Evangelical Church in Stuttgart, and heard from Martin Niemöller, Otto Dibelius, and others—those who had themselves suffered for their witness under Nazism—their remarkable declaration admitting, on behalf of church and people, guilt for the evils wrought by Nazism. The Stuttgart Declaration was a pivotal event in the process of post-war reconciliation and healing. Over the next few years Bell kept a very close eye on the work of the Allied Control Commission in Germany, making recommendations where he considered the commission weak and voicing criticisms where he thought its actions unjust or unhelpful to the rehabilitation of Germans and Germany in the family of nations.

Then, in 1948, at last, ten years after its constitution had been laid down, came the full inauguration of the World Council of Churches at its first assembly in Amsterdam. George Bell was appointed first chairman of the central committee, and served until the next assembly in Evanston 1954. To be chairman (or moderator, to use today's term) of a central committee may not sound a very glamorous title. In fact it is the crucial role in the life of the WCC. The central committee comprises over 100 members, all representatives of member churches and elected by the assembly. It meets every year or so between assemblies. It is where decisions are made on priorities and policies, where the work of staff and particular committees is scrutinised. Here is where real encounter takes place. Here east meets west, protestant meets Orthodox, lay meets clerical, youth meets age, south meets north, male meets female, traditionalist meets liberal... and so it is often the place of impassioned debate. Here you see ecumenism often at its finest—and sometimes, inevitably, at its worst. The final message of the Amsterdam assembly had included a notable phrase, penned by a young English woman, Kathleen Bliss: "We intend to stay together." That this commitment was fulfilled in those first years of the WCC, facing as it did the new division in Europe and the world between east and west, crises such as the Korean war and the new atomic age, and the steady emergence to prominence of the so-called younger churches of the south and east, owed an immense amount to George Bell and his steady, mediating, and compassionate discharge of his role. Particularly crucial were the central committee meetings in Toronto, Canada (1950), which laid down a strong policy on religious freedom and adopted a statement on the basis on which churches join and accept each other within the WCC, and Lucknow, India

(1953) the first time such a gathering had taken place in Asia. This was a deliberate attempt by the WCC to combat the idea of its being a western-based and western-oriented organisation, and an attempt to call the "older" churches into a new relationship of partnership with the "younger" churches. And Bell really did lead. As Visser 't Hooft said of him, he always came to the meeting "with something in his pocket" (the bane of life for a general secretary!) whether a proposal concerning refugees, or a persecuted church, or some new idea to increase understanding or co-operation between the churches.[9] Visser 't Hooft says of Bell that his chairmanship "was that of father of a family rather than a keeper of hard and fast rules of procedure." As Bell's term of office concluded in 1954, he could report on "the steady growth of mutual trust" among the central committee members. Nor was Bell only a chairman; he was an ecumenical pastor as well, and made a special point of visiting, in company with Wim Visser 't Hooft, the churches of Eastern Europe under the new totalitarianism, not least the Eastern Orthodox churches, most of which had not yet joined the WCC.

When the second WCC assembly met in Evanston, near Chicago, in 1954, it was in a thoroughly confident, forward-looking, and outward looking spirit. For Evanston Bell wrote another short book, *The Kingship of Christ*, dedicated to the members of the central committee with whom he had served those six years. The book is a further telling of the ecumenical story and the work of the WCC, but also a wide-ranging survey of the challenges facing the world and the world church's responses to them, both at the global level and on the local scene. The churches had not just stayed together, they were now more conscious of their common mission. The WCC was a growing family, and would grow still further with the arrival of more of the Orthodox Churches—most notably the Russian Orthodox Church—at the next assembly in 1961, a development Bell had longed to see happen but, like Moses on the top of Mount Pisgah, had only been able to envision from afar.

This is where Bell had led the ecumenical family, and the WCC signalled its gratitude to him by electing him to be one of its presidents, and as such he died four years later in 1958. That, in briefest summary, is a sketch of *what* Bell did to deserve the title "Apostle for Unity," or in the more prosaic epitaph in Chichester Cathedral, "tireless worker for Christian unity." Many things worth mentioning have had to be left out, and give place to a highlighting features of the *spirit* that drove him, the why and how of his apostleship. I select four main marks of Bell's ecumenism.

---

9. See Ronald C. D. Jasper, *George Bell: Bishop of Chichester* (London: Oxford University Press, 1967), 337; see also the many references to Bell in W.A. Visser 't Hooft, *Memoirs*, 2nd ed. (Geneva: WCC Publications, 1987).

An Ecumenism Theologically Grounded in the Kingship of Christ

"I believe that God is a Living God. I believe that Christ is the Lord of all life. I believe that Christianity is the one true way. I believe that the Church of Christ is the supreme fellowship."[10] So George Bell states his personal credo at the start of his 1940 book *Christianity and World Order*. His quest for unity was motivated not by any purely pragmatic considerations of tidying up the unruly church scene so that it might act more efficiently, nor so that the wagons of the churches might form a defensive circle against the world as the secularist night falls. For him unity came as an imperative because, as declared in his hymn, "Christ is the King!" The king has only one kingdom, to be foreshadowed and declared by one church. It is therefore no accident that Bell's 1954 summary of the whole ecumenical story and what it means, and what he himself has experienced of it, is given this title *The Kingship of Christ*. "The Church ... is not itself the realisation of the Kingdom of God on earth. It serves the Kingdom, and is not an end in itself... But the Church charged by its Lord with this mission was one Church. It is now divided... There is disunion and division, even conflict and antagonism. Therefore the work of the whole body of Christ suffers. The witness to the Kingship of Jesus suffers."[11] Bell's focusing on the kingship of Christ, Christ's sovereign lordship *over and above and in command of* all that is human, gave his witness its prophetic cutting edge in challenging the status quo in both church and society. "To accept Christ as the Hope of the World is to follow Christ's way in the world. To recognize Christ as King is to accept his rule for oneself and for society, and to be active in obedience to his will. The Church as the pilgrim people of God is called to proclaim this Kingship, and to strive to be true to it in its own life."[12] Admittedly, to view the world of the day against that kingly horizon might only deepen the sense of its failure, crisis and tragedy. "Cheer up, Jeremiah!" was the gist of a letter to Bell from Hensley Henson, the idiosyncratic bishop of Durham, commenting on *Christianity and World Order*.[13] But if belief in the kingship of Christ threw the shadows of the world into deeper relief, for Bell it also and even more so heightened the brightness of the hope given to the world, for "the future is Jesus Christ" who transcends death and in whom the new world *has begun*.[14] And so Bell concludes *The Kingship of Christ* not with a litany of despair but an anthem of hope.

All Bell's work for unity has to be seen as an expression of this fundamental theological conviction of the kingship of Christ.

---

10. Bell, *Christianity and World Order*, vii.
11. Bell, *The Kingship of Christ* (London: Penguin, 1954), 14ff.
12. Ibid., 173.
13. Jasper, *George Bell*, 248ff.
14. Bell, *The Kingship of Christ*, 174ff.

An Ecumenism Expressed in Personal Relationships

If Christ is the King, we are but his "unworthy servants," to allude to one of Bell's favourite gospel texts. Consistent with the theological conviction of the kingship of Christ, Bell's style of ecumenism was one of humility seen in a rare gift for building personal relationships of trust and respect. *Unshakeable Friend*[15] is the apt title of Edwin Robertson's account of George Bell and the German churches before, during, and after world war II (and expressed eloquently in the cover photograph of Bell talking with Bishop Otto Dibelius, with Russian guards behind them). It is not reducing ecumenism to simplistics, but rather going to its heart, to say that ecumenism is about building friendships. If Bell often had to rely on interpreters for conversing with Germans, he compensated by being able to converse with his ears and eyes as well as his mouth, for he was above all a good listener. Nathan Söderblom recorded his impressions of Bell at one of the early Life and Work meetings:

> He sat just opposite me. He said hardly anything except when he was asked. Then, after consideration, he gave a thoughtful answer which always proved to be reliable. The face is dominated by two large, round eyes, which shine with the life and soul behind and indicate a rich inner life. In my opinion, no man means more for the ecumenical awakening than this silent Bell. This Bell never rings unnecessarily. But when it sounds, the tone is silvery clear. It is heard. It penetrates more than many boisterous voices. He does not speak without having something to say. The strong spirituality of his personality marks everything that he does.[16]

It hardly needs saying that this was in contrast to that well-known type at ecumenical gatherings, always anxious not only to speak but to make the same speech we have all heard umpteen times before, and more eager to champion one's own church or group's position than to understand that of others. Bell never pretended to be other than Anglican, and indeed did much to promote an understanding of the Church of England within the ecumenical family. But he was free of the kind of prejudice shown by Hensley Henson, who on one occasion wondered how such an intelligent person as T.R. Glover, Cambridge classicist and university orator, could be a Baptist. He was above all always ready to *learn* from others, which is the key to forming relationships with them. A striking instance is in one of his early exchanges with Dietrich Bonhoeffer. It was in the spring of 1934. Hitler had been in power for just over a year and the German Church Struggle was growing fiercer by the day.

---

15. Edwin Robertson, *Unshakeable Friend: George Bell and the German Churches* (London: CCBI, 1995).
16. Jasper, *George Bell*, 60.

Hitler's appointee for church affairs, *Reischsbishof* Josef Müller, was using heavy-handed methods to browbeat those pastors opposing the nazification of church life. There was increased bullying by the storm-troopers, searches by the Gestapo and many arrests were made. An appeal was made to Bell, in his capacity as chairman of the Universal Council of Life and Work, to speak out on behalf of the church opposition. One important mediator of this appeal was Bonhoeffer, who had been in London since the previous October. He and Bell had met in London several times, Bonhoeffer had been entertained by the Bells at the palace in Chichester, and a valued friendship had begun. Bell decided to issue his statement in the form of an Ascension Day message to all the member churches of Life and Work, highlighting the plight of the German Church and calling for solidarity with those being persecuted. Typically, he first circulated a draft of his proposed statements to a number of trusted advisers, including Bonhoeffer. In referring to the persecuted pastors, his draft spoke of the loyalty of the persecuted pastors "to what they believe to be Christian truth." Bonhoeffer was deeply grateful for the message as a whole, but respectfully took issue with Bell over his wording at this point. In his reply to Bell he states:

> You speak "of the loyalty (of the pastors) to what they believe to be Christian truth." Could you not say perhaps: to what *is* the Christian truth—or "what we believe with them to be the Christian truth"? It sounds as if you want to take distance from their belief. I think even the Reichsbishop would be right in taking disciplinary measures against ministers, if they stand for something else but the truth of the Gospel (even if they believe it to be the truth)—the real issue is that they are under coercion on account of their loyalty to what *is* the true Gospel— namely their opposition against the *racial and political element as constituent for the Church* of Christ.[17]

Bell duly took note, and his final text spoke of disciplinary measures against pastors "on account of their loyalty to the fundamental principles of Christian truth." This was more than a verbal quibble. Continually in the English speaking-world the German Church Struggle was seen as a fight about "religious freedom." To the Confessing Christians themselves, especially such as Barth and Bonhoeffer, it was not about the general principle of religious freedom (a very "Anglo-Saxon" notion, they said!) but obedience to the gospel as was expressed in the Barmen theological declaration at the end of May 1934. Bell, from Bonhoeffer, learned about this vital

---

17. Dietrich Bonhoeffer, *Dietrich Bonhoeffer Works*, vol. 13, *London 1933-35* (Minneapolis: Fortress, 2007), 140.

distinction very early on, and this proved crucial in securing his enduring under-standing of and support for the Confessing Church. His was an ecumenism which was prepared to travel contextually—not just geographically, but mentally and cul-turally, into the actual scene of others, and to view that scene as those involved actually see it and experience it, and understand more of it from within their own mind-set. In other words, to live in more than one place at once. Such is an ecumen-ism free of presumptions, vital in building relationships of understanding and no less creating opportunities for reconciliation. On that October evening in 1945 in bombed-out Stuttgart, sitting in the room of the Markuskirche, and seeing Bell sit-ting there, Niemöller and the other Evangelical leaders would have known beyond doubt that their confession of guilt, no less than their confession of the gospel a decade earlier, would be truly heard and understood.

An Ecumenism concerned with the World as Much as the Church

To George Bell, the coming together of the churches in cooperation, common wit-ness, deeper fellowship and—so he hoped—ultimately in reunion mattered deeply. If Christ is King, then as Lord he transcends all the forms of the churches in their present divided state and calls into question any contentment with the status quo. But such unity could never be an end in itself and already, as the pilgrim people of God, the church is called to witness to the kingship of Christ over all humanity, the whole world and every aspect of life. You do not find much mention of "religion" in Bell, as if faith were one compartment of life and the secular, everyday world the other. Christ is Lord of all life, all realms, whether we call them religious, sacred, secular, political, or by any other name. Bell would be aghast at so much of the current debates in the media on whether or not faith or religion had a role in the public sphere.

For George Bell, to speak of the kingship of Christ in the public, political and international realm did not mean that the church has, or should claim to have, an instant answer to every problem that arises in the public domain, still less that the church should try to impose its will directly on society through force or legislation. When Bell speaks of "Christianity and World Order" he does not have in view a theocracy, for that is to anticipate the end when, and not before, God shall be all in all. What he does mean, however, is that that the kingship of Christ sets two crucial bearings for Christian witness in the secular sphere.

The first is that to confess the kingship of Christ implies a challenge to the claims of other sovereignties in the world. Just as the earliest Christian baptismal confession, *Iesous Christos Kurios*, "Jesus Christ is Lord," conveyed a potential challenge to the absolutist claims of the Roman Caesar, ultimately to the point of martyrdom, so too all worldly claimants to human allegiance are questioned by the kingship of Christ.

In the 1930s and 1940s, obviously, the most evident contemporary equivalents were the Nazi state and other totalitarian regimes which demanded unequivocal allegiance from their subjects. "By making the State an absolute, they subordinate truth, goodness, mercy, justice to the supposed interests of the State as interpreted by the contemporary leader and party."[18] As such they were essentially godless. But Bell saw that the challenge of the kingship of Christ reaches much further than the fascist and communist states. Under the sovereignty of Christ, all assumed human sovereignties are laid open to being relativized including, and perhaps especially, that of the nation-state even in its "democratic" form. So there is a negative or at least critical impact of the kingship of Christ in the public realm. Just *what* is to be rendered to Caesar?

Second, there is the positive bearing of the kingship of Christ in the ordering of society. Bell acknowledged but disagreed with those idealistic Christian traditions which claimed that Christ's law of love could and should be perfectly applied in the world. Equally, he rejected the idea that Christianity was totally inapplicable to secular life. He took the mediating position which affirmed that an incorrigibly imperfect world is nevertheless malleable by *justice*, a position in keeping both with much of the thinking of the Oxford 1937 conference and indeed with much Roman Catholic social teaching. This is not to downgrade the place of love as the heart of the gospel and the will of Christ, but to maintain the framework of life and thought within which alone there can be hope of love. Bell summarises it thus:

Justice and Order are in effect the necessary groundwork on which Love is to build. Those who undermine or violate Justice and Order are making the rule of Love immensely, if not impossibly, difficult to secure or continue. By itself Justice is insufficient. It is regulative, not creative. It is not a Gospel. It cannot, being without religious devotion, do what religious devotion alone makes possible. But its discipline is essential to the ordering of all social life.[19]

Seeking justice, then, is the form which obeying the kingship of Christ must take in present-day society. In recognizing both the negative or critical and the positive aspects of the kingship of Christ, questioning claims to sovereignty and pursuing justice, Bell was drawing on much contemporary theological and social ethics, especially in the ecumenical circles. Deeply and widely read, he made no claim to originality and his writings gratefully abound in quotations from other writers. What was significant about Bell, however, was his unusual readiness not just to quote, but

18. Bell, *Christianity and World Order*, 68.
19. Ibid., 63.

to act, and in such a way that united the challenge to assumed sovereignty with the pursuit of justice. To care so deeply, as he did, for the waves of refugees from Nazi Germany was not just altruistic sentiment. It was a matter of *justice*, challenging the assumed national attitudes and selective policies towards foreigners. It made Bell deeply unpopular with sections of public opinion hostile to all foreigners, and especially when after the outbreak of war so many of them—even including such as Dietrich Bonhoeffer's brother-in-law Gerhard Leibholz—were interned as "enemy aliens." Bell was both seeking justice for vulnerable people in need and challenging the assumed sovereignty of national feeling that sought to dictate who deserved help and who did not. It was the same concern for justice which motivated his House of Lords speeches, and letters in the press, against the area bombing of German civilian populations. Bell was not a pacifist, and his carefully stated position on the Christian citizen in wartime was that the Christian should serve his or her country in uniform unless there is compelling reason why *this* war was wrong.[20] Bell had no doubt that Hitler had to be defeated. But the means had to be "just" and his speeches against the area bombing (which incidentally he always prefaced with tributes to the personal courage and sacrifice of the aircrews involved) were careful expositions of the traditional just war criteria and the reasons why in this particular instance he believed those criteria to be violated, and indeed inimical to the valid aims of the war. But in this, too, he was challenging the accepted idea that the supposed sovereignty of national interest could override the claims of justice, which for him meant the claims of the kingship of Christ. He rigorously maintained the capacity to imagine himself into the world beyond narrow national self-interest or churchly self-concern. His protests against the bombing policy meant living under the law of Chjrist as manifest in principles of justice, and an imagined living in a post-war Germany wrecked beyond hope of self-reconstruction.

An Ecumenism Both Serious and Risk-Taking

To an unusual degree George Bell's work for Christian unity combined seriousness and risk-taking, sobriety and dare-devilry.

First of all the seriousness. In his letter of 1940, Hensley Henson gently mocked Bell for his narrative in *Christianity and World Order* of "the solemn procession of Conferences, etc, which you picture so reverently" and suggested that he had "lived too much in the heated atmosphere of committees, conferences, congresses, and the like debased outcrops of modern democracy."[21] Bell did indeed take with unmiti-

---

20. Ibid., 81.
21. Jasper, *George Bell*, 248.

gated seriousness the ecumenical institutions and organisations, not because he liked institutions and organisations, but because these were the actual means of meeting, the means of encounter where relationships developed and where decisions were taken on common action. That is what is so well seen in that little postcard sent by Bell to Henry-Louis Henriod in the summer of 1933: Friedrich Siegmund-Schultze, leading German Protestant social theologian and peace-worker, was being attacked by the Nazi authorities and in fact soon would be hounded out of Germany. Bell was seeking to mobilise Life and Work, together with the World Alliance for Promoting International Friendship through the Churches, and as many church leaders as possible in Britain, to protest not only on Siegmund-Schultze's behalf but against all the Nazi government's actions against freedom of speech. It was therefore out of real experience that he wrote in 1940, "Conferences are not ends in themselves. They are means towards unity and action, and their initial expression."[22] By then Bell had in view especially the Oxford and Edinburgh conferences of 1937, where the decisive steps were taken towards forming the WCC. For Bell, the ecumenical bodies were not the be-all and end-all of the ecumenical movement, but the means whereby the Universal Church was being rediscovered and even beginning to take visible form. He would be the first to repudiate "committee ecumenism."

Hensley Henson could have gone further and teased Bell about his series of publications *Documents on Christian Unity* which he published in three series from 1924 to 1948.[23] Denominational responses to the Lambeth Appeal of 1920, papal encyclicals, relevant statements whether of the Free Churches or Eastern Orthodox, the Oxford and Edinburgh resolutions and those of the International Missionary Conferences of Jerusalem and Tambaram, the South India reunion scheme—all and much else is there: a labour of love, careful work, tedious work, donkey work. Today such collation and publication is done by the Faith and Order Commission in Geneva, but for over 20 years Bell was doing it single-handedly, and it is remarkable that he started it so early, even before the Stockholm 1925 conference. He did it because he recognised that the ecumenical movement is a story of its own which has to be chronicled properly if it is to be known, understood and above all carried forward by the churches.

So much for the seriousness. All the more remarkable is that this same serious student, this bell that never rang unnecessarily, should more than any other British church leader of his time have taken risks and hazarded his reputation, status, and perhaps even his career, all in faithfulness to his vision of the kingship of Christ and

---

22. Bell, *Christianity and World Order*, 124.
23. Published by Oxford University Press in three series: 1928, 1930, 1948.

the unity and order which that required in both church and world. Bell took the risk of taking sides in the German Church Struggle. He went far beyond the call of what many considered to be the duty of an English diocesan bishop in arousing the national conscience on the plight of German refugees, being abused in one newspaper as "the self-appointed champion of captive Nazis and Fascists."[24] During the war, after his meeting with Bonhoeffer in Sweden in 1942, he took the risk of pleading the cause of the German resistance to Hitler, the risk of being proved wrong and being seen by the British Foreign Office as a tool of the German propaganda machine. His public protests against the area bombing policy, in the opinion of some, cost him the succession to the see of London and perhaps even to Canterbury itself on the death of William Temple in 1944. In his leading role for the WCC, as the Cold War took hold, Bell took the risk of looking eastwards and going eastwards in solidarity with the churches there, at a time when many in the west saw any approaches to eastern Europe as befriending communism. As late as 1956, two years after retiring from the WCC central committee chairmanship, he made himself unpopular in the House of Lords by supporting the WCC's criticism of the British government's deportation of Archbishop Makarios of Cyprus, incurring the rebuke even of Archbishop Fisher, and being accused of serving the interests of the WCC rather than those of Britain. Bell never minded that kind of accusation; in fact, he said on at least one occasion when arriving for a WCC central committee meeting that he was glad to be where he was *not* expected to be just a voice for Britain.

Bell's combination of seriousness and risk-taking is a reflection of the Christian belief in the way of death and resurrection. There is no more powerful and moving utterance of this from George Bell than in the sermon he preached in London on 27 July 1945, at the memorial service for Dietrich Bonhoeffer and his brother Klaus, executed a month before the war had ended. Here we see gathered together all those distinctive features of Bell's passionate concern for ecumenism, an ecumenism for the world as much as for the church, his personal devotion to those he had known and loved in the fellowship of Christ that crosses all national boundaries, and his sense of history and his hope for the future, all fused in his hope in Christ crucified and risen:

> Our Lord said, "Except a grain of wheat fall into the ground and die, it abideth alone; but if it die, it bringeth forth much fruit. He that loveth his life shall lose it, and he that hateth his life in this world shall keep it unto life eternal." To our earthly view Dietrich is dead. Deep and unfathomable as our sorrow seems, let us comfort one another with these words. For him and Klaus, and for the countless multitudes of their fellow victims through these terrible years of war, there is the resurrection

24. Jasper, *George Bell*, 151.

from the dead: for Germany redemption and resurrection, if God please to lead the nation through men animated by his spirit: for the Church, not only in that Germany which he loved, but the Church Universal which was greater to him than nations, the hope of a new life. "The blood of the martyrs is the seed of the Church."[25]

Bell's Meaning for Today? Creative Dissent

George Bell has been described as "the paradigm of creative dissent."[26] As one who formally stands within the English nonconformist church tradition, I find that description especially challenging. For George Bell inhabited and wore the robes of the Anglican establishment; for 44 years he lived in the heart of that establishment, at Lambeth Palace, in the deanery at Canterbury, and in the Palace at Chichester. Yet no one in the 20th century stood against many of the assumptions of that establishment more provocatively than he did—no Anglican and moreover no Free Church leader either. That is what makes Bell so significant an ecumenical figure. What is more, his dissent and his ecumenism were two sides of the same coin of his allegiance to the kingship of Christ. George Bell will be a constant reminder that the unity we seek is the unity of the universal church, the church of the *oikoumene* which means "the whole inhabited earth." The needs of that whole inhabited earth, for bread, for justice, for true freedom, for peace and reconciliation, must ever be central in the witness of the church as it seeks to proclaim, serve and manifest in its own life the kingship of Christ. People who take seriously the calling to serve the whole *oikoumene* will always be controversial at some points because they challenge both the domestication of the church to suit lesser interests (whether denominational, national, racial, or related to any other division) and the absolutisation of the state. They risk incurring the wrath heaped upon the prophet in his hometown (Luke 4:24), for speaking of God's reign being received elsewhere than there. Living in more than one place at once, they will be accused of betraying their home.

In the more than half century since George Bell died, much has happened to separate his world from ours. There is a nice irony in that less than four weeks after his death, on 28 October 1958 in Rome, Cardinal Angelo Roncalli was elected Pope and took the name John XXIII, and just three months later announced "an ecumenical council for the universal church." Bell would have rejoiced to see that day, and so much else that followed from Vatican II. Perhaps, too, he would share the sense of

---

25. *Bonhoeffer Gedenkheft*, ed. Eberhard Bethge (Berlin: Verlag Haus und Schule GMBH, 1947). See also Keith Clements, *Bonhoeffer and Britain* (London: CTBI, 2006), 136ff.
26. John Munsey Turner, "Bell, George Kennedy Allen," in *Dictionary of the Ecumenical Movement*, ed. Nicholas Lossky et al., 2nd ed. (Geneva: WCC Publications, 2002), 104.

frustration that many of us now feel about the ecumenical scene both at home and abroad. We can identify particular points where we feel he would still speak prophetically: the failure of the churches either to take the ecumenical bodies as seriously as he did or to take any risks for unity. He would surely also be aghast at the lack of a really positive vision for Europe being expressed by any British political or church leader at the moment, not to mention the lack of a counter to the continual drip-feed of poison about Europe from many political and media circles.

At the same time, it must be acknowledged that our context is now markedly different from Bell's in important respects. It will be pointed out for example that the divisive issues today are not so much between churches and confessions as within them, on issues like gender, sexuality and authority. Moreover, one finds in Bell relatively little on relations between Christianity and other world faiths,[27] whereas today we face a multifaith and pluralistic world both abroad and at home. Many will argue that it is interfaith relations, not "old-style" Christian ecumenism, that is item number one on the agenda now. Many will not feel quite comfortable in speaking as confidently as Bell did about the kingship of Christ since it seems to have imperialistic overtones.

But it is precisely *how* Bell saw the Kingship of Christ that matters. For nearly two millennia, the sovereignty of Christ has been tied to one or other sovereignty of this world, of one empire or another, being protected by it, imposed by it, controlled by it, or exploited by it and thus mistaken for it. George Bell is outstanding among 20th century Christian leaders for detaching the sovereignty of Christ from the interests of worldly sovereignty, insisting that worldy sovereignty—even British sovereignty and even in wartime—be made accountable to the kingship of Christ, and not vice versa. This both requires and enables the unity of the body of Christ on earth, as a sign of the new creation in the midst of the old. The apostle for unity is one who speaks out of the source and points us towards the end and exemplifies in his own life, to the point of suffering, the reality of the unity that is God's gift and our calling. Such an apostle both has a contemporary message and foresees that the agenda will change and develop on the way into the unknown future. That is why Bell is important. In the concluding words of his hymn:

So shall God's will on earth be done,
new lamps be lit, new tasks begun,
and the whole Church at last be one.
Alleluia!

---

27. In fact, in late 1943 Bell presided over a meeting of the World Congress of Faiths, and shortly afterwards proposed the formation of an interreligious body to advise governments and related bodies on the ethical aspects of international issues. J.H. Oldham expressed marked scepticism about this idea in *Christian News-Letter* 197 (15 December 1943).

Chapter 8

"Perfectly Mad Adventure"

J.H. Oldham's "Moot" and a Post-Christendom Social Order

Illustrating the dynamic of living in more than one place at once, much of the ecumenical story that we have looked at so far has involved large-scale events and prominent figures. Not surprisingly, the episodes and actors have been on the international stage of the *oikoumene*, the inhabited earth. But the dynamic operates wherever and whenever, even on the smallest numerical scale, through personal encounter and venturesome imagination, people mentally migrate from the immediate here and now to another world—whether another part of the world than their own or another possible version of the world that is "home" to them. In this chapter we shall look at one such example of a small group which for a decade, discreetly and almost unknown except to its members, accompanied the more public and dramatic side of the ecumenical movement and in significant ways helped to service the wider cause. In so looking, we shall for a time have to focus our attention quite narrowly on what was happening in mid-20th century Britain—a focus, however, which throws into sharp relief the global crisis of the time and the questions being put to the churches everywhere. The group was known as the "Moot."

The Moot[1]

The Moot was a group of intellectuals in Britain, mostly but not all confessedly Christian, which met three times a year over nearly a decade, from 1938 to 1947, to explore the role of Christian belief in modern society, the nature of modern society itself, and what kind of society could legitimately be called "Christian" or at any rate meet with the approval of Christian faith. It was convened, chaired and managed throughout by the ecumenical pioneer and social thinker J.H. Oldham.[2] In his

---

1. The main source for this chapter is Keith Clements, ed., *The Moot Papers: Faith, Freedom and Society 1938-1944* (London: T. & T. Clark, 2010), hereafter referred to as *MP*.
2. See Keith Clements, *Faith on the Frontier: A Life of J.H. Oldham* (London: T. & T. Clark and Geneva: WCC Publications, 1999).

capacity as secretary of the International Missionary Council, "Joe" Oldham had already done much to stimulate theological reflection and concerted action on issues as varied as race, education and British colonial policy in Africa. Oldham's crowning achievement—alongside his laying the foundation for the future World Council of Churches—was his masterminding of the study programme and agenda for the 1937 Oxford conference on "Church, Community and State," one of the great landmark ecumenical events of the 20th century. In face of the impending crisis of a second world war, Oxford 1937 brought together representatives of the worldwide family of churches to study and debate the urgent social and international issues of the day, and it laid down solid guidelines for future work and witness in these areas.

In many ways Oxford 1937 was a triumph for Oldham, then in his 63rd year. But Oldham himself regarded the Oxford conference as the merest beginning of a programme which, he maintained, should occupy the churches for the next thirty years. It would surprise people to know that Oldham, who had first come to ecumenical fame as the secretary of the World Missionary Conference of 1910, in fact always looked askance at large gatherings. Far more useful, in his view, was the meeting of minds, and moreover "the best minds," as he called them, in small-scale encounter and in-depth study. The Moot was conceived by Oldham as a means of pursuing in this way the post-Oxford agenda in Britain, and he deliberately borrowed the term "Moot" from the Old English vocabulary, where it designated a local meeting, or meeting-place. The Moot was nothing more, and nothing less, than that. It had its particular place in what for Oldham was "the perfectly mad adventure" of the missionary enterprise,[3] an enterprise which was now in his view requiring of Christians and churches a vast reorientation from the clerical and ecclesiastical sphere to the perspective of those who work in and for the world.

But what helped make it extraordinary, indeed unique, was the diversity and calibre of the minds it brought together (whether they were actually the "best minds" or not is of course, we might say, "a moot point"). On the theological side, as well as Oldham himself, there were the Scottish theologian John Baillie and Alec Vidler, an Anglo-Catholic theologian becoming strongly influenced by Karl Barth. The borderland between theology and philosophy was straddled by H.A. Hodges, professor of philosophy at Reading University. T.S. Eliot, foremost modernist poet and literary critic of the time, and future Nobel laureate, was there to represent High Tory conservatism, and in colourful contrast to him, but equally immersed in the literary world, was John Middleton Murry, writer, pacifist and passionate Christian communist. Education was well represented: Walter Moberly, chairman of the University

---

3. See Clements, *Faith on the Frontier*, 453.

Grants Committee; Hector Hetherington, Vice-Chancellor of Glasgow University; Fred Clarke, director of the Institute of Education, London University; and Walter Oakeshott, High Master of St Paul's School and later Vice-Chancellor of Oxford University. If by now it is being wondered if anyone in the Moot was in touch with so-called ordinary people, it is a relief to meet Gilbert Shaw, Anglican priest working among the poor of London's East End and a kind of chaplain to grassroots working-class movements, but far from "normal" in many of his stances. There were only three women in the Moot: Joe Oldham's wife Mary; Eleonora Iredale, researcher and expert fund-raiser; and, later on, Kathleen Bliss, Anglican lay theologian and educationist. But Oldham cast his net wider than the usual Anglican-Protestant ecumenical scene. The Roman Catholic scholar Christopher Dawson was a committed member, his few actual attendances being supplemented by several important discussion papers that he wrote. But in particular, there were also two recruits from the many Jewish refugees who arrived on the British academic scene from 1933 onwards. The first was the economist and philosopher Adolf Löwe. The second, who was to prove the most decisive intellectual force in the Moot right from his debut at the second meeting in 1938, was the sociologist Karl Mannheim, expelled by the Nazis from his chair at Frankfurt and now teaching at the London School of Economics. It was Mannheim's analysis of the nature of the crisis in Western society, developed in his works *Ideology and Utopia*[4] and *Man and Society in an Age of Reconstruction*,[5] which set much of the framework for the Moot's perspectives on society, and his motto "planning for freedom" denoted his prescription for responsible politics. In all, some 23 persons were registered as members of the Moot, though the actual attendance rarely exceeded 12 at any one meeting. Later on, younger blood was introduced with such recruits as Kathleen Bliss (already mentioned), the Welsh Congregational theologian Daniel Jenkins, Alex ("Lex") Miller, sometime deputy leader of the Iona Community, the Oxford philosopher Donald Mackinnon, and yet another notable refugee from the continent, Michael Polanyi. Not to be overlooked throughout was Eric Fenn, English Presbyterian minister who had been Oldham's assistant at the Oxford conference and was now entering upon a new career in religious broadcasting with the BBC. It was Fenn who dutifully took the minutes of nearly all the Moot discussions, virtually verbatim. At several meetings there were also guests and visitors, among the notables being Reinhold Niebuhr on two occasions, and once, in 1943, the Labour politician Frank Pakenham, later better known as Lord Longford, who came to talk about the

---

4. Karl Mannheim, *Ideology and Utopia*, rev. Eng. ed. (London: Routledge, 1991) (original German ed. 1929).

5. Karl Mannheim, *Man and Society in an Age of Reconstruction* (London: Routledge & Kegan Paul, 1944).

Beveridge Report, charter of the the post-war British welfare state, since he was assistant to the author of the report, Sir William Beveridge.

It should be emphasised that while at first sight the Moot might appear to constitute an ivory tower of ethereal, academic debate, by far the great majority of its participants were actively involved in public responsibilities through either their professional work or their special interests. Oldham's previous activities have already been mentioned. In addition, for example, Iredale, Moberly, Oakeshott, and Oldham had all been involved with the Pilgrim Trust project on unemployment and its visionary report *Men Without Work* (1938))—described by one social historian, C.L. Mowat, as "the best social study of unemployment made in the thirties."[6] In Scotland Hector Hetherington's record of service on committees and tribunals embracing industrial disputes, employment legislation, social services, health policy, and education is truly awesome. These were intellectuals, certainly, but *engaged* intellectuals, and by engaging with each other they helped reshape each other's outlook in important respects.

What the Moot Did

As far as outcomes go, it is easier to say, first, what the Moot did *not* do, or try to do. It did not produce any collective writing of its own for public consumption. The nearest it came to doing so was in preparing a draft for a lengthy statement by Archbishop William Temple in 1943 on "What Christians Stand for in the Secular World."[7] Nor did it succeed in generating what Oldham and others, particularly Mannheim, long hoped for: an "Order" of people committed to defending and advancing the values of freedom and justice in society, in face of what was feared to a creeping totalitarianism from within. We shall return to that later.

What the Moot *did* do was to provide a crucial resource for its members in the outworking of their varied interests and engagements. From 1940 John Baillie was chairman of the Church of Scotland's wartime Commission on "The Interpretation of God's Will in the Present Crisis," which covered a whole range of contemporary social, economic and international issues.[8] Alec Vidler was acting as a theological midwife in his editing of the journal *Theology*. T.S. Eliot was deeply into his writing on society and culture. Moberly and Clarke were heavily engaged with the future of educational policy—especially with the coming into view of the Butler Educa-

---

6. See Adrian Hastings, *A History of English Christianity 1920-1985* (London: Collins 1985), 258f.
7. Published as Supplement to *Christian News-Letter* 198 (29 December 1943). See Clements, *Faith on the Frontier*, 401ff.
8. See Andrew Morton, ed., *God's Will in a Time of Crisis: A Colloquium Celebrating the 50th Anniversary of the Baillie Commission* (CTPI, 1994).

tion Act of 1944. They were especially influential in the formation of the University Teachers' Group, while Moberly's book *The Crisis in the University* (1949) would prove to be one of the most challenging essays, with longer-term influence, on post-war higher education. Hetherington's heavy agenda of social and industrial, no less than academic, concerns have already been noted. To all such, it mattered being in the Moot; perhaps the very fact of their *not* being required to produce reports to order, but simply given precious space to explore new ways of thinking, added to its appeal. The Moot has justly been described as "a catalyst for the thinking of an extraordinarily diverse group of people."[9] Michael Polanyi, although he arrived only late in the day, was later to say that the Moot discussions "changed our lives."[10] Above all, that debt was felt by Karl Mannheim who, having arrived as an outsider to the British intellectual scene, found in the Moot a sympathetic *entrée* to it and an invaluable sounding-board for his ideas. It was largely Mannheim's death in early 1947 that prompted Oldham to terminate the Moot, and there is no more powerful and moving testimony to what the group signified than the letter that Mannheim's widow Julia wrote to the Moot members: "It was the spot for him to be as he was without the slightest reservations because he knew that you all wanted and do not mind if he gives himself as he is... Until the formation of the Moot he was longing for that safe and free place for the mind, soul and spirit and your circle has given that to him and I should like to bless everyone of you for having taken him in so completely."[11] But equally, the Moot was in Mannheim's debt. It is significant that the most influential intellectual force in the group, the one who most effectively helped its members to view their own society from a new perspective, was this refugee figure who was himself having to live in two places at once, that is, in Britain while still very much mentally a continental European; and in retaining much of his Jewish background while seeking to understand, and to be understood by, his Christian hosts.

But neither was the outcome purely at the individual level. For example, one of Oldham's wartime projects, begun in autumn 1939 just weeks after the outbreak of war, was the extraordinarily effective weekly *Christian News-Letter*, which reached a subscription level of over 10,000 and a still wider actual readership. Several members of the Moot, including Vidler and Eliot, assisted Oldham in editing the *News-Letter*, which covered all manner of topics from industry to education, family life to

---

9. William Taylor and Marjorie Reeves, "Intellectuals in Debate: The Moot," in *Christian Thinking and Social Order: Conviction Politics from the 1930s to the Present Day*, ed. Marjorie Reeves (London: Cassell, 1999), 42. This chapter and the book as a whole form an additional valuable source on the Moot and its context. See also *MP*, 15.
10. Reeves, *Christian Thinking and Social Order*, 42.
11. *MP*, 23.

reconstruction in Europe, the church under persecution to the future of democracy, from spirituality to the role of Britain in the world,. and much more, including genuine news from all over the world. For many people in Britain, hard-pressed by the anxieties and dangers of war, the *News-Letter* was a window onto the wider scene, in many cases one of far greater sufferings than their own; and a vantage-point onto a post-war future which could be glimpsed by faith and hope, and built through justice and compassion. "What holds us back," wrote Oldham in the first issue in October 1939, "more than anything is fear—fear not only of death but of life."[12] People were learning they could and should live in more than one place at once, even when their own homes were under threat. Discussions in the Moot often reinforced and contributed to, as well as reflected, what appeared in the *News-Letter*, and the same was true of another wartime brainchild of Oldham, the Christian Frontier Council, formed in 1942.

A Legacy for Today

Thanks to Eric Fenn's painstakingly recorded minutes, typed up and mimeographed each time by Mary Oldham, the Moot has bequeathed us a virtually verbatim record of the exchanges at 19 of these meetings, from 1938 to 1944, amounting to some 400 sides of foolscap, virtually unique in the annals of British intellectual life. Added to this are the copious papers prepared for almost every meeting, for which Mannheim, Hodges, and Oldham himself were the most prolific writers but to which others contributed also, notably Murry and Dawson.

The basic question with which the Moot repeatedly wrestled may be summarised as: How do we love our neighbour not only at the immediate personal level, but in the increasingly dominant, complex world of impersonal social organisation, economic policies, and welfare provision? The fact that this is still our issue in many countries today should prompt us to ask whether the Moot may still be our contemporary too. The quest for a public theology today, as then, is a quest for dialogue with all in society, on what society is and should be according to the vision of the reign of God, and how the values we derive from that vision impinge upon and challenge our political discourse. We can readily admit the huge changes that have intervened in these sixty-plus years, to create a context increasingly secularised, yet also multicultural and multifaith. But ponder: "A new situation is now arising, in which Christians are neither a small minority in a pagan world nor in control, but an influential minority in a world with a Christian past." That may sounds like a contemporary church leader of some insight. In fact it is John Baillie, speaking at the 15th meeting of the Moot in 1942.[13]

---

12. Clements, *Faith on the Frontier*, 193.
13. *MP*, 537.

Oldham and most of his Moot colleagues, like Baillie, were prophetic in discerning that Christendom, in the sense of the centuries-long marriage between official Christianity and the organs of power, political and cultural, in society, was rapidly coming to an end in Britain, and indeed had already disappeared to a far greater extent than most church leaders and sentimentalist exponents of traditional opinion were willing to admit. It might cause some surprise, therefore, to note the title of Oldham's 1940 book, the first in the Christian News-Letter series: *The Resurrection of Christendom.*[14] The title conveyed a recognition that the *old* Christendom lay dead. The contents gave a glimpse of what a new Christendom might look like—or at least what would be required of those working towards it. It reflected much of Oldham's concerns following the 1937 Oxford conference and the themes of the Moot discussions in the first 18 months of the Moot. It succinctly stated the need for a re-engagement of faith in the gospel with the contemporary social challenges, holding in unity two truths of human existence: "The one is that the true home of man's spirit is not in this world, and the other that it is in the here and now, in the dust and heat of the conflicts of this world, that he is called to fulfil his responsibility as a son of God."[15] It makes clear that what is envisaged in this new Christendom is *not* a society controlled by Christian institutions but nevertheless one guided by "Christian principles," a society of diversified centres of action, culture, and commitment at both local and national levels, and above all a shared set of values. "What is meant is a body of assumptions, purposes and ways of behaviour which are shared by the great majority of the people and are the common foundation of different party programmes and varying intellectual formulations."[16] Not, then, a society controlled by or under the immediate impress of the church, but rather one permeated by Christian values as lived out in the world by the lay members of the church. It was a vision calling for a "Christian heroism" by multitudes of individual men and women serving God in their citizenship. Oldham's founding of the Christian Frontier Council in 1942 was a further effort this direction.

A Selection of Themes

During those long weekends at retreat houses or conference centres in the home counties, the Moot discussions embraced a kaleidoscope of topics: what is meant by a "Christian" society? a personalist and communal view of society; response to the war; facing the educational challenge; the universities and their purpose; nationality and nationalism; pacifism; whether the state has a conscience; religion and power;

---

14. London: Sheldon, 1940.
15. Ibid., 8.
16. Ibid, 22.

religion and science; socialism; the nature of democracy ... and so on. All these were dealt with under the overall rubric of the question, "How can society be re-directed from its mindless slide into utilitarian bureaucracy, if not totalitarianism, towards a society consciously aiming at what may broadly be considered to be 'Christian'?" In Oldham's own words, this would mean:

1. A social environment in which the gospel of God's love for men is reflected at last fitfully in the actual conditions of their lives and does not appear in relation to those conditions a hollow mockery.
2. A society in which men can live as those who are responsible to God and conse- quently to one another, and who have, therefore, the opportunity of responsible choice.
3. A society in which there is a growing realisation of our membership one of another.
4. A society which has a respect for the claims and rights of all men, as created by God and the objects of His redeeming love, and has as its purpose the service and well-being of mankind.

The fact that the present state of society is for the most part a complete denial of these aims and that contrary aims for society are publicly proclaimed in various quarters is evidence that the Christian faith, if men are guided by it in their public conduct, is very far from being otiose or irrelevant in modern society.[17]

Later (at the 17th meeting) some socialistic flesh was put on this outline, with an emphasis on a general public awakening and education as the means towards this end rather than direct, compulsive or revolutionary action. Four themes may be selected which were of major concern to the Moot which still resonate powerfully today.

The Divorce Between "Organised Religion" and Society at Large

A German colleague who has reviewed *The Moot Papers*[18] said to me in a personal comment that he was struck by how, in contrast to most continental theological dis- cussions of the mid-20th century, there is relatively little said in the Moot about the institutional church and its place in society. This is a pertinent observation, but in this respect the Moot also stands out in relief against its own British background—now as then. In some quarters, as soon as "the role of faith in public life" or "public theology" is mentioned, the assumption is made that what is being talked about is the place of the institutional church in society and the direct influence of the church, and more

---

17. *MP*, 76.
18. The late Hans Pfeifer, review in *Theology* 114 no. 1 (Jan.-Feb. 2011): 61-64.

particularly its leadership, on the political process and the lives of citizens. This assumption may be an approving one from within the churches, or a disapproving one from secularist circles. In our present context, we know how the return of religion—especially in fundamentalist forms—as a political force has become a new factor.[19] But it is an assumption from which the Moot was remarkably free. At the Moot's first meeting in April 1938, Oldham opened up discussion on "the increasing divorce between the life of the Church and the life of the community."[20] Virtually all the members agreed that this was indeed the situation from which they were starting, as Walter Moberly put it: "The whole traditional relation between Church and Community had become unreal—e.g. the Coronation or the contrast between a Cathedral city and a new housing area." Around this time there had been a lot of wishful and sentimental talk at church leadership level about "a return to religion" signified by the coronation of King George VI the previous year. The Moot from the beginning was unimpressed by this, and believed that what was at issue was not "a return to religion" or increased respect for the churches, but what was happening within society itself. These social changes the churches were not addressing, and probably not capable of addressing; indeed, as some trenchant critics like Middleton Murry and Alec Vidler were wont to say, the churches themselves were a major part of the problem. The focus of the Moot was almost entirely on what was happening in society, how people were treating each other there, how the state was treating people, and the values by which people and society as a whole were living. Interestingly it was the largely secular Jew Karl Mannheim who saw Europe's problem as the "divorce" between "traditional Christianity" and the modern world, resulting from the difficulty of translating the "primary" ethics of the New Testament, centred on personal love of neighbour, into the demands of an increasingly complex and impersonal society. Mannheim called upon the churches to help meet what he called "the crisis in valuation." In working with *this* perspective, of focusing on what the kingdom of God means in the secular world, and of seeing the churches' salvation as lying in addressing *this* issue, not their own survival, the Moot was prophetic of much that was to come in ecumenical life and thought after the second world war. Moreover, the Moot recognised the perennial tendency to self-deception whenever the churches try to plead their social significance too quickly, and Middleton Murry's remarks in response to William Paton at the second Moot meeting can still bite: Murry "felt it necessary to preserve a profound scepticism because the Christian mind did not realise the effect of its connection with economic privilege. Our liberties were not Christian liberties *won*, but natural liberties *given* by economic privilege."[21]

19. See below, chapter 11.
20. *MP*, 39.
21. *MP*, 95.

Diagnosis and Prescription: "Planning for Freedom"

In convening the Moot, Joe Oldham was prescient about the coming crisis of war in Europe. By the time of the Munich crisis of September 1938, the Moot had already met three times. In a famous letter to the *Times* just after Munich, Oldham warned that while the immediate crisis of war had been averted, the deeper questions remained unaddressed: namely, precisely what was the difference in moral basis between our society and that of the totalitarian states?[22] When war actually broke out, he pressed further the question of just what Britain thought it was fighting for, apart from its national survival. The stock answer in public discourse was: democracy good, fascism bad, Soviet communism worse still. For Oldham and the Moot this would not do, and here is where Karl Mannheim became so important, on account of both his socio-political analysis and his background on the continent, where the battle between democracy and totalitarianism had been joined— and seemingly won by the dictators. Mannheim repeatedly argued in the Moot, as in his published works, that while western liberals might not like either fascism or Soviet communism, it was important to see that these had been responses, albeit inadequate ones, to a genuine crisis in capitalist industrial societies, and the worst mistake would be to pretend that this crisis was not real or could be left to solve itself. The crisis was one of how societies fragmenting under the disintegrative impact of *laissez-faire* economics could retain any kind of social coherence, could avoid sliding into a jungle warfare of individualistic acquisitiveness and deprivation, of moral relativism and nihilism: in short, into chaos. To this undeniable challenge, Hitler and Stalin had their own answers, which consisted of enforcing a unity based respectively on nation and race or on an imposed materialist ideology, but in both cases rejecting the concept of freedom which had prospered since the Enlightenment. No doubt today Mannheim would be warning that it is not enough simply to react in horror to religiously-inspired political extremism, whether Islamic or any other, without probing deeper into the crises to which they are, however perversely, seeking to respond.

Mannheim was fascinated by the evident stability of British society, which was apparently resistant to such traumas as experienced on the continent. But Oldham had already warned that, especially under wartime conditions, Britain too might drift towards totalitarianism by default, under an omnicompetent state regulating and directing all aspects of life according to secular, utilitarian ends and denying that element of freedom which is essential to moral responsibility. Mannheim agreed, as did most of the Moot members, and his prescription was embodied in his concept "planning for freedom" (the "third way" as he called it, between totalitarianism and

---

22. See Clements, *Faith on the Frontier*, 364.

laissez-faire). If an increasingly complex society was not to break down there had to be planning, from housing to health care, from industrial production to education, from cultural needs to scientific research. But *planning*, for Mannheim, did not equate simply with *regulation*—that was the mistake of the dictatorships. Rather, planning had to be undertaken democratically and, moreover, had consciously to *include* in its purview those areas where freedom for individuals and communities had to be preserved. It would not be diktat from on high, but would involve coordination between already existing groups at every level in society, with whatever would enhance communal life and voluntary social cohesion—what today we would no doubt call "civil society." In this "planning for freedom" the churches as real communities and bearers of values would have a vital role.

Values: Common and Christian

Central to Mannheim's thesis was that to be cohesive, a society which planned for freedom needed shared moral values adequate to the changing situation. This provided the Moot with one of its most persistent and taxing subjects, which still besets us today. It is the perennial tension generated by, on the one hand, the specific claims of the Christian gospel, and on the other, the need to find a workable ethic for the whole of society irrespective of whether that gospel is consciously accepted by all: or put another way, the coexistence, if not competition, between revelation and "natural law." The Moot spent hours on this, and to setters of examinations on ethics its minutes can be commended as a rich resource for the sort of question which consists of an aphorism in quotation marks followed by "Discuss." Now we might expect that with the Moot including such a strong contingent of Oxford-trained classicists and philosophers, and such a devotee of Anglo-Catholic High Toryism as T.S. Eliot, there would be an overwhelming affirmation of "natural law." Such, however, was not the case. The discussions tended to end up each time with the concept of natural law heavily battered from several directions, but with the question remaining not fully answered as to how the gospel and the teaching of Christ relate to the matters of everyday social ethics, politics, and economics. For example, at the ninth meeting, H.A. Hodges led off with a strong critique of natural law as developed in medieval Catholicism: while claiming to be derived from first principles, natural law was in fact historically conditioned, and while purporting to conform to objective reality, its acceptance was a matter of choice. This we now realise, says Hodges: "This meant a new conception of thinking; you could not now 'just know' anything; you had to make a choice."[23] Mannheim agrees, but points out that that this leaves us with the problem

---

23. *MP*, 327.

of relativism, product of the scientific revolution, and comments ruefully that back in Germany his own earlier work *Ideology and Utopia* had proved capable of Fascist interpretation: "We [have] to face realities and the fact of a deep relativism in knowledge; but some other basis was required for immediate social action." This leads to a discussion about functional rules and utilitarianism, in which Walter Moberly joins with his special interest in criminal law arguing that certain "working principles" can be looked for that derive neither from sheer retributive impulses nor utilitarianism. Catholic natural law, according to Moberly, built up a complete system and in the end failed for that very reason; but at the same time "there was more in it than merely the will of considerable number of people imposing itself on others. There was some correspondence to human nature and the law of the universe. It had its anthropological and theological aspects."[24] T.S. Eliot agrees that the medieval Catholic concept was far too abstract, and limited in its historically conditioned nature, and then intriguingly says also that it "set a premium on ingenuity rather than wisdom. The content of natural law lay in the field of wisdom rather than logical argument. We were always brought back to this in some form ... You could not defend Natural Law, but it would turn up again and again. It was the characteristic of something objective that it should turn up again and again!" Middleton Murry then seizes approvingly upon Eliot's linking of Natural Law to "wisdom," saying that "Life-wisdom, a flair for fullness of existence in immediate experience, was the only category he could use."[25] Beginning with Oliver Cromwell's "any order is better than none" as axiomatic, Murry argues that we could on to say some orders are better than others (which was where traditional Catholicism stopped), but then go on further still to identify which particular order was better than any other. But, he suggests, contemporary Christianity seemed incapable of making any declaration on this level. Moberly asked whether this was wisdom or incompetence of the part of Christianity—and Murry replied that it was impotence.[26] This, incidentally, is typical of the kind of rapid-fire Moot conversation which one finds oneself wanting to join in as it goes along This, incidentally, is typical of the kind of rapid-fire Moot conversation which one finds oneself wanting to join in as it goes along. That this discussion, incidentally, took place in July 1940, right at the most perilous juncture of the war for Britain, when the threat of invasion seemed so real, is testimony to the remarkable degree of intellectual concentration which the Moot members were determined to maintain in face of immediate crisis and anxiety.

During other meetings, natural law was questioned much more from the theological side by Alec Vidler who, echoing Karl Barth, suggested that secular people

24. *MP*, 330.
25. *MP*, 332.
26. *MP*, 333.

were far more likely to be impressed by the church uttering a distinctive, theologically based word than by a reiteration of what the world believed already; and by Lex Miller, who brought both Barth and another notable, Karl Marx, into the discussion and asked whether the group, in looking for social reform, was pre-empting the case for revolution. There were also long and fascinating explorations led by Hodges on "social archetypes" as carriers of values, a concept which would merit revisiting especially for its potential in our present multicultural context.

Effecting Change: Mobilising an "Order"

This theme is the one on which the Moot seemed to spend an unwarrantable amount of time, leading to frustrating arguments and profound disagreements—and finally getting nowhere. The frustration was born out of an unresolved ambiguity about the very nature and purpose of the Moot itself: was it primarily for intellectual discussion (faith seeking understanding) or was it itself to generate action in order to fulfil the understanding of society which it was achieving? Oldham clearly wanted it to be both, as did Mannheim and Middleton Murry. In fact Murry grew so frustrated at the lack of progress towards action that he withdrew his attendance after the 15th meeting. The action which Oldham had in mind from the beginning was the creation of an "Order" (or, as he later called it, a "Fraternity of the Spirit") of about 300 persons in key positions in society who would commit themselves to working for resistance to the creeping totalitarianism which Oldham saw as threatening society, and promoting the cause of human dignity, just relationships, and freedom at every level of society wherever decisions affecting the lives of citizens were being made. But there never was full clarity on what this Order would aim at, how it would be set up and its members be recruited, and what the relation of the Moot itself to it would be. It has to be reckoned one of the least viable products of Oldham's fertile mind.

At the same time, what Oldham envisaged has to be seen as but one part of the overall vision that he and his ecumenical contemporaries had for Christian social transformation. In the preparatory material for the 1937 Oxford conference, he and W.A. Visser 't Hooft had emphasized the decisive role of the laity as the main instruments of God's mission in the world, and moreover advocated the spontaneous activity of small "cells" meeting for mutual encouragement, fellowship and common effort: "May not the formation of such cells of Christian witness and service be the distinctive contribution to the social and political struggles of our time? To be effectively changed a social system must be changed from within and in all its parts."[27] Perhaps

---

27. J.H. Oldham and W.A. Visser 't Hooft, *The Church and Its Function in Society* (London: George Allen & Unwin, 1937), 365. See also *MP*, 8.

more than Oldham realised, during and immediately after the second world war, this was already happening, not least stimulated by his own *Christian News-Letter*, his Christian Frontier Council, the University Teachers' Group, the new growth of industrial mission, not to mention the continued life—for a time at least—of the student movements. How impoverished so much of our so-called ecumenical life today (in the West at least) appears by comparison! Oldham and his Moot may be sixty years in the past, but as far as seeing ecumenical life as a liberating, participatory movement for the whole people of God we are now miles to the rear of those pioneers. Ecumenism has been clericalised, bureaucratised, made the prisoner of church structures which claim to "own" it and do just that, to the extent of locking it away from the people while disempowering the ecumenical instruments they have set up. Meanwhile we complain that our voice is not listened to in the public forum, but less often ask whether we have anything worthwhile to say. Whatever else it was or was not, whatever it achieved or failed to achieve, the Moot exemplified the effort to find something distinctively critical and constructive to say, to engage with all the costly seriousness involved in spiritual and intellectual effort, and to bring into the enterprise as wide a variety of people and experiences as possible.

A Resource to Be Pondered

The Moot indeed served as a resource for the personal endeavours and engagements of its members. In turn, it can be a resource for those today who are engaged in a faith seeking social transformation, especially in a context which is increasingly described as "post-Christendom." By "resource" is not meant an authoritative textbook of ideas to be accepted, or even guidelines on how the task is to be carried on in our time and our context, which indeed in many ways is very different. But only an arrogance devoid of any imagination will presume that nothing is to be gained from the past and no inspiration to be received from the sense of continuing an endeavour already begun, of joining in a conversation started and as yet unfinished.

In any case, there are many gems awaiting the reader's discovery in the Moot minutes, and not only by those setting examination questions. There is John Baillie's dry comment on the deep separation in the minds of people at large between public life and religion: to wit, that people "are equally horrified at hearing Christianity doubted and at seeing it practised."[28] One can almost hear Alec Vidler growling in consternation on being told by Frank Pakenham that William Beveridge had received not a single representation from the churches while preparing his report. There are poignant exchanges between, on the one hand, Löwe and Mannheim representing the

---

28. *MP*, 94.

Jewish perspective, and on the other hand those speaking out of Christian tradition: as for example when Mannheim, following a deeply thoughtful and well-argued presentation of Christian apologetics by Hodges, suggests that not only as a sociologist does he see things otherwise, but that there is a real difference of religious experience too: "For him [Mannheim], God was more real in search and disquietude than in peace and certainty. This might go back at bottom to the Jewish experience which found suffering more important than redemption."[29] The poignancy is only deepened by noting that that remark, during the 14th meeting in March 1942, was made not knowing that just weeks earlier there had taken place the secret Wannsee Conference at which the Nazi leadership had decided on the "Final Solution." There are intriguingly provocative statements like that of the eminent economist Noel Hall, guest at the fourth meeting, who said: "Christian belief provided the only possible reconciliation of politics and economics in its reaffirmation of essential values."[30] There is Kathleen Bliss's brief diatribe against the "gadget mind" in the "new fangled house" being held out as the promise to solve all the problems of the housewife after the war. And if one wishes to hear a word which could indeed be spoken as well now as then, there is Fred Clarke, in the midst of a discussion about Britain's anticipated role in the post-war world, and speaking out of his long and sometimes disillusioning experience as an educator in British territories overseas: "We knew where we would like to go but grudged the cost. That was where the need for repentance came in. One of our national weaknesses was that of taking on commitments under the impulse of duty without counting the cost and then failing to fulfil them."[31] Enough said.

We shall return to Oldham in chapter 11 to ponder the continuing relevance of his "middle axioms" concept for social ethics. Much else flowed from the cauldron of ideas for which the Moot supplied much of the heat. It was Oldham, recalled W.A. Visser 't Hooft, who in 1948 suggested to him the phrase "the responsible society" as a title for the WCC's long-term agenda to follow the inaugural assembly at Amsterdam.[32] "The responsible society" indeed became the motif for much ecumenical work, effectively until the 4th WCC Assembly at Uppsala in 1968. It is still worth attending to. Nor should the Moot be thought of in total isolation from other study groups that were meeting before, during and after the war in the USA, on the continent of Europe and even in Nazi Germany—some of the themes and thinking of the Moot show striking parallels, for example, with the work of the Kreisau Circle of

---

29. *MP*, 522.
30. *MP*, 202.
31. *MP*, 633.
32. W.A. Visser't Hooft, *Memoirs* (London: SCM, 1973), 205. See also Clements, *Faith on the Frontier*, 432.

German resisters around Helmut von Moltke and Adam von Trott. Visser 't Hooft at the WCC office in Geneva was in touch with both Oldham and von Trott, was able to give to von Trott some copies of the *Christian News-Letter* on his visit to Geneva in 1941; and it is interesting to speculate whether any of the Moot discussion papers may also have found their way to Kreisau.[33] Visser 't Hooft likewise showed Dietrich Bonhoeffer Oldham's *News-Letter* and writings of other British ecumenicals. He and Bonhoeffer wrote and sent to London a response to William Paton's 1941 book *The Church and the New Order*. There was therefore at this time when Europe and the world were savagely torn by battle-lines a network of thinkers who nevertheless were able to communicate from context to context, living elsewhere than just their immediate situation, and trying to envisage together a coming world of peace and justice.

Finally, two points should be re-emphasized about the Moot and what it signifies for creative ecumenical life. First, as we have noted, while the Moot included some clergy and academic theologians, it mostly comprised lay people who were in fact experts in their own fields. But there is more to it than that. The recruits were not all necessarily recognised as "ecumenical" beforehand. They *became* ecumenical by involvement in the group and its concern for the *oikoumene*. The ecumenical movement thrives not by creating or recognizing a distinct and separate class of ecumenical or "ecumenically-minded" persons but by drawing into the enterprise any and all who have something important to give in the perfectly mad adventure of serving the *oikoumene* in the light of the gospel and in seeking quite new ways of doing so.

Second, the Moot provided *space and time* for such people to meet and to explore specific issues in a persistent and open-ended way, without the pressure (other than any they imposed on themselves) to produce results. Indeed, as an adventure, mad or otherwise, it could not guarantee results and had to risk failure. Inside the cover of his pocket-diary for 1945, Oldham wrote a verse by the ill-fated Scotsman James Graham, Marquess of Montrose (1612-1650):

He either fears his fate too much,
Or his deserts are small,
That puts it not unto the touch
To win or lose it all.[34]

That would well serve as a motto for the ecumenical way, for to live elsewhere than just at home is always to invite risk, and that will always be part of the dynamic.

---

33. On these linkages via Geneva see Clements, *Faith on the Frontier*, 397f, and "Oldham and Baillie: A Creative Relationship" in Morton, op. cit. (see n8 above).
34. Clements, *Faith on the Frontier*, 415.

Chapter 9
European Journey of Hope
From Creed to Charter

In a world of border controls and passports, visa requirements and work permits, immigration quotas and xenophobia, "living in more than one place at once" does not always seem a very practicable idea. Across much of Europe for the four decades of the Cold War, it seemed especially unrealistic. The political and military divide between East and West was so deeply entrenched and seemingly, until the late 1980s, permanent. Today, a whole generation has grown up for whom the Berlin Wall is a piece of pre-history and the map of Europe almost unrecognizably different, with countries of the Soviet Bloc, from Poland to Bulgaria, and even former parts of the Soviet Union itself (the Baltic States) now members of the European Union. Because so much has changed in Europe since 1989, the landscape before that scene-change now seems like foreign territory. Yet much of what we now take for granted in ecumenical life was forged in that very different and often forbidding environment. The Conference of European Churches (CEC) began modestly in 1959 as a means primarily of enabling the churches of east and west to meet across the Cold War divide and manifest their oneness in the Body of Christ, and soon grew into a fellowship of over 125 churches—Protestant, Orthodox, Anglican, and Old Catholic.

In those early days, even just to meet across the East-West divide was a mighty achievement, and the first few years' activities of CEC were, outwardly, little more than a series of annual conferences usually held at Nyborg in Denmark. Not until 'Nyborg IV' in 1964 did CEC even have a formal constitution. But Nyborg IV was notable in another way, for the manner of its meeting which has passed into CEC legend. In 1962 several delegates from the East had missed the assembly because of passport problems. As far as travel from the East was concerned, it was often visitors from the communist German Democratic Republic (GDR) who faced the greatest difficulties. GDR passports were not recognized in the West, and GDR citizens who wanted to travel to NATO countries had to obtain a special "passport" from the Allied Travel Board in West Berlin. But they first had to obtain permission from the GDR authorities even to apply for such documents, and in 1964 this permission was refused. Undaunted by this diplomatic and bureaucratic stand-off, in order to save the face of GDR officialdom and to spare the Danes embarrassment, CEC chartered a ship, the *Bornholm*. With most of the assembly on board, the vessel sailed from Copenhagen into the Baltic, to the incontrovertibly neutral demarcation line between Denmark and Sweden. There it took on board the delegates from the GDR who had been brought out on another vessel from the East German port of Rostock.[1] So this decisive assembly took place. Appropriately, as well as the constitutional issues its main theme was "Living together as continents and generations." In face of the divisive ideologies and politics of the day, the reality of a European Christian fellowship transcending borders was affirmed both symbolically and practically. It is small wonder that while the image of a boat is a widely used ecumenical symbol, for CEC it became an especially apt and precious logo. "The walls of separation do not reach to heaven," it was frequently said in those and subsequent days.

Other significant developments were also afoot. The year of CEC's birth, 1959, also saw the calling by Pope John XXIII of the Second Vatican Council, one of the European fruits of which was the creation of the Council of Catholic Episcopal Conferences in Europe (CCEE)—again, a determinedly pan-European body despite the hugely oppressive context for the Roman Catholic Church in many parts of Eastern Europe. CEC and CCEE soon found themselves as partners in promoting a Christian dialogue and common witness across Europe. The particular piece of history to be related here is their common venture, over a twenty-year period from the mid-1980s, to express a common hope for the churches and peoples of Europe as a whole. This involved, on every side, an attempt to see the world not only from within one's own tradition, and not only from one side of the East-West divide, but in anticipation of what a "common home" in Europe might be like.

Daring to Hope: Riva del Garda 1984

Our starting point is the Ecumenical Encounter organised jointly in 1984 by CEC and CCEE at Riva del Garda, near Trento in Italy. As one who was not present at Riva del Garda, my own pictures of that event have been formed by reading the accounts and documents,[2] but no less by the vivid recollections passed on by some who did participate. They tell how moving it was for many Protestants to come to Trento, a city whose name is inevitably associated with the hardening of dogmatic and ecclesiastical divisions in the aftermath of the 16th century Reformation. They tell of the

---

1. See Robin Gurney, *CEC at 40* (Geneva: Conference of European Churches 1999), 17.
2. *Confessing the Faith Together—A Source of Hope*, Report of the Third European Ecumenical Encounter, 3-8 October 1984, Riva del Garda, Italy (Geneva and St Gallen: CEC and CCEE, 1985).

inspirational worship services of common prayer, including prayers of repentance. They speak of the richly informative theological lectures by Dr R.P.C. Hanson and Professor Werner Löser, and other addresses. They record the sense of real achievement in the production of the text "Our Credo–Source of Hope"—and much else.

Riva del Garda 1984 must be set in its historical context. It was the third ecumenical encounter organised jointly by CEC and CCEE, following those at Chantilly, France, in 1978 and at Logumkloster, Denmark, in 1981. It should be borne in mind that both CEC and CCEE at that time were still relatively young organisations, still feeling their way in promoting ecumenical dialogue. It was, moreover, humanly speaking, a very bleak climate in which they dared to speak about unity among the churches and peace in Europe. Not only was Europe still politically—and seemingly for ever—divided between east and west, but the Cold War was now entering a newly alarming phase of military confrontation. The threat of nuclear warfare hung over all. As yet *glasnost* and *perestroika*[3] were unknown words.

Chantilly and Logumkloster had focused on the calling of the churches to unity in one hope, that the world might believe. It was a bold and decisive step that was taken, to make the theme of Riva del Garda not the production of a new statement about unity, but a return to a study of the ancient confession of faith common to all trinitarian Christians: the Niceno-Constantinopolitan Creed of 381. This choice of topic should not be seen in isolation from the wider awakening of interest in the creed around that time. The Faith and Order Commission of the WCC was launching the study process "Towards the Common Expression of the Apostolic Faith Today" based on a new ecumenical explication of the creed.[4] Both the WCC and the Vatican Secretariat for Unity had proposed that this study also be implemented in continental, regional contexts. Riva del Garda can therefore be seen as a venture in Europeanizing the wider programme. But it also had a momentum and a specific motivation of its own. Divided churches in a dangerously divided continent; churches which by their divisions had historically contributed to the wider human divisions, churches which seemed powerless in face of the ideological divides and the nuclear arsenals: what had they to say, what *could* they say, with integrity? How could they bring hope into a seemingly hopeless situation? What common witness could they bring?

---

3. *Glasnost* (openness) and *perestroika* (restructuring) emerged as watchwords in the mid-1980s in Mikhail Gorbachev's time as general secretary of the Communist Party in the Soviet Union, as the country moved toward political and economic change at the turn of the decade.
4. For the summary results of this study process, see *Confessing the One Faith: An Ecumenical Explication of the Apostolic Faith as It Is Confessed in the Nicene-Constantinopolitan Creed (381)*, Faith and Order Paper No. 153 (Geneva: WCC Publications, 1991).

At first sight, it must have seemed that to return to an ancient creed was an escape from the brutal and fearful realities of the present day. The architects of Riva del Garda were under no illusions that the project might be laughed at and dismissed. What is remarkable is that they refused to see the creed as merely a historical monument, or even just as a liturgical text enshrined in tradition, but as a sign and source of hope: it still had a future, and it offered a future. As the "Message to the Christians of Europe" from Riva del Garda stated: "This common confession of our faith is certainly not the immediate answer to the questions nor is it the solution to all the problems which arise today in a divided Europe. It does however remind us of God's love for all men; and it encourages us to go further together along the road which will lead Europe and the world to peace and reconciliation."[5] This was a recognition that if the churches *do* have anything of relevance to say to one another in their search for unity and to the world in its longing for peace, it must arise from the faith confessed in this creed. The churches' witness cannot just be a recasting of one form or another of human philosophy or political ideology. It has to have a specific theological grounding in the Trinitarian faith. This was a decisive clearing of the ground and a laying of the foundations for so much which was to come in the two following decades. The churches of Europe were recovering a truly theological confidence for their witness, even if at that time many aspects of that witness remained unclear and uncertain. Above all, it was a witness *in hope* which was being recovered. As the theological text says in its concluding paragraph on the resurrection and new creation: "We realize that this patient expectation of the new creation does not exonerate us from working with others for the establishment of a more just and human world. Indeed, this liberates us for this task... The courage to live has its source in the hope of eternal life."[6]

Riva del Garda reverberated with a two-fold harmony: the faith confessed in the creed as the source of hope, and the calling for that hope to be translated into concrete action in responsibility for Europe:

> Our common confession of the faith challenges us to find new ways of responding together to the questions raised by the modern world and of providing together the service of aid and sharing which Christ commands. Peace, disarmament, human rights, the place of women in church and society, unemployment, poverty, the environment—these are some of the difficult questions to which we as Christians should seek answers together.[7]

---

5. *Confessing the Faith Together*, 8.
6. Ibid., 26.
7. Ibid., 8.

Hope Widens: Peace with Justice—Basel 1989

The recognition of this agenda was indeed to prove prophetic, as further developments from the mid-1980s showed. Again, these developments cannot be isolated from the wider ecumenical world scene but in Europe they were to take a dramatic turn. The sixth assembly of the World Council of Churches in Vancouver, 1983, had recommended that the churches enter into a "conciliar process of mutual commitment to justice, peace and the integrity of creation." It was in Europe that this call was to be taken up in an especially important way, and the initiative was to be provided by the churches in the two countries which represented the division of Europe in its starkest form: the German Democratic Republic and the Federal Republic of Germany. It should be noted too that the European churches had already been accompanying very closely the implementation of the Helsinki Final Act and the work of the Conference on Security and Cooperation in Europe (CSCE) which at that time represented the only real hope on the political level of countering the Cold War divide. But the German initiative, especially on the GDR side, came with a particular challenge to the churches themselves. In part it was because among German Protestants, the memory had been kept alive of what had happened in 1934 at the conference of the Universal Christian Council for Life and Work on the Danish island of Fanø. There, Dietrich Bonhoeffer had spoken on the need for a universal ecumenical council of the churches to be summoned, to declare God's will of peace among the nations and to outlaw war.[8]

At the ninth assembly of the Conference of European Churches in Stirling, Scotland, in 1986, representatives of the churches in the two German republics presented resolutions calling for a European assembly as part of the worldwide process for justice, peace, and the integrity of creation. The assembly itself adopted a resolution proposing that CEC and CCEE together should call an ecumenical Peace assembly for all the churches in states which were signatories to the Helsinki Final Act. Thus was set in train the process that led to the First European Ecumenical Assembly, organised by CEC and CCEE, which met in Basel, Switzerland in May 1989, under the theme "Peace with Justice."[9] The assembly was an epoch-making event in several respects. Not since the great East-West schism of 1054 had Christians from all over Europe met in such numbers—Catholics, Orthodox, Protestants, and Anglicans— as the 700 official church delegates and hundreds more gathered for that week of prayer, celebration, study, and affirmation of faith and responsibility. But it was also of course significant in the more immediate historical context. The tremors of change were already being felt across Europe. In the west there was increasing criticism of

---

8. See above, chapters 2, 4, and 5.
9. See *Peace with Justice*, the official documentation of the European Ecumenical Assembly, Basel, Switzerland, 15-21 May, 1989 (Geneva: Conference of European Churches, 1989).

the military standoff. In the east, Poland had been transformed by Solidarity[10] while *glasnost* and *perestroika* were now familiar terms. Basel took up many of the items spelled out for the Christian agenda at Riva del Garda: peace, disarmament, human rights, reconciliation. But one concern which received relatively little attention at Riva del Garda now took at least an equal place with all the others: the integrity of creation, to be made concrete in the care of the environment and its preservation for future generations. This new recognition of creation was quite decisive in giving European Christians a sense that they belonged to one continent, which was part of the one interdependent world of nature and humanity. The Chernobyl disaster of 1986 had spread radioactivity far beyond the borders of the Soviet Union. There was a new realization of the significance that land and soil, sea and air, are held by all in common. The Danube rises in western Germany and flows through Romania into the Black Sea. Whose river is it?

Basel celebrated the one faith of all European Christians, and Christians celebrated that unity—the unity they already had and the unity they still hoped for. They went on pilgrimage across the three borders between Switzerland, France and Germany to symbolize their vision of a new Europe *sans frontières*. A new language was being spoken, heard for example in one of the prayers prepared for Basel that echoed words of Pope John Paul II: "We thank you that the peoples of the East and the peoples of the West share a common home in Europe. Lord, help us to know that peace between East and West in Europe will help to solve many conflicts outside Europe. Keep us from accepting division and tension."[11] If Basel in May 1989 took place at a time of rising excitement and hope, few could have anticipated that by the end of that same year the Berlin Wall would have collapsed, and change would have swept through Hungary, Romania, Czechoslovakia, and other countries in the east. But it is important to acknowledge that the churches of Europe, while taken by surprise at the speed of events, were not simply following in their train. Just as the revival in the Russian Orthodox Church did not wait for the events of 1990-91, nor even for the policies of President Gorbachev, but was already under way in preparation for the celebrations in 1988 of the 1000th anniversary of the conversion of Russia, so too Basel anticipated much of what was to come in Europe as a whole. The European churches were finding each other anew, and realising they had a common responsibility for Europe, their common home.

---

10. Solidarity (*Solidarinóść*), whose full name was the Independent Self-governing Trade Union "Solidarity," began at the Gdansk Shipyard under the leadership of Lech Walesa and was the first trade union not affiliated with the Communist Party in a Warsaw Pact country. During a decade of (often persecuted) activism on both labour and broader social issues, Solidarity contributed to political change in Poland and to the broader movement of change in Eastern Europe and Russia. Walesa was elected President of Poland in 1990.

11. *Peace with Justice*, 15.

As Wordsworth said of the early days of the French revolution, "Bliss was it in that dawn to be alive." But the full light of day challenged the euphoria. While Basel had declared that there were no problems or tensions in Europe which justified violence as a solution, soon we had the bloody conflicts attending the break-up of the former Yugoslavia, conflicts which tragically did have a religious dimension to them. It seemed that with the breakdown of the political and ideological divide between east and west the ancient historic fault-line between Orthodox east and Latin west was re-emerging. This did not run only through present-day Bosnia-Hercegovina, but more widely from the Baltic to the Mediterranean. It had cultural elements. It was also taking on new economic aspects, as it became clear that many of the countries in the east were entering not a new paradise of prosperity but a chaos of industrial disintegration, unemployment and breakdown of social welfare. And what of the churches? For many of them, the new scenery was bewildering. The totalitarian regimes had imposed a kind of *de facto* ecumenism where Protestant, Catholic, and Orthodox found themselves in natural solidarity, and in which belonging to wider ecumenical bodies like CEC or the WCC had served to enable contact with the western world. Those who had endured or resisted communism found that the new situation of freedom posed new questions to them as to their identity, in relation both to society and to other churches. Who were they meant to be, and to whom should they now relate? The churches in the west, for their part, found that their partners in the east often had quite other priorities than theirs, in for example the need to rebuild their life and ministry in their basic essentials.

In the early 1990s there was talk of the emergence of a "new confessionalism." It was certainly significant that during 1991 and 1992 three major confessional gatherings took place: the First Synod of European Catholic Bishops in Rome, the "Protestant Synod" in Budapest, and the Synod of Orthodox Bishops in Constantinople. This in itself was hardly remarkable. It was only to be expected that those with a shared tradition and identity should seek to reflect on their particular role and responsibility in a quite changed situation. What was more alarming was that at the same time new suspicions and disputes were arising interconfessionally. Orthodox were angered at what they saw as invasions by proselytising Protestant missionaries from the west, or new Catholic designs on their territory. Equally, some churches in minority situations felt that the majority historical churches were seeking to restore their old pre-communist priviledged positions in state and society, without regard for religious freedom and democratic rights. All this, however, did not prevent CEC and CCEE from holding another ecumenical encounter in Santiago Compostela in 1991 on the theme "Mission and Evangelism in Europe Today."

Costly Hope and Reconciliation—Graz 1997

It was becoming clear that the call made at Riva del Garda in 1984, for the churches to seek again reconciliation and unity as the basis for a credible witness in Europe, was taking on a new urgency in these years. In fact, in addition to their regular annual meetings of the CEC-CCEE Joint Committee, CEC and CCEE maintained a joint working group specifically to monitor the follow-up to the Basel Assembly and to see that its vision was not lost. It was at the meeting of the Joint CEC-CCEE Committee in Leanyfalu, Hungary, in 1994 that the decision was taken to start preparing for a second European ecumenical assembly. The final decision was taken at the Ecumenical encounter in Assisi in May 1995 to hold the assembly in 1997 and to focus on the theme of "reconciliation." This was chosen deliberately as a way of continuing the central concerns of Basel but also to open up new dimensions. The experiences since Basel had made the churches aware that reconciliation was what they needed among themselves, and that the gospel of reconciliation was the most precious gift they could offer to the world.

This brings us to Graz, July 1997, where 10,000 Christians from all traditions and from all over Europe came to pray, celebrate, and study together under the theme "Reconciliation—Gift of God and Source of New Life."[12] It was the largest ever pan-European gathering of this kind, where for the first time east Europeans were together on truly equal terms with the west. But it was noteworthy not only for its breadth but for its depth as well. It was one of those rare occasions when not only the public issues of peacemaking, economic justice, and environmental care were studied and debated, but where the need for spiritual formation of those who would be peacemakers and reconcilers was made clear. As the final message states:

> We came to this ecumenical gathering not just to exchange ideas and share experiences, but to go beyond words to specific measures, aware that our divisions and enmities still provoke conflict and are a serious obstacle to making visible the gift of reconciliation. For this we seek God's forgiveness and express our repentance to those we have harmed. We are sadly aware that these divisions exist not only between our churches but also between members of our churches and between women and men. Since these exist in us as individuals and in our churches, reconciliation must start by the Spirit of God in Christ changing our hearts and minds.[13]

---

12. See *Reconciliation—Gift of God and Source of New Life*, Documents from the Second European Ecumenical Assembly (Graz: Verlag Styria for CEC and CCEE, 1998).
13. Ibid., 32.

"To go beyond words to specific measures." Among the recommendations of Graz was:

> We recommend that the churches develop a common study document containing basic ecumenical duties and rights. From this a series of ecumenical guidelines, rules and criteria could be developed which would help the churches, those in positions of responsibility and all members, to distinguish between proselytism and Christian witness, as well as between fundamentalism and genuine faithfulness, and help to shape the relationships between majority and minority churches in an ecumenical spirit.[14]

Equally significant was the stated rationale for this: "The ecumenical fellowship is currently in a difficult situation as a result of various factors. This requires conscious counter-strategies. It seems necessary to foster an ecumenical culture of living and working together, and to create a firm basis for it."[15]

The *Charta Oecumenica*

Thus was conceived what was born and became known as the *Charta Oecumenica. Guidelines for the Growing Cooperation among the Churches in Europe*.[16] The *Charta* is an attempt to set out in concrete terms what growing together in dialogue, cooperation, fellowship and shared responsibility towards Europe mean for the European churches today. No less than its content, the way it was produced was an effort to exemplify these values. The process was launched at the annual meeting of the CEC-CCEE Joint Committee in Rome in January 1998. Its drafting was entrusted to a joint group of Protestant, Orthodox and Roman Catholic theologians who laboured through much encounter and debate to produce a first text which was circulated to all the Bishops' Conferences and CEC member churches in the summer of 1999, giving them more than a year in which to respond with their comments, criticisms and suggestions. A large number these were received, in the light of which the text was revised and submitted for final amendment and approval by the CEC-CCEE Joint Committee in January 2001. It was launched upon the world at the ecumenical encounter held by CEC and CCEE in Strasbourg just after Easter 2001. This was an encounter between 100 European church leaders and an equal number of young

---

14. *Reconciliation*, p.49.
15. Ibid.49,
16. Council of European Churches and Council of European Episcopal Conferences, *Charta Oecumenica. Guidelines for the Growing Cooperation among the Churches in Europe* (St Gallen and Geneva: CCEE and CEC, 2001). Text of the *Charta* available online at http://www.ceceurope.org/current-issues/charta-oecumenica/. For a discussion of the *Charta* and its reception see Viorel Ionita and Sara Numico, eds., *Charta Oecumenica: A Text, Process and a Dream of the Churches in Europe* (Geneva: WCC Publications, 2003).

people, who gathered to celebrate and affirm the meaning of Christ for the new millennium under the theme "Lo, I am with you always, to the end of the age." Many of those present for the ceremony at which it was signed by the then Presidents of CEC and CCE, Metropolitan Jérémie Caligiorgis and Cardinal Miloslav Vlk respectively, felt not so much that they had come to the end of a process but to a new beginning, a new stage on the ecumenical pilgrimage.

For an ecumenical document, the *Charta* is a relatively short text; perhaps that is one reason why it has become so popular. It has been translated into at least 30 languages and been studied and discussed all over Europe, and officially adopted by a number of churches. It comprises three main sections: "We believe in 'One Holy Catholic and Apostolic Church'"; "On the Way Towards the Visible Fellowship of the Churches in Europe"; and "Our Common Responsibility in Europe." It states both the obstacles towards unity and the means of grace by which alone they can be overcome, the renewing power of God's Spirit in our hearts and lives. It lays down the importance of meeting together, struggling on difficult ethical and theological issues together, praying together. It sets out Europe's reality as a diversity of peoples and cultures and religions, in which peace is to be sought through dialogue, and the needs and rights of all to be respected. Thus it implicitly recognises the process of European integration in which the enlarging European Union is playing a key role but at the same time seeks to provoke questions about the values which must sustain a united Europe. But the core of this text, what makes it unique, lies in the *commitments* which it invites the churches and Christians to make their own: from recognising freedom of conscience to praying for one another and for Christian unity; from counteracting any form of oppressive nationalism to adopting a lifestyle free of consumerism; from strengthening the position of women and equal rights of women to dialogue with Jews and Muslims. In some circles, the *Charta* has been criticised for allegedly saying little that is new, and in one sense that is true, for it gathers up much of the thought and experience on the ecumenical journey from Riva del Garda onwards. What is new, is the series of commitments which churches are challenged to make in specific directions. It is a mirror against which they can look at themselves and their real actions, or lack of action. Certain churches, once they have started to do this, have admitted that while they think they may know and already do what is in the *Charta*, when measured against the actual praxis called for by the *Charta* they are found wanting. It indicates the direction in which they still have to walk.

From Riva del Garda to the *Charta Oecumenica* was one journey. The starting point of the *Charta Oecumenica* is the same as the theme of Riva del Garda, for the *Charta* opens its first section by declaring: "With the Gospel of Christ, according to the witness if Holy Scripture and as expressed in the ecumenical Nicene-Constantinopolitan Creed of 381, we believe in the triune God: the Father, Son and Holy Spirit." Much had happened since Riva del Garda. There in 1984 the churches of Europe were brought together. Since then they have journeyed together. And if in some ways new problems have arisen between the churches, it is precisely because they have been brought so much closer together. You only really *argue* with people next to you, not those far away. At Riva del Garda the churches came together on the basis of a given text, the ecumenical creed. With the *Charta* they have created a text of their own. At Riva del Garda they looked forward in broad terms to a greater unity in a more united Europe. With the *Charta Oecumenica* they were committing themselves to concrete acts of cooperation and common responsibility. So it is a journey from confession to actions which are themselves new forms of confession. It cannot claim to have left dialogue behind. The *Charta* in fact it calls for still deeper dialogue. While at Riva del Garda the churches of Europe expressed their longing to be together, they now know they cannot do without each other, cannot get away from each other, and cannot understand themselves without one another. At Riva del Garda in 1984 it was said: "Our creed supports our hope in a quite special way. It witnesses to God the Holy Trinity who gives a future and hope to all, and at the same time commits each of us to perform acts of hope." The *Charta Oecumenica* is but the continuation of this way, being itself an act of hope, and specifying those actions which here and now lead us towards visible unity, towards peace and human dignity for all, towards reconciliation and the care of creation, and all to the glory of the one God, Father, Son, and Holy Spirit.

Promising Past—Uncertain Future?

These two and a half decades of European ecumenism indeed constitute a promising past. But the future of the story is uncertain, even following the third European ecumenical assembly held in Sibiu, Romania, in 2007 under the theme "The Light of Christ Shines Upon All—Hope for Renewal and Unity in Europe." It is a truism now to say that the ecumenical movement is more beset by questions and doubts than driven by confident expectations. What has to be asked is whether the journeying of the kind undertaken thus far has enough energy to ride these uncertainties and find answers. Or, to put it another way, does the *Charta Oecumenica* with its repeated emphasis on dialogue represent simply a contentment to mark time, or a determination to push ahead? It must at least be a positive sign that the *Charta Oecumenica* itself is still generating interest, as remains a reference point for churches in ecumenical pilgrimage as became clear in events marking its tenth anniversary in 2011.[17]

---

17. A joint statement by CEC and CCEE (CEC Press Release No. 11/09e) on 5 May 2011 reports:

Continuing commitment?

The European ecumenical movement of the past sought to build bridges across the ideological, political and military division of Europe. That divide has gone, so has that sort of ecumenism and its relevance gone too? But Europe still has divisions to challenge, old bridges to mend and new ones to build. Each country is conscious of its own internal challenges to justice and social cohesion, through migration for example. It is not so much that migration is happening into and across Europe. Much more profoundly, it is simply that Europe is part of a newly (and unprecedentedly) migratory world, and is meeting that world within its own member states, its own cities and neigbourhoods. And at the time of writing (May 2012) the European Union thanks to economic pressures is itself now in turmoil and in great uncertainty about its future. Does all this herald a new phase in European fragmentation of interests, political, social cultural—and religious? A new time of withdrawals into the seemingly safe but narrow confines of separatist nationalisms, rigid cultural identities and absolutist confessional loyalties? This is a critical moment for the churches, since they are already highly self-conscious bearers of traditions and identities. They can be tempted either simply to assert these for the sake of their own survival, or to allow them to be used and exploited by political interests (as has happened in the Balkans). Alternatively, and, more creatively, they can remember that they have a vocation to reconciliation, and that is where the *Charta Oecumenica* remains pertinent.

There can be no question that faith is received and lived out in particular, concrete forms, confessional and cultural. There is no abstract, disembodied Christianity. One believes and worships and lives as a Russian Orthodox, or a Polish Catholic, or an English Baptist, and so on. But what the ecumenical movement stands for is the *active relating between* these forms, and the basis on which they recognise that in all their diversity they do belong to one other, in Christ. Put most fundamentally, ecumenism is about people embodied in these particular, diverse forms loving one another through identification with the other and accepting each other as part of the whole which claims them all. It means learning what it is to live

---

"The *Charta Oecumenica* is a continual process of construction which, in one way or another, has already marked the ecumenical journey of various church communities in Europe as testified by the numerous translations (more than thirty: from Arabic to Castilian, from Greek to Esperanto) and the scores of churches, communities, church associations and movements which have signed the document.

The penetration of the *Charta Oecumenica* into the European church and social institutional fabric is such that it is now also quoted in documents by lay institutions as testified by the frequent recourse to it on the part of PACE (the Parliamentary Assembly of the Council of Europe) in its 25 March 2011 report on *The religious dimension of intercultural dialogue (cf. doc 12553 nn. 93, 94 ff.).*"

where the other lives. The *Charta Oecumenica*, in two of its sets of commitments, states very clearly what must surely be the minimum ecumenical duty here:

> to pray for one another and for Christian unity;
>
> to learn to know and appreciate the worship and other forms of spiritual life practiced by other churches;
>
> to move towards the goal of eucharistic fellowship, to continue in conscientious, intensive dialogue at different levels between our churches, and to examine the question of how official church bodies can receive and implement the findings gained in dialogue;
>
> in the event of controversies, particularly when divisions threaten in questions of faith and ethics, to seek dialogue and discuss the issues together in the light of the Gospel.

Such invitations to commitment signal that a decisive point on the journey has been reached. It is now a matter of nerve as to whether it will be pursued further: whether the European churches will retreat once more into their own enclaves of nation and tradition or, with no less courage than they showed during the Cold War, discover what it means to live as the one body of Christ in more than one place at once.

Part Three

The Dynamic Continues

Chapter 10
Community
Promise or Danger?

Amid all the social confusion of the present day, with its clamour of conflicting voices, the churches also are making their voice heard. These social conflicts are due in part to the growth of large modern unified States, with their democratic tendencies and their party struggles. They are also the outcome of modern industrialization, the development of the proletariat, and the emancipation of the masses in many lands. These problems do not merely concern politicians, political economists, specialists in social science, and modern independent philosophers of culture; they are also the concern of the churches, whose roots are entwined with traditions of great historical importance and vital energy.[1]

These words were written just over 100 years ago by one of Germany's most famous philosopher-theologians, Ernst Troeltsch (1865-1923), at the start of his monumental work *The Social Teaching of the Christian Churches*. While his language obviously reflects something of his time and place, it is equally clear how little we would need to change it in order to express our contemporary Christian concerns early in the 21st century. We might wish, as well as industrialization, to speak of globalization; as well as emancipation of the masses, to talk about racial equality; as well as or instead of development of the proletariat, to raise gender issues. But these would be further variations on the same basic theme. What Christians believe about human society, and how they view themselves as a society or community within that human society, is one of the perennial issues of modern times.

Community: A Word Whose Time Has Come?
That is hardly surprising, since how Christians understand themselves as a community, and how they relate this to the world around them, has marked their history

---

1. Ernst Troeltsch, *The Social Teaching of the Christian Churches*, vol. 1, (London: George Allen and Unwin, 1931), 23. (Original German ed. 1911.)

from the beginning. Jesus calls and gathers twelve apostles "to be with him" and to proclaim the message (Mark 3:14) as a sign of a new Israel being formed in the midst of the old. One of the striking features in the gospels is how, on the one hand, this community of disciples is called and set apart for a special quality of life, the life of humble, serving love one to another; and on the other, how the compassionate love of Jesus and his community is to embrace the whole people, whether they belong to his inner group or not, and especially the poor, the sick, the "unclean" and marginalised in every way. The disciples live in more than one place at the same time. For the apostle Paul, the community of Christians is a new humanity in place of the old humanity divided between gentile and Jew, slave and free, male and female (Gal. 3:28, Eph. 2:14-16, etc.). It is in fact the body of the risen Christ, with its many diverse members making up one whole in mutual service and upward growth (Eph. 4:15ff)—as we saw, a mutuality spanning distances as well as diversity at home.[2] Ever since the apostolic era, Christians have sought to understand how their life together should be both different in quality from human society at large and also serve and be a sign of hope to that wider society, a pointer to what—by the grace of God—humanity can be like. In addition, not always but very often, Christians have believed that the word of God, as well as governing their own community, speaks to society as a whole about matters essential to its health, and especially about justice, peace, and human dignity. One of the crucially important events in the 20th century ecumenical story was the Oxford 1937 conference on Church, Community and State,[3] which faced the threats of widespread social disintegration and chaos under the pressures of competing totalitarianisms and impending war. "In the midst of such a world, torn and disrupted and feverishly seeking a way out of its troubles, the Christian Church stands and must fulfil its task. What is it to say? How is it to act? What is its understanding of the deeper meaning of the present situation of mankind? What, if any, is its wisdom for the healing of corporate disintegration and the restoration of sound and lasting community? What are individual Christians to believe and to do?"[4] In fact, in the conference report, the section "Church and Community" is by far the longest.

In recent years, especially in ecumenical discussion, theology has taken up the term *koinonia* from the New Testament and the early church in order to express the peculiar quality of life in Christian community. Often, for example in the words of "The Grace" based on 2 Corinthians 13:13, *koinonia* is translated as "fellowship"

---

2. See chapter 3 above.
3. See chapter 8 above.
4. *The Churches Survey Their Task: The Report of the Conference at Oxford, July 1937, on Church, Community and State* (London: George Allen & Unwin, 1937), 189.

or "communion," but no one word does justice to it. It is about the richness of life together in dynamic relationship with God and with one another; the message of the World Council of Churches' 1993 conference on Faith and Order speaks of "community, communion, sharing, fellowship, participation, solidarity... This koinonia which we share is nothing less than the reconciling presence of the love of God." [5] In its deepening of koinonia the church is called to be "sign and instrument" of the all-encompassing will of God for all people and all creation. Such an understanding of *koinonia* is in fact one of the most precious emphases of the modern ecumenical movement, to which we will return later in this chapter.

As well as there being "normal" congregations and parishes, over the centuries we repeatedly find Christians forming communities with a distinct identity and purpose and an unusually intense common life, seen most famously of course in communal monasticism in the Roman Catholic and Orthodox traditions, but not unknown in Protestantism (the Moravian community at Herrnhut, for example) and in High Church Anglicanism. Ernst Troeltsch includes many such examples in his great survey of Christian communities, but he died in 1923, and there is one great feature of our experience that he was in no position to foresee: how from the late 1920s down to the present there has been all over the world, and among all confessional families, an explosion of new communities and communes. In Protestantism we see some of its first stirrings in Dietrich Bonhoeffer and the rigorous communal life he established in his seminary for the Confessing Church at Finkenwalde on the Baltic coast in 1935, which caused some fellow Protestants to wonder whether he was "catholicizing" his students. Bonhoeffer's little book, *Life Together*, written for and out of his Finkenwalde project, has become a classic reflection on Christian community and its theology and practice and has inspired and guided many other experiments in turn.[6] There are the famous communities and movements such as Taizé, Bruderhof, Focolare, Laurentius, Sant'Egidio, Iona, and Corrymeela, but also countless other smaller experiments in community life, some that have proved relatively ephemeral, others still established and fruitful after half a century. Not only so, but these developments have fed back into "normal" church life a new emphasis upon church as a community: not just a place where people go to worship, not even just a congregational meeting for decision-making, but an actual organism of mutual relation, participation, *koinonia*.

---

5. "On the Way to Fuller Koinonia: The Message of the World Conference" in *On the Way to Fuller Koinonia: Official Report of the Fifth World Conference on Faith and Order* (Geneva: WCC Publications, 1994), 225.

6. Dietrich Bonhoeffer, *Dietrich Bonhoeffer Works*, vol. 5, *Life Together* and *Prayerbook of the Bible* (Minneapolis: Fortress, 1996).

So if community is an idea whose time has come, why do we need to look at it any further? Perhaps it is just *because* it is so in vogue, both in church and in wider society, that we should look at it more deeply, both theologically and by means of analysis of our contemporary human situation.

Individuals, Freedom, and Society

One of the remarks famously attributed to Margaret Thatcher, British Prime Minister 1979-90, was "There's no such thing as society, only individuals and families." Critics were quick to point out that this was a very odd view for a prime minister to take since if true, this would make government impossible. Yes, democracy, as understood in the west at least, involves free choices by individual citizens and voters. But democracy, if it is not to be chaos, requires many other things too: the rule of law and its enforcement, education, systems of communication, the organization of labour, and not least, political parties. There is freedom of individual conscience and also freedom of association. Society is not a homogeneous entity, but at the same time it comprises a mass of interconnecting mini-societies, including families (to be sure, and foundationally important), informal or organised neighbourhood groups, school parents' associations, clubs, football team supporters clubs, gardening clubs, women's institutes, trades unions, political parties, churches, and so on—all that today we mean by "civil society." The story of modern western society is that of attempting to find a balance between individual autonomy and liberty on the one hand and communitarian existence on the other.

During the cold war period, in a politically, ideologically and militarily divided Europe (but also in a world where super-powers played out their rivalries in the global South), the west was seen as the standard-bearer of individual liberty and the east was held to represent the assertion of communitarianism over individualism. The breakdown of Marxist-Leninist socialism and the end of the Soviet era were at first hailed as the complete triumph of liberal democracy and the free market economy. Some, like the American Francis Fukuyama, announced this as the "end of history."[7] The time of ideological blocs and communal identities was over. We were now to see the unlimited worldwide spread of capitalism, the market economy, and free consumer choice. People would now be free to select what they wished to be, make, do, and buy. History as the competition between ideologically, culturally, racially, or religiously distinct collective blocs was over. The age of the free individual, everywhere, had arrived. But it did not take long for this announcement to prove premature, as the Balkans were plunged into the most appalling ethnically-linked conflict since the second world war. On the world scale, radical Islamist movements

---

7. Francis Fukuyama, *The End of History and the Last Man* (London: Penguin, 1992).

arose precisely—in part—in opposition to that very same western neo-conservative vision of what the world could and should now become.

Fukuyama has now apparently, to some degree, repented of his over-hasty prophecy. It is not just that events on the international and global political level challenged it. There has also been a realisation that a philosophy of individual autonomy and freedom by itself is not adequate to the human condition: if you emphasize individual freedom alone as the highest good, it is difficult then to affirm equality and dignity. The British theologian Richard Bauckham goes further and asks "whether freedom is sustainable, whether it does not become a kind of slavery, demeaning human life and destroying human community, without a context of other values and practices in which human life is related to God."[8] Further, not just in theory but in practice, humans seek to *belong* as well as to be free. They look for solidarity as well as autonomy; they want to be part of a larger identity as well as to be themselves. And one of the permanent insights of the biblical tradition, backed up by sheer observation, is that it is only in some form of social or communal context that human beings can actually enjoy their freedom. There is evidence from within Britain that emphasis upon freedom of choice in, for example, the national health service, far from creating increased consumer confidence in health care, is in fact eroding trust in the very institutions responsible for health care delivery and in the values of universal care and the paramountcy of patients' interests that the institutions were created to embody.[9]

So community does matter, as does the wider concept of society. Small wonder that Europeans and North Americans look enviously at Africa when they hear about *Ubuntu*, that attitude of natural, assumed togetherness and mutual obligation—"I am what I am because of who we all are"—that is held to be the bond of traditional society. Too often, though, "community" in the West is spoken of in an unexamined way. Broken families, delinquent children, widespread crime and drug abuse (the two often closely related) and other societal wounds are grim realities today. In face of them, politicians, newspaper editors, and preachers are prone to speak of "the breakdown of society" or "social disintegration," the "lack of community" that is apparent all around us. The picture is that of a well-designed, attractive, and hitherto structurally sound building now in a state of rapid and total collapse—society fragmenting into a chaos of atomised individualism. The reality is somewhat dif-

---

8. Richard Bauckham, "Freedom in the Crisis of Modernity," in *Public Theology for the 21st Century: Essays in Honour of Duncan B. Forrester*, ed. William F. Storrar and Andrew R. Morton (London: Continuum, 2004) 77.

9. See letter in *The Guardian* (UK), 5 March 2007, by Professor Peter Taylor-Gooby (University of Kent).

ferent. In the first place, we must not idealize what has been, or what actually is, in apparently stable conditions of community. So much of the peace and harmony of apparently stable communities is due to *non-contact* between neighbours. Second, what of the other extreme, of violently dangerous neighbourhoods? While this may be described as a symptom of communal breakdown into individual, lawless selfishness, from another point of view manifests thje formation of an alternative communal restructuring of a certain (if perverse) kind born of desperation. During 2006-07, in London and other cities in England, there was a spate of horrifying shootings of young teenagers by other teenagers. Many, but not all, occurred in the young black communities. Those who know the scene well (including pastors and other church workers) spoke of a highly organized gang culture among disaffected, unemployed, and poorly educated youngsters. Each gang has its own hierarchy of leadership. One such leader, a white 17 year old on a Manchester municipal housing estate, an area of great social deprivation, says: "My gang's the Benchill Man Dem. We've always lived round here. We all went to school together. *We're all really close. We look after each other. We keep an eye out for other gangs and look after our area.*" There's "community" for you! The journalist who interviewed this young man on the street says: "Despite their bravado and criminal lifestyles, the boys appear almost endearingly eager to please, desperate for attention as most teenagers are. They shout greetings to some of the residents who walk past." And what of their future? "Their plans ... revolve around having lots of money, owning big cars or motorbikes and the latest mobile phones."[10] But, one may ask, how different are such aspirations from those of the great majority in the consumer society where life is often assumed to be much more "stable"? Apparent social stability does not equal community. Equally, some forms of evidently close community are destructive, and ultimately self-destructive, through their implicit or overt violence and their impossible ambitions. The riots which broke out in a number of English cities in 2011 predictably prompted a spate of comment about a "breakdown in community." In fact, in the immediate aftermath of the riots, there were many examples of people in the local areas affected turning out to work together in cleaning up, repairing, and rebuilding destroyed and looted properties, reclaiming the area as their own and thus showing real community spirit. Politicians are prone to diagnosing an abstract "breakdown in community" as a pretext for imposing their own ideologically-driven remedies, without pausing to reflect on the varying forms, beneficial and otherwise, that community can assume, and *where* they are to be found.

---

10. Report by Nicola Woodcock in *The Times of London*, 24 February 2007.

People in our societies know that in one way or another they are social animals and indeed in many cases dread utter isolation and loneliness. It is also the case that many of the pressures affecting people in their daily lives are the end-results of forces and developments operating globally today. We live in an ever-expanding global market economy. Ours is a migratory world. It is an increasingly technological world, and especially an interconnected world through instant means of global communication. As such it is a world of confusions and paradoxes, depending who you are and where you are. Some people find it exciting to travel and experience people and distant places in ways their parents never dreamed of. Others find it rather threatening that people of other cultures are now living in their cities and neighbourhoods, that the mosque is now at least as prominent on the skyline as the church spire or chapel roof. For many people, the world as a whole has grown smaller, while their immediate neighbourhood has grown bigger, more complex, more puzzling, and often more frightening. The term "glocal" has been coined to express this new kind of contextual awareness.

People instinctively want to express their sociality—but how? On the broadest level, they want to feel part of something bigger than their individual selves. That is why for most the family is still the most defining unit. Even if more and more adults are living on their own, the sense of belonging to a family circle, even if it is widely dispersed physically, still matters. But it does not usually stop there; people have many circles of belonging from their work place to their football team, from networks of friends to much vaguer ideas such as country. If there is a *Leitmotiv* of our time in western society, it is the phrase "only connect." I shall return to look more closely at this phrase, but it does express what many people see as important for their well-being: only connect—connect into another reality or a bigger world than just yourself. Where people cannot connect, they feel unimportant and disempowered. Take for instance the issue of climate change. One reason why it has risen so prominently to the top of the public agenda is not just because scientists and governments and the UN have produced reports on it, full of warnings about the future of the planet. It is also because people's perceptions are not only that something must be done, but that it *can* be done, and by selves, in the form of quite specific actions: using the car less, flying less, recycling rubbish. It is an agenda that people feel they can connect into in everyday actions and decisions.

The Connecting Culture: Contrasts with Community

The instinct for sociality through connecting can in fact be highly ambiguous and is capable of being exploited and manipulated in the interests of profit and control at the expense of real community. What people today are aspiring to, or think they are acquiring, is often not real community but a virtual sociableness. Five ways can be recognized in which this deception and manipulation operate in our time, and to which we who see community as part of Christian vocation must be alert.

Connecting to the Consumer Market

In the market economy, goods are advertised with an appeal to people's instinct to belong to the circles of those who somehow matter: those in the know, the successful, the powerful, and the status-rich. One only has to see how cars, in particular, are advertised, but also many everyday household goods: buy this cleaner, use this brand of cereal, and you will be among the housewives and mothers who really know how to manage their kitchens and care for their children. Use this coffee, and you will be living like the rich, beautiful, and famous who spend half the year at Cannes and the rest at Hollywood. At least as much as the actual usefulness of the product, it is the status in your own eyes and the eyes of others that, by implication, is being offered. But there is a contradiction built into this. You are being offered entrance into the imaginary circle of "people who matter" by acquiring something that will (apparently) make others look up to you. You are in fact being drawn into a game of imaginary belonging which is working against actual community and real belonging with others. Promising connection, it is in fact reinforcing an individualism in which any notion of *sharing* material goods is implicitly devalued as something abnormal. Further, as Rowan Williams observes, when this consumerism is identified with freedom of choice elevated to an absolute, abstract value and a purely individual good, then it becomes the prime seducer of a sense of responsibility, for it blinds us to the *consequences* of our choices, for both others and ourselves: "Real choice both expresses and curtails freedom—or rather it should lead us further and further away from a picture of choice that presupposes a blank will looking at a bundles of options like goods on a supermarket shelf."[11]

The consumerist culture, fed by the global economy, manipulates our belief in freedom of choice in a way that diverts our attention from the need to build community in a shared space with others. To exercise freedom of choice is indeed precious and essential to our humanity. The problem comes with two deceptive and dangerous related myths: first, that we are only consumers and not producers, and second, that for us as consumers there can be an infinite variety of choices, one marvellous life-enhancing invention after another, a denial of the hard truth that we live in a world of finite resources. Nicholas Boyle, an English Catholic scholar, correctly

---

11. Rowan Williams, *Lost Icons: Reflections on Cultural Bereavement* (London: Continuum, 2003), 38.

states: "Recognizing ourselves as self-constraining consumer-producers we recognize not only our finitude but that of the world we inhabit. There is one world and it is not endless and we have to work out among ourselves how we are to live in it together or we shall die in it separately."[12] *There is one world—one* OIKOUMENE—*and* ⋊ *it is not endless.* That is a simple yet profound insight, and every refusal to face it, every diversion round it, is inimical to community.

Connecting to Well-Being

Health keeps us all busy these days. Of course it has always been of prime concern to humans. But today in western society it comes as a commodity. Out there is something called "health," or as it is often called in English these days, "wellness," to which we have to connect. Our bookshops and magazine stalls are full of advice and advertisements on how to connect into this thing called wellness—or, more accurately, how we are to join the society of those who are well. Quite clearly, the impression is that there is somewhere some kind of land of health, inhabited by the fit and well who have discovered the secret of feeling well and especially of *looking* well. They smile at us from the glossy pages with their perfect profiles and beautifully tanned skins, in almost obscene contrast to the degradation of so many bodies through malnutrition, disease, and war in the world at large.

There are two ways in which we can, apparently, join the society of the healthy.

The first is by submitting our bodies to the prescriptions, decided by fashion and commercial interest, for what is healthy and beautiful. We see this form of slavery at its most extreme in the harm being done to young women, even girls in their early teens, by the dictates of fashion according to which only the slimmest can really be considered beautiful. Often this results in serious eating disorders. But even where this extreme is not reached, it is still the case that we are caught in a culture of health-consumerism that is breeding a new kind of anxiety for both women and men. The body is under continual threat and debate. Every day some new dangerous food component is discovered, or some new wonder-working formula claimed to have been invented. Health then becomes not a gift for us all to share, but a competition. Health is to be got individualistically. It further creates the paradox, which is really a contradiction, that you can acquire health only if you give up your body as your own and hand it over to those who claim really to know what is good for it.

The second way is even more individualistic. You connect to psychological well-being by disconnecting from anything that might disturb you. Well-being is equated

---

12. Nicholas Boyle, *Who Are We Now? Christian Humanism and the Global Market from Hegel to Heaney* (Edinburgh: T. & T. Clark, 1998), 119.

with individualistic self-fulfilment. That requires insulation from emotional upset and pain of any kind. Well-being is equated with "peace of mind," getting in tune with your body, letting your feelings get into balance with each other, getting the world in perspective, and not letting others' problems burden you too much. It need hardly be said that true community cannot be built where such individualistic assumptions hold sway in what constitutes well-being. It is the philosophy that would have nicely counselled the priest and the Levite on the Jericho road, needing reassurance that it was quite all right to hurry past the bleeding victim on their path. It is the ultimate in living in only one place at one time: one's own private, individual world, sealed and cocooned from every outside disturbance and potentially damaging contact. By contrast, someone who through his work as an international television journalist has more than most of us seen at first-hand human misery, violence, and the cruelty of war is BBC World Affairs Editor John Simpson. He writes tellingly:

> But what if ... the point of living isn't to be placid and happy and untouched by the world, but to be deeply, painfully sensitive to it, to see its cruelty and savagery for what they are, and accept all this as readily as we accept its beauty? To be touched by it, loved by it, hurt by it even, but not to be indifferent to it?[13]

Simpson, incidentally, also relates how after many years, his own Christian affiliation came alive again through witnessing at first hand the "miracle" of the ending of apartheid in South Africa and especially the role of Archbishop Desmond Tutu and others as agents of reconciliation.

"Only Connect": The Reign of Technology

Back in the 19th century, the great artist and social critic John Ruskin, on hearing that the first telephone cable had been laid across the Atlantic, so connecting people in America and Britain, asked, "Will they have they anything to say to each other?"

Here we come to the heart of the problem of speaking about community in westernized culture today. It is worth pausing for a moment on this English word "connect" that we use a thousand times every day in normal life as we go about our work, travel, communicate, cook, write... and so on. The English word has two Latin roots, *con* (together with) and *nectere* (bind). It appeared first in late Middle English, i.e. around 1400. But interestingly it only became common in the 18th century: it is a word of the machine age and the industrial revolution founded on the joining together of moving parts—most iconically, the connecting rod of the steam engine. It is a technological

---

13. John Simpson, *Not Quite World's End: A Traveller's Tales* (London: Macmillan, 2007), 460ff.

term, *the* term of the technological age. So much of our life now, in so many ways, and especially electronically, consists in "making connections." Indeed in the age of the internet and mobile phone, we might be tempted to say that life *is* connectibility.

Technological control provides much of the infrastructure of our lives. We cannot go back to a pre-technological age, but we do have to be aware of how unchecked technological assumptions subvert authentic human relationships. The danger is that "connection" becomes a superficial substitute for true relationship.[14] We all know that at the end of the day, no matter how marvellous our internet facilities and other forms of electronic communication may be, including helping us discover new networks and potential friendships, there is no substitute for physical, face to face meeting for developing human understanding. Literally sitting where others sit is the only way real community can develop. When we rely solely on technological instruments to communicate with others, there is an inevitable tendency to instrumentalize those we are trying to "connect with" and regard them as less than fully human. Christine Ledger, an Australian theologian and writer on Christianity and culture, speaks of *recognition* and *respect* as hallmarks of genuine relationships, and she states: "The instrumentalism and idolatry implicit in a technological culture are the opposite of recognition and respect. Instrumentalism involves a lack of respect, an objectification and an exploitation of the other. The idolizing of our technological capabilities is a failure of recognition of God and our contingency upon God."[15] Using terms of another writer, Albert Borgman, she speaks of "regardless power" over against "careful power": "Regardless power has no regard, recognition or respect for God, other people and the world. It is driven by selfishness, self-absorption and self-glorification. Careful power arises from recognition and respect for the other."[16] Our technological culture, Ledger argues, leads to erosion of relationships with other people and the world around us. "Apathy, the inability to suffer, flows from a withdrawal from relationship, from an avoidance of the risk and vulnerability that comes with relationship. It is tightly linked, therefore, with a technological culture built on ease and convenience."[17]

The necessary risk and vulnerability in relating, as distinct from simply connecting, lies in our being unable to instrumentalize or objectify *ourselves* in the presence

---

14. The source for the oft-quoted phrase "Only connect!" is chapter 22 of E.M. Forster's novel *Howards End* (1910). But note that Forster was not in fact here referring to inter-personal or social relations, but to connecting "the prose and the passion" for the expression of human love at its height.
15. Christine Ledger, "Seeking *Koinonia* in a Technological Culture," in *Windows into Ecumenism: Essays in Honour of Ahn Jae Wong* (Hong Kong: Christian Conference of Asia, 2005), 250.
16. Ibid.,
17. Ibid., 256.

of other people. I have to be open to being changed in my encounter no less than I might wish to influence the other person. Even more so, in real encounter I have to be open to discovering more of who I actually am, as distinct from what I imagine or would like myself to be.

Virtual Relatedness

A concomitant result of the dominance of technology in the infrastructure of our life is the increased possibility of fictional or even fantasy life as an alternative to real existence. Of course the capacity for story-telling, myth, drama, and visual art is one of the marks of essential humanity, and one of the signs of civilization of any sort. But there is always an ambiguity in such work. It can either illuminate our human condition or provide sheer escape from it. Today, the situation is such that some are claiming that the former distinction between reality and fiction, the actual and virtual reality, no longer applies. The eventual logical outcome would appear to be that, in the English-speaking televisual world for example, the latest doings on *Neighbours* are as much "news" as what is happening on the stock exchange or in Iraq.

This is not a pretext to mount an all-out attack on the fictional world as such. Unless one were to be wilfully elitist, it would be hard to do this without dismissing Shakespeare and Thomas Mann along with pulp fiction and television soap opera. The point is that the fictional—or, if preferred, virtual—world presents and explores human relationships that may mirror or go beyond the experience of actual everyday life. That is part of its fascination, and indeed of its value. But precisely for that reason, it also allows people to connect with a virtual realm at the expense of relating to real neighbours. (This is not only a phenomenon of the technological age: Tolstoy tells of the duchess who shed floods of compassionate tears at a stage melodrama, while her coachman froze to death on her carriage outside the theatre.[18]) It is second-hand, virtual community that people then live in, rather than their own world, where, by contrast, relationships are often too messy, too difficult, and too insecure. Relatedness appears to be "out there," beyond our actual mundane experience, but deceptively accessible given our present technology. Again, the paradox is that one enters this virtual world of relatedness only on one's own. You go in, and come out, with your individuality confirmed, but not your capacity for forming personal relationships. It is the recipe for reinforcing individualism.

Closely allied to this second-hand, virtual relatedness is the huge growth industry in "spirituality." Surveys show that many people in western society say they have given up on organized religion, Christian or otherwise, but are on a "spiritual quest."

---

18. Quoted in Alec R. Vidler, *Christ's Strange Work* (London: SCM, 1963), 102.

They feel the need to be in touch with a reality larger than themselves, to connect with "the spirit" within them and around them, or to "tune in" to the cosmos. Again, we must not decry such aspirations, which are often genuine expressions of dissatisfaction with the superficiality of a culture increasingly disillusioned by the gods of material progress. It is, rather, what is typically on offer to meet this felt need that requires examination. I have a CD with a selection of music from down the ages, under the title "Voices of Silence." The blurb on the cover commends this as music of great beauty, peace, and relaxation which has "the special ability to transport the listener on a mental journey to a mystical place where nature, emotion and cultural interchange both past and present are brought together in a distinctive listening experience. Allow yourself to sit back, relax, experience and dream along with 'Voices of Silence.'" It is of course debatable whether it was with the intention to produce such feelings that Schubert, Brahms, Messiaen, and Walford Davies and others actually composed these pieces, and it is typical of the current new-age-type commercialism to ransack everything from Gregorian chant to birdsong as a way of "tuning in" to a realm of nice feelings. It is, again, a second-hand experience of peace (there is no need to know the actual words in Schubert's "German Mass") that people are invited to connect with, instantly, painlessly, and individualistically. It is also a travesty of the genuine mystical Christian tradition to suggest that the goal of mysticism is a purely individual, insular encounter with the divine in which relations to others, to society, and to the earth slip away.[19]

Insulating Identity

It is a truism to say that, being social animals, we humans group ourselves into distinct communities with their specific corporate ethos, rules and identities—ethnic, linguistic, class-related, religious, and so on. Often our sense of collective identity is marked out by saying how we differ from other groups, or from society as a whole. The question facing any social group, however, and especially those groups with a strong sense of moral or religious distinction, is how they do in fact relate to the overall society in which they are set. Do the groups' identities in fact enable them to live "there" as well as "here"? Or does group identity merely confirm the preference to live inside one's own tradition and immediate community, at the expense of any wider imagination and interest?

One of the most illuminating and thought-provoking studies on communities and society has been that on Northern Ireland carried out by Joseph Liechty

---

19. For a succinct and useful corrective to this view, see Melvyn Matthews, *Awake to God: Explorations in the Mystical Way* (London: SPCK, 2006).

(a Mennonite) and Cecelia Clegg (a Roman Catholic sister) and published as *Moving Beyond Sectarianism: Religion, Conflict and Reconciliation in Northern Ireland*.[20] The religious-political sectarian divide between Roman Catholics and nationalists on the one hand, and Protestants and Unionists other has, as all know, resulted in over thirty years of violence and bloodshed that we now hope and pray is a thing of the past. In their study, Liechty and Clegg approached the issue of sectarianism in a quite novel way. They looked at it not so much as the attitudes and actions of certain individuals or even certain groups, but as a systemic feature of the Northern Ireland society as a whole. In effect, whether people admitted to being sectarian or not, all people were located somewhere on the grid or map of sectarianism. Liechty and Clegg pictured society as a kind of pyramid. At the top of the pyramid were the most overtly violent groups and gangs who robbed and murdered at will, the "mad dogs" who were scarcely related to any political group but were usually identified as Protestant or Catholic. Beneath them were the organized paramilitary groups, like the Provisional Irish Republican Army and the Ulster Defence Force, who carried out targeted acts of violence for clear political ends. Next layer down came the political and religious leaders on all sides, who generally disowned violence and publicly condemned it, but nevertheless on occasion would deliver highly provocative and inflammatory statements or sermons. The broad base of the pyramid comprised the mass of people, the "ordinary, decent, citizens," Protestant and Catholic, some of whom would be committed members of one political party or another, many not, and nearly all denying any connection with the violence, condemning it and indeed repelled by it, and often critical of the extremist politicians too.

What Liechty and Clegg demonstrate, however, is that all these layers of the pyramid are interconnected, directly or indirectly. Each feeds into the layer above it, and each of the upper three layers justifies itself by appeal to the layer beneath. The "mad dogs" at the top would not deny that they act purely out of self-interest, but would say that if paramilitaries on the layer below are acting out of political self-interest they are entitled to operate for purely economic self-interest. (The troubles have indeed produced a Mafia-like society in some quarters.) The paramilitaries say to the political and religious leaders on the level below, "Your words are fine, for a united Ireland or an Ireland free from Rome, but we who are actually delivering. We are simply getting the results you call for, while scared of getting your hands dirty." The leaders say to the broad mass of citizens beneath them, "You say we are too outspoken and extremist in our language—but we are only articulating what you as

---

20. Joseph Liechty and Cecelia Clegg, *Moving beyond Sectarianism: Religion, Conflict, and Reconciliation in Northern Ireland* (Dublin: Columba Press, 2001).

good Protestants or Catholics deep down feel but daren't express openly." Citizens who may consciously and sincerely distance themselves from both extremist rhetoric and actual violence cannot therefore totally extricate themselves from the systemic sectarianism unless they are doing something much more positive to counter any exploitation of their passivity. Liechty and Clegg refer to the "false allure of benign apartheid" as a soft option to actual peacemaking and reconciliation: "simple coexistence of communities, as separate as ever, but living without violence."[21] Benign apartheid has obvious attractions. It allows one to continue in a detached but still real distaste for the other side. "Such people," the authors write, "long for the violence to end, but they never cared much for the other community."[22] Religious communities, they point out, can be very tempted to benign apartheid, which at a very basic level can take the apparently innocent form of merely overlooking or disregarding the presence of the other community or tradition (as when Catholics talk as if only they took the eucharist seriously, or when Protestants do not take Catholic study of the Bible into account). In these benign, seemingly innocent ways, there may not be overt hostility, but elements are created that can become building blocks in deeper separation and therefore eventually actual division, and thus the ultimate possibility of conflict and violence.

In short, it is not enough to be a community defined purely in its own terms, even if those terms speak about harmony, peace, and goodwill. The location of the community in relation to other communities and on the total grid of society has to be examined. Christine Ledger's hallmark tests of *recognition* and *respect* have to be applied to inter-communal and well as to intra-communal relations. Just as "connecting" can be deceptive, so too can "disconnecting."

Community: Checking Our Bearings

In a context where there are so many signs of breakdown in social life, from personal isolation and loneliness on the one hand to conflict or actual violence on the other, it is right and good that churches should feel called both to exemplify community in their life and to contribute to community-building in society at large. But as I have tried to indicate, there are ways in which our present western society and its cultural fashions can divert attention from what is really involved in community-building by offering cheap, superficially attractive substitutes. These manipulate people's well-founded desires for sociality, for belonging, and for relationships, but in the end only connect them to imaginary circles that leave them as individualistically isolated as ever, or leave them in communities that camouflage their complicity in discord in

---

21. Ibid., 195.
22. Ibid., 196.

the wider society. It is not enough for Christians and churches simply to wish to offer "community," any more than the need for food is answered simply by opening a fast-food store. We need to be sure that what we offer in the name of Christ is not just another form of the sort of pseudo-community already available in society, not just another consumerist commodity in religious guise. Which is where ecumenical responsibility comes in.

There can be many motivations for wanting to be in community, build community, offer community. Christian community always has to check its theological bearings. It is *koinonia*, participation in Christ through the Holy Spirit, participation in one another through Christ, becoming members one of another, bearing one another's burdens (that is, one another's sins, Gal. 6:2). It means living where the other person or community is living as well as one's home. It means believing, according to that gloriously mistaken rendering of the Apostles' Creed, in the communion of sins and the forgiveness of saints. There is a cost to *koinonia*, for it is a community of the cross. (Some years ago at an ecumenical meeting I heard a Mediterranean bishop mutter that people were always willing to talk about community but not to pay the price that had to be paid for it.) It is continually orientated by gathering under the word of God and meeting around the Lord's table in the eucharistic fellowship that Christ establishes with us in his broken body and poured out blood, and issues in the ministry of humblest service and witness. It is in the world, for the world, on behalf of the world, and as such always counter to the world and its individualism, its competitiveness, its power-seeking, its self-seeking, and its self-advertisement. It is a sign and instrument of the world to come. Texan Baptist theologian Barry Harvey uses well the term "re-membering" to describe the new-birthed sociality of members of the body of Christ to one another and to the world, and states:

> Through our confession of Christ's Lordship—sealed by baptism, celebrated in the Eucharistic feast, and lived out in a holy life of service and fellowship—we announce to the world in both word and deed that the end toward which history is moving is not determined by those whom this age calls powerful, but by the one who gathers together all things in heaven and on earth in the crucified Messiah of Israel.[23]

At the same time, being the community of Jesus who is the incarnate one, it is always a very human community of real people. It is never an ideal community of perfect

---

23. Barry Harvey, *Can These Bones Live? A Catholic Baptist Engagement with Ecclesiology, Hermeneutics, and Social Theory* (Grand Rapids: Brazos, 2008), 229.

people. It is the community of forgiven and forgiving sinners. But even there it runs counter to one of the world's most seductive tendencies: that of idealizing community and so banishing it to the sphere only of fiction and virtual reality. Dietrich Bonhoeffer sums it up: "First, Christian community is not an ideal, but a divine reality; second, Christian community is a spiritual [*pneumatische*] and not a psychic [*psychische*] reality."[24] In his earliest theological writings Bonhoeffer had already spoken of the church as "Christ existing as community" and thus living by Christ's forgiveness,[25] a continual learning experience of unconditional love. The Orthodox theologian John Zizioulas in not dissimilar way speaks of biological existence as that which in the end is marked by individualism, in contrast to "ecclesial existence" given in baptism, marked by "the capacity of the person to love without exclusiveness."[26] This means, also, that in a world where communities typically are obsessed with their boundaries and with border-controls and exclusion so as to maintain their identity, Christian community is more concerned with its centre, the Christ who establishes his communion with us and who calls all people to himself.

It is at this point that true ecumenism and ecclesiology meet each other in the dynamic of true community. The ecumenical movement has not just been about "church unity" but about "church *comm*unity," *koinonia*. It is no accident that the Oxford 1937 conference coined as its unofficial slogan "Let the Church be the Church!" in face of all the disintegrative forces that were threatening human society and scheming to draw religion itself into their designs. The conference was already anticipating our contemporary concerns with globalization when it declared "The world has become a unity and for this high destiny mankind is not yet fit."[27] It marked a resistance point of identity and mission. There is therefore no better way to conclude this chapter than to cite in full the practical suggestions for immediate steps with which the 1937 Oxford conference section report on "Church and Community" concluded. Due allowance being made for the language of its time and other reflections of its context—including the colonial ethos—far from representing a dated ecumenism, the statement vibrates with the dynamic that has yet to make its full impact upon the churches. Here it is:

---

24. Bonhoeffer, *Life Together* and *Prayerbook of the Bible*, 35.
25. See, e.g., Dietrich Bonhoeffer, *Dietrich Bonhoeffer Works*, vol. 2, *Act and Being* (Minneapolis: Fortress Press 1996), 112. See also above, chapter 2.
26. John D. Zizioulas (Metropolitan John of Pergamon), *Being as Communion: Studies in Personhood and the Church* (London: Darton, Longman and Todd, 1985), 57.
27. *The Churches Survey Their Task*, 190.

There is a call from God today:

1. To every local congregation—to realize in its own self at any cost that unity transcending all differences and barriers of class, social status, race, nation, which the Holy Spirit can and will create in those who are ready to be led by Him.

2. To the different Churches in any district—to come together for local ecumenical witness in worship and work.

3. To all Christians—to a more passionate and costly concern for the outcast, the under-privileged, the persecuted, the despised in the community and beyond the community; just as Jesus Himself was "moved with compassion" for the multitude and spent most of His life in ministering to their needs by healing and preaching. The recrudescence of pitiless cruelty, hatred and race-discrimination in the modern world (including most notably anti-Semitism) is one of the major signs of its social disintegration. To these must be brought not only the weak rebuke of words but the powerful rebuke of deeds. Thus the unity of the Church is advanced. For the Church has been called into existence by God not for itself but for the world; and only by going out of itself in the work of Christ can it find unity in itself.

4. To the Church—to extend its concern to the particular areas of life where existing conditions continually undo its work and thwart the will of God for His children; such as misunderstandings between old and young, tension between men and women, health, housing, employment, recreation in their distinctive rural and urban forms. Thus the Church should seek to express God's concern for every man in his own neighbourhood and vocation.

5. To the Church, and particularly to the younger Churches—to show a deeper interest in, and concern for, the rural community through whose labour and toil mankind is clothed and fed, and which is in many parts of the world the most important unit of social life. The Christian Church must learn from the strong non-Christian religions to take root in these little communities, conserving what is best in their traditional life but demonstrating a quality of communal living, inspired by faith in Jesus Christ and by Christ-like love, that shall both judge and transform the existing social environment, from these may come examples of Christian group life and of a fellowship in common labour and worship which will be a priceless contribution to the common life of the world.

6. To the Church—to undertake new, prophetic, and daring social experiments in local communities through which the general level of conscience may be raised.

7. To the Church—to play a healing and reconciling part in the conflicts, misunderstandings, and hatreds which arise between interests or classes within the local community or nation.

8. To those Churches which have predominant influence in any country—to set their faces against any persecution of other Churches or the raising of communal barriers to their free development.

9. To the Churches—to promote united study, fellowship, and action; and in particular to arrange that successful experiments within various Churches in finding new channels for the message of Christ to the people of this generation shall be made known in other Churches also.

10. To Christian men and women in the same vocation or industry—to meet together for prayerful discussion as to how, in their particular sphere of the common life, the practical problems which arise can be dealt with as God would require. Herein is a special responsibility of the laity.

11. To members of the Christian Church—to be ready to undertake responsibilities in local and national government. The Church should seek to guide and support these its representatives in their efforts to solve the problems by which they are faced in the light of Christian principles.

12. To all Christians—to seek by simplicity and discipline in personal living to go beyond the accepted standards of the community in the direction of the love of Christ.

Finally there is laid on the Christian Church in all lands the obligation to create and to foster a solidarity and co-operation with one another that are stronger than all the divisions which now disrupt the family of mankind. The ecumenical movement which has found expression in the Conference at Oxford should become an integral part of the life of every Church, every local congregation, every individual Christian. To help to create it, to support it, to develop it, is a solemn responsibility to God, who so loved the *world* that he gave His lonely-begotten Son for its sin. Thus shall be plainly manifested to mankind in its chaos and division something of that peace and order of brotherly love which come only from God and from Jesus Christ His Son, our Lord.

This was not committee-ecumenism but community-ecumenism, and it was prophetic in marking the way ahead for the churches then. Can it honestly be said that the agenda set out then has been completed and can be left behind?

Chapter 11

Translating Faith into Public Policy

"Middle Axioms" Revisited

The previous chapter argued that *community* is a word central to Christian life and mission, yet one whose meaning must ever be theologically grounded and clarified if it is not to be distorted by interests other than, or even opposed to, the gospel of Christ. After all, "community" is part of the currency of all people in society, and all kinds of societies. Peoples at local and national levels aspire to being not just "societies" or associations of people but "real communities." The older English word *commonwealth* expresses the sense that in society at large there should be a set of shared values, above all the belief that all people have a right to and obligation towards the public good. Further, most Christians and churches will assert that somehow or other the existence of the specifically Christian community or the church is a benefit to the public good. Quite how that benefit is transmitted is not so straightforwardly obvious, however. It is one thing, and comparatively easy, to assert that community in Christ is quite distinct from all other kinds of community in human society and even to state what the distinction is—as I tried to do in the concluding paragraphs of the previous chapter. It is quite another to identify what positive bearing community in Christ should have upon the wider human community. The 1937 Oxford conference spoke much about Christian concern, interest and responsibility for the conditions under which people at large were living. In what was still largely a western gathering, there was assumed a capability and competence in the churches, and moreover a recognized authority which would guarantee the churches a hearing in the public sphere. It is precisely this assumption, however, which is under question from many quarters today, especially when Christian concern moves beyond charitable activity into the realms of policy and legislation. Can, or even should, faith be translatable into public policy?

Not so long ago there was indeed confidence that this was so:

God send us men alert and quick
His lofty precepts to translate,
Until the laws of Christ become
The habits of the state.[1]

That hymn reflects the energy and confidence of the Social Gospel movement, which at the time was a real power in the land of North American Protestantism and had its counterparts in Britain up until about the time of the First World War. The belief that heavenly precepts can or should be translated into "habits of the state," into public policy and into legislation if necessary, is today a highly contested idea, not least in Britain. It was raised to a new level by the visit of Pope Benedict XVI to Britain in September 2010. In a number of addresses, especially one delivered in the most historic parliamentary building, Westminster Hall, the pope pleaded for a recognition of the positive role that religion can and should play in the public sphere, much to the anger of secularist opinion. But this had been a contentious issue since long before his visit, as a look at the national press almost any week for the past few years would show.

In fact we have an odd situation in which some representatives of churches and other faith groups claim to feel persecuted, or at any rate increasingly marginalised, in a steadily secularising society, while the secularists in turn feel to be victims of the iron grip of religion on society. On a wider European level this polarisation also fuelled the debates surrounding the Preamble to the European Treaty drafted in 2003. No issue excited more attention than whether the Preamble should specifically mention Christianity—or indeed God—as the prime spiritual and cultural root of Europe. Even the churches were divided on this issue. Many were disappointed, but some relieved, that the final text speaks in a generalistic way about drawing inspiration "from the cultural, religious and humanist inheritance of Europe." Each side obviously feels very insecure in face of the other, and that is a recipe for a shouting match instead of a proper dialogue. Where each side feels to be a victim of the other side's machinations and ambitions, this at the very least points to a need for greater clarity. Suffice it to say that there is immense pressure from secularist quarters to have religion regarded as something to be confined entirely to the personal, inward and private sphere with no bearing on public life at all. Here the situation after 11 September 2001 has of course done no one any favours, and it almost seems at times as though in secularist eyes any manifestation of religious belief is regarded as being on the slope towards a terrorist atrocity. No less, in response it is tempting for reli-

---

1. Hymn by Frederick J. Gillman, 1909.

gious leaders to make declamations which imply that if only political power and government were in their hands the world would be a better place—exactly the kind of authority-mongering that confirms the secularists' worst fears.

The polarization can be found in very different contexts. The notorious constitution of apartheid South Africa began with a very specific religious reference indeed: to God as the providential bringer of the various races to South Africa. Even the transitional constitution of 1992 began "In humble submission to Almighty God . . ." By contrast the Preamble of the post-apartheid constitution opens, "We, the people of South Africa, recognize the injustices of our past . . ." But the Preamble also includes the prayerful statement "May God protect our people" and cites the two hymnic national anthems of the new republic which invoke God's blessing on South Africa. In fact the public sphere in post-apartheid South Africa has witnessed a noticeable tension between secular and religious motivations. The Truth and Reconciliation Commission (TRC) which played an important role in encouraging both perpetrators and victims of oppression and violence to come to terms with the grim past of apartheid, was chaired by Archbishop Desmond Tutu for whom there could be no doubt that reconciliation reached its most profound understanding and was given its strongest motivation by the gospel of Christ, and who opened each session of the commission with prayer. Others, however—including some Christians—were uneasy about too closely identifying the TRC and its work with religious conviction or a "theological" understanding of reconciliation. To speak religiously, it was argued, ran the danger of overly pathologizing both individuals and society with a sense of guilt, or even of emotionally blackmailing people into forgiving. As an essentially political process, it should not be laden with religious or romantic overtones about forgiveness. By contrast Allan Boesak, theologian and a foremost campaigner against apartheid in the 1980s, strongly critiques the idea that "our process of political reconciliation and transformation is purely secular and should be purged of all spiritual elements"[2] on the grounds, first, that Africans *are* profoundly spiritual people whether that spirituality is rooted in African traditional religion or in the Christian tradition, and this makes a purely secular understanding of the TRC alien to the African spirit; second, the TRC *was* about reconciliation at deeply personal levels, going beyond purely legal concepts, and took people into the realms where the language of repentance and forgiveness became unavoidable. This reluctance to concede the reality of the spiritual dimension, Boesak argues, is of a piece with the reluctance of elements in the post-apartheid political leadership to acknowledge the part that faith commitment played in the anti-apartheid struggle itself.

---

2. Allan Boesak, *The Tenderness of Conscience* (Glasgow: Wild Goose, 2008), 186.

Middle Axioms

It was in fact in South Africa that my interest in this matter was reignited. During a conference at the University of Stellenboschin October 2009 commemorating the 500th anniversary of the birth of John Calvin, following a presentation by Professor John de Gruchy on "Calvin, Barth and Christian Humanism" the discussion turned to the question of how the church, on the basis of its theology, can meaningfully address the issues of human welfare and social justice which are the concern of society as a whole and not just of the church. During this discussion there came up the concept of "middle axioms" as a way of bridging the divide between the fundamental tenets of faith in God's self-revelation on the one hand, and the particular social and ethical problems that a human society is facing at the moment on the other. "Middle axioms" was a term coined by J.H. Oldham[3] and in view of my specialist interest in him, the discussion at Stellenbosch particularly aroused my attention. This was not least because the notion of middle axioms obviously did not find favour with everyone there—or at any rate, at least one voice strongly queried the need for them in the church's address of social issues. As I recall, it was argued that surely it was enough for the church, in its prophetic role, simply to convey the biblical demand for justice, peace, and so forth. Why does it need translating into anything else? For my part, I would wish to argue that middle axioms—or something like them—are necessary if there is to be a translation of faith into public policy. Before so arguing, however, some further reflection on our contemporary situation is called for.

In order to justify their existence, it is not surprising that western democracies today often give the impression that it is enough for them to be contrasted with the alternative *theo*cracies aspired after by Islamic fundamentalists or actually found in a country like Iran. In a theocracy there is no question of religion operating in the public realm, since there is no public realm outside the religious authority. But the secularist opposition to any role of religion in the public realm does not rely simply on the nightmare scenario that, given a centimetre, religion will take a kilometre. It argues rather that faith-based values of whatever kind are inimical to the very nature of an open, democratic society, unless they are confined to the most private areas of individual life. The public sphere, being public, can only operate only under the norms of universally accepted canons of reason, not the unproveable, non-rational tenets of faith. Religion is thus an alien intruder into the body politic. Looking at pitches as varied as Northern Ireland, the former Yugoslavia, Sri Lanka, Israel-Palestine, and Nigeria, where religious differences have been primary factors in igniting or inflaming social and ethnic conflict, it is not hard to find sympathy with such a

---

3. See above, chapter 8.

view. It recalls how the European Enlightenment was in part born out of weariness with the 17th century Wars of Religion that had wrought so much havoc and misery across central Europe.

Faith-Based Values and the Public Forum

The view that in modern society religious belief is only, and must only be, a matter of private opinion and should be barred from the public forum, finds powerful philosophical support, as expressed by one of its leading American exponents, John Rawls.[4] Rawls at most concedes that religious views may be admitted to the public forum "provided that they meet the commonly accepted criteria of public reasoning,"[5] as may happen for example with the Catholic teaching of natural law. This has been challenged by, for example, the Scottish theologian Duncan Forrester who points out that this may, by debarring what *cannot* be so easily translated, exclude from the public discourse uncomfortable ideas—to the eventual impoverishment of that discourse.[6] And who is to decide what are "the commonly accepted criteria of public reasoning"? Who are to be the gatekeepers of this forum? In turn, is the conscious role of religion only to be that of endorsing the liberal, democratic consensus? Duncan Forrester is describing the debate in the immediate American context of John Rawls, but the debate is increasingly similar to that in Britain and elsewhere, wherever we find "liberal democratic societies."[7] There is indeed a problem which the Rawls-type argument, left to itself, cannot solve; for within the public forum even certain apparently "secular" values may prove extremely vulnerable precisely in face of an unexamined and oppressive consensus and will need determined advocacy, from faith quarters if nowhere else. In a recent essay "In Pursuit of Egalitarianism: And Why Social Mobility Cannot Get Us There,"[8] Rebecca Hickman writes:

---

4. John Rawls, *The Law of Peoples, with "The Idea of Public Reason Revisited"* (Cambridge: Harvard University Press, 1999).

5. Ibid., 142.

6. Duncan Forrester, *Apocalypse Now? Reflections on Faith in a Time of Terror* (Aldershot: Ashgate, 2005), 46-48.

7. For a carefully argued British statement of the case that religion, since it claims an authority apart from reason, should not exercise influence in formulating public policy and legislation on ethical matters, see Mary Warnock, *Dishonest to God* (London: Continuum, 2010). Warnock, it should be noted, does not make a secularist dismissal of religion *tout court* and indeed adopts what might be called a traditional Anglican-romantic view of its interiority and cultural effects.

8. Rebecca Hickman, "In Pursuit of Egalitarianism: And Why Social Mobility Cannot Get Us There" (London: Compass–Directions for the Democratic Left, n.d.) (www.compassonline. org.uk). The essay is available online at http://www.compassonline.org.uk/publications/item. asp?d=1440 and in PDF form directly at http://clients.squareeye.net/uploads/compass/documents/compass%20egalitarianism%20WEB.pdf.

To help the most marginalised, and help them gladly, we need an ethic born of love, kindness, sympathy and generosity. *These words currently reside at the outermost fringes of political discourse.* Qualities that we praise and seek in our personal relationships and conduct, we dismiss as sentimental or sources of inefficiency in the design of public services and the organisation of the economy.[9]

The "commonly accepted criteria of public reasoning" may in fact prove to be as elusively unsubstantiated, or as irrationally motivated, or as unjust in their effects, as anything generated by religious belief. This does not by itself, of course, give religious belief an entry ticket into the public forum. Faith, if it is to be translated into public discourse or even as far as public policy, will have to be able to demonstrate that it is offering something positive to the *public bonum*, and that its wares can be recognised as such by a constituency wider than the faith community itself. In former times when the church wielded political power, or was in close alliance with political power, or had unquestioned historical and continuing influence upon a society's life, ethos and culture, it was not a problem for the church to be in the public forum. It was the time of Christendom, the time when the church towered over the market place symbolically as well as literally and the church was naturally looked up to by the market place as supplying its ethics and mores. Part of the debate in present-day Europe is whether Christendom has gone, and whether it should go if it has not done so already, or if it is not yet wholly disappeared and whether remnants of it can be clung to. It is in this situation, where the role of the church in the public sphere is at the very least highly contested, that the concept of "middle axioms" deserves renewed consideration.

Middle Axioms: Content and Context

The founding statement of "middle axioms" was set out by J.H. Oldham in his preparatory essay for the 1937 Oxford conference on "Church, Community and State." In a section dealing with "The Ethical Implications of the Gospel," Oldham writes that broad assertions about the law of love or striving for social justice do not go far in helping the individual to know what to do in particular cases. On the other hand, to give him or her "precise instructions" to be followed literally is to deny the individual's moral responsbility as a person. Further:

It is not the function of the clergy to tell the laity how to act in public affairs, but to confront then with the demand and to encourage them to discover its application for themselves. Hence between purely general statements of the ethical demands

---

9. Ibid., 9. (Emphasis mine.)

of the Gospel and the decisions that have to be made in concrete situations there is need for what might be described as middle axioms. It is these that give relevance and point to the Christian ethic. They are an attempt to define the directions in which, in a particular state of society, Christian faith must express itself. They are not binding for all time, but are provisional definitions of the type of behaviour required of Christians at a given period and in given circumstances.[10]

Later in the same book, Oldham states:

If action is to be effective in the social sphere it is, of course, essential that there should be definite objects of attack and pursuit. Without specific programmes nothing will be done. It is not for one moment suggested that the response of the Church to God's call should not issue in the adoption by the Church, or by groups within the Church, of particular policies for the redress of social evils. It has already been urged that the formulation of middle axioms, defining the forms in which at a given period and in given circumstances the Christian law of love can find most appropriate expression, is an urgent need at the present time. Such collective judgments of the requirements of Christian conduct are not only permissible but imperative.[11]

Note that while Oldham is speaking in terms of the actions of individual Christians, this for him includes their responsibility for formulating and implementing social policy. For illustrations of what he means, Oldham cites his contemporary, the social ethicist R.H. Tawney, on the need for greater equality in society, based on the equal value of all people and that any differences as will still exist in a more just social order must be made "not on the externals of class, income, sex, colour, or nationality, but on the real needs of the different members of the human family," requiring "the removal of *all* adventitious advantages and disabilities which have their origins in social institutions."[12] While not explicitly named as such, middle axioms featured in the discussions of Oldham's "Moot" group of intellectuals considered in chapter 8 and in Oldham's notion of a "Christian society."[13]

The question, of course, was how to move beyond such generalities towards more specific objectives and policies. That attempt can perhaps be best illustrated by the

---

10. J.H. Oldham and W.A. Visser't Hooft, *The Church and Its Function in Society* (London: George Allen and Unwin, 1937), 209ff.
11. Ibid., 238.
12. Ibid., 211.
13. See above, chapter 8.

work of another group, chaired by a member of The Moot, John Baillie. The Church of Scotland had responded to the second world war by commissioning a group to work and report on the theme "The Interpretation of God's Will in a Time of Crisis." The Baillie Commission, as it was called, discussed and reported on the whole range of contemporary national and international life, and in doing so exemplified at several points what was meant by "middle axioms." For example:

> Economic power must be made objectively responsible to the community as a whole. The possession of economic power must be answerable for the use of that power, not only to their own consciences, but to appropriate social organs—as the possessors of military or police power are so answerable.[14]

Such was the meaning and, as illustrated, the kind of content envisaged for "middle axioms." To understand more fully both the concept and the motivations of their advocates like Oldham and Baillie, however, we need to appreciate the specific context in which they arose in the ecumenical discussion of the late 1930s. It was a situation when many felt that the West was in moral chaos and that the supposedly Christian, democratic societies had no real answer to the threats posed by the fascist and Marxist totalitarianisms entrenched in continental Europe and menacing much of the rest of the world. As the delegates assembled in Oxford in July 1937, few really believed that another major war could be postponed indefinitely. China was already experiencing the Japanese onslaught. Oldham was already voicing his fear that if Britain went to war with Nazi Germany it would not be clear what values Britain would really be fighting for apart from national survival. It was a prophetic insight which was already seeing the need not for preservation of the existing social order, but for its reconstruction. But what tools would be available for the rebuilding work, and what plans should be followed for the new architecture? Theologically, there was not a lot in view. The tradition of natural law appeared to be largely discredited because it was precisely that which the totalitarian ideologies had been able to appropriate and exploit in their fashion and for their own ends, as fulfilling the supposed laws of biology and the historical process, to bring about the triumph of either the master-race or the dictatorship of the proletariat (for which read "party"). In Protestant tradition there had long been reverence for the "orders of creation," features of human existence instituted by God for the fulfilment and proper functioning of human life and society; but the more enlightened ecumenicals had seen what nation-

---

14. See A. Morton, ed., *God's Will in a Time of Crisis: The Baillie Commission* (Edinburgh: CTPI, 1994), 48.

alist Protestantism in Germany had now made of these orders of creation, turning nation, race, and *Volk* into absolute tenets of a new pagan creed. Karl Barth had in any case demolished any basis for ethics beginning with this world as we know it, and it was not yet clear how his theology of revelation through the Word of God would yield a positive social ethic (though his fellow Swiss theologian of the Word, Emil Brunner, was already at work on this). It was a situation soon to be characterised by Dietrich Bonhoeffer as one where people "had so little ground under their feet," where the traditional tools of reason, principles, conscience, duty, personal freedom and private virtue, however noble, were no longer adequate in themselves.[15] How could there be action both grounded in faith yet also concrete and purposeful for human community? Middle axioms were an attempt to relate faith to the messy unpredictability of the human scene under reconstruction, a projecting into that scene of provisional but seriously thought out ideas, based on the biblical faith but not *expressed* in biblical terms which might mean nothing to those not versed in that tradition, which would make sense to responsible people whether or not they for themselves consciously adhered to Christian belief. J.H. Oldham himself, in 1942, gave further substance to this attempt by creating the Christian Frontier, a movement which drew together people who called themselves Christians, humanists, or of no particular label but who shared a common concern to address the problems of responsibility in secular life and society.

There was, however, another feature of that context which needs to be appreciated. Today we take for granted the existence of what I would call "intermediary organisations" at both national and international level. Perhaps indeed one should call them "middle organisations" corresponding to "middle axioms." They represent a certain consolidation, codification, indeed at times a legislation, of ethical concerns. Not to be confused with or substituted for the church (though in some cases owing a lot to Christian instigation) and rarely if ever wholly capable of meeting the criteria of love, justice, and peacemaking as called for by the gospel itself, they nevertheless offer vital ways of transmitting responsible faith-based action into the world. They function to promote justice, human rights, and peace, to combat poverty and to aid human development in terms of healthcare, education, cultural enrichment, protection of labour and, more recently, the environment. On the widest international level these of course include the United Nations, the International Court of Justice at the Hague, the UN High Commission for Human Rights, UNESCO, and so on, and in Europe the European Court of Human Rights. We take for granted too the importance of what we now

---

15. Dietrich Bonhoeffer, *Dietrich Bonhoeffer Works*, vol, 6, *Ethics* (Minneapolis: Fortress, 2005), esp. "Ethics as Formation," 76ff.

call "civil society" alongside the state, defined as "the space where both the diverse needs and the will for a constructive linkage of differences are expressed"[16] and where Non-Governmental Organisations (NGOs) play a crucial part. From the point of view of churches and other faith groups, the "middle organisations" themselves can provide means of translating into society their concerns, but in 1937 there was by comparison very little of all this. The League of Nations had been totally discredited, the UN had yet to be born, even the notion of a Universal Declaration of Human Rights was but an idealistic talking point and much of it—including church-related aid and development bodies—had to be shocked into existence by the calamities of the second world war. Middle axioms were pioneering attempts to map the unfamiliar territory as yet uninhabited by the intermediary institutions that today we take for granted.

Middle Axioms: Still Relevant?

If, however, that was the context in which "middle axioms" emerged, are they now redundant? That is a question which could be addressed from two different angles. One angle would be to look at the actual "intermediary landscape" of governmental, intergovernmental, and non-governmental institutions that we have today, and its adequacy or otherwise for the tasks we face as the human community in the 21st century. The other is, as theologians, to focus our attention nearer home and to ask whether, regardless of the change in context, "middle axioms" represent something that is always needed in our theological armoury, or toolkit if you prefer. It is interesting that it is a Latin American liberation theologian, José Miguez Bonino, who points out that middle axioms are like anchors and compasses, which are required for successful, navigation: "Compasses help those at sea to get their bearings and anchors help to minimize drift in troubled waters; and that while there may be little overt reference to middle axioms in recent ecumenical discussion the question which this category addresses is still present, and the distinction and relation which liberation theology establishes between the terms 'utopia', 'historical project' and 'political programmer' point, in a different theological context, to an analogous question."[17] Given the constraints of space, I will take this second option.

Briefly, four positive theological approaches to the public sphere carry weight, at any rate in the present European context.

First, *the Roman Catholic tradition of social teaching*. No one can fail to be impressed by the body of social doctrine with which the Roman Catholic Church has sought to address the social, political, and international conditions of the modern

---

16. H. Gallardo, "Civil Society," in *Dictionary of the Ecumenical Movement*, ed. Nicholas Lossky et al., 2d. ed. (Geneva: WCC Publications, 2002), 211-12.
17. José Míguez Bonino, "Middle Axioms," in Lossky, *Dictionary of the Ecumenical Movement*, 761

world, beginning with the encyclical of Pope Leo XIII *Rerum Novarum* (1891), continuing through many others such as Pope John XXIII's *Pacem in Terris* (1963), Pope Paul VI's *Populorum Progressio* (1967), and the document marking the centenary of *Rerum Novarum*, John Paul II's *Centesimus Annus* (1991). Whatever particular points of disagreement there may be with Catholic social teaching (such as on birth control or its rejection of Latin American liberation theology), there must surely be welcome for its tremendous emphasis on the essentially social, communal, and relational nature of being human, which opposes itself to capitalist individualism no less than Marxist totalitarianism. The question arises as to how this corpus of thought is to be related to particular situations in society. There is a very interesting paragraph in the 1971 Apostolic Letter of Pope Paul VI *Octogesima Adveniens* marking the 80th anniversary of *Rerum Novarum*:

> It is with all its dynamism that the social teaching of the Church accompanies men in their search. If it does not intervene to authenticate a given structure or to propose a ready-made model, it does not thereby limit itself to recalling general principles. It develops through reflection applied to the changing situations of this world, under the driving force of the gospel as the source of renewal when its message is accepted in its totality and with all its demands. It also develops with the sensitivity proper to the Church which is characterized by a disinterested will to serve and by attention to the poorest. Finally, it draws upon its rich experience of many centuries which enables it, while continuing its permanent preoccupations, to undertake the daring and creative innovations which the present state of the world requires.[18]

One can almost imagine Oldham smiling and nodding in agreement, because what is being advocated sounds so very close to "middle axioms": "reflection applied to the changing situations of this world." What is not clear, however, is whether it is only the conscious acceptance of the totality of the gospel which can make such reflections effective in society; or, again, whether acceptance of them implicitly depends upon acknowledgment of the status of the church by society. There is, one might feel, a Christendom model lurking here.

Second, there is *the approach of "political theology,"* represented over the past four decades in Europe by such German figures as the Protestant Jürgen Moltmann and the Catholic Johann Baptist Metz. Here the question is not so much about what the church can say to the world about God's will, but how it can discern and catch up

---

18. *Octogesima Adveniens* 42, in *Proclaiming Justice and Peace: Documents from John XXIII to John Paul II*, ed. Michael Walsh and Brian Davies (London: Collins Flame/CAFOD, 1991).

with what God is already doing in the world in the public realm where the struggle is joined for justice and the liberation of the oppressed, and where the church's role is to become part of God's transforming work in history, alongside the poor. As Moltmann says, "The church always belongs *within the context of the world*, whether it likes it or not."[19] The church is forever placed at the point where the lordship of Christ is in battle with the principalities and powers of this world. The question is how this point in practice is to be identified in relation to current political processes. One commentator speaks of a tension here, "which works itself out in several ways, [and] has to do with the inherent difficulties of combining the way one reads the Christian story about Israel, Jesus and the church with a hermeneutics that makes the politics of the world, interpreted in a certain emancipator tradition, the primary horizon."[20] To hook the church to a particular political hermeneutic can make it hostage to the fortunes of that particular cause, manifesto or group, in which case it is not so much translating faith into public policy as translating public policy into faith. Moltmann has evidently seen this problem and has in his more mature theology focussed on the particular nature of the church in relation to God's ongoing salvific work, having become critical of those aspects of modernity—gleaned from his dialogue with the neo-Marxist philosopher Ernst Bloch—to which he was attracted earlier. The question therefore arises of how the church can speak concretely of purposes to be achieved within the world without committing itself to a particular political loyalty and thus surrendering its critical and prophetic freedom vis-à-vis the worldly powers. Middle axioms, aiming at the concrete yet not claiming to be more than provisional, can claim a role here.

Third, still today, within the European context, the American *Reinhold Niebuhr* (1892-1971) is listened to especially by those who fear that Christian social ethics is always in danger of losing touch with "reality" and floating off into the stratosphere of utopian idealism.[21] For Niebuhr there is no final solution to the problem of justice. Slow progress is possible, but so endemic is the self-seeking propensity of "moral man and immoral society"[22] that there is always the threat of a collapse into chaos: "The twin perils of tyranny and anarchy can never be completely overcome in any political achievement."[23] Therefore a primary function of the church in the public

19. Jürgen Moltmann, *The Power of the Powerless* (London: SCM, 1981), 156.

20. Arne Rasmussen, *The Church as Polis: From Political Theology to Theological Politics as Exemplified by Jürgen Moltmann and Stanley Hauerwas* (Lund: Lund University Press, 1994), 14.

21. See, e.g., the essays in *Reinhold Niebuhr and the Issues of Our Time*, ed. Richard Harries (London and Oxford: Mowbray, 1986).

22. The expression is taken from the title of one of Niebuhr's books: Reinhold Niebuhr, *Moral Man and Immoral Society: A Study of Ethics and Politics* (New York: Charles Scribner's Sons, 1932).

23. Reinhold Niebuhr, *The Nature and Destiny of Man*, vol. 2 (London: Nisbet 1943), 294.

sphere is to prick the pretensions and vanities of those who, whether they be politicians or religious leaders, believe that their cause is absolutely righteous and that on its success the kingdom of God depends. Optimism is permissible, provided it is cautious. The problem with the Niebuhrian approach is that while Niebuhr himself was a deeply committed Christian Socialist, his thinking can be misused as a justification for the church not doing or saying anything in the public realm except to apply the brakes when things start moving too quickly. Perhaps it is indeed a political theology for the energetic land of the free where it is believed that all things are possible and that America has a grand mission to the rest of the world, and where a critical and cautionary note always needs to be on hand. But in contexts like those we Europeans inhabit at the moment, breathing a lack of political and social imagination, the primary need is the spur rather than the bridle. There is a need for re-envisioning our representative politics itself, and for this some middle axioms will not come amiss. If they are the kind of axioms Oldham envisaged, concrete but provisional and not claiming to do more than mark the next steps to be taken by society, we need not fear that they will make Niebuhr turn in his grave.

Fourth and finally, there is the American theologian who perhaps more than any other has been exciting attention on both sides of the Atlantic for the past decade: *Stanley Hauerwas.*[24] Hauerwas owes something, whether in agreement or otherwise, to all the previous three approaches, but above all he has been indebted, Methodist though he is, to the Radical Reformation and Mennonite tradition as developed by John Howard Yoder. For Hauerwas, theological ethics must centre on the church as the new *polis* of God, the community of Jesus Christ which is in sharpest contradiction to the world, especially the postmodern world, which in its delight in its own fragmentariness is simply witnessing to the destructive divisiveness of capitalism. Furthermore, for Hauerwas it is theological politics rather than political theology which is the proper Christian concern. Where Moltmann aims at underscoring the participation of Christians in the politics of this world, Hauerwas (like Yoder) warns against Christians wanting to run the world, or even to run America. Their task is to be the cross-shattered and cross-shaped church, the alternative *polis* to the politics of this world, a community of virtue, and it is precisely by being this church that the church's primary political witness is made. The church confronts the world with the world's own unintelligibility apart from God's self-revelation in Christ and his

---

24. A more complete survey would refer also to the British "Radical Orthodoxy" school in which John Milbank is preeminent, and which is both indebted to Hauerwas and has certain important affinities with him (see e.g. Milbank, *The Word Made Strange. Theology, Language, Culture* (Oxford: Blackwell 1997)). However, Hauerwas serves as representative figure for all contemporary approaches which contrast the Christian community and its way with the ways of this world, and of all such theologians, he commands the widest attention internationally and interconfessionally.

way of peace. Christians are called to be "resident aliens," a recognition that became muted when "Christianity became a civilizational religion. That project ... was to turn the world into the kingdom. It was the attempt to force God's kingdom into being by making the worship of God unavoidable."[25] Hauerwas adds: "No one listens to a church which speaks the same truths than can be heard anywhere other than church."[26] The separateness of the church is for the sake of the world. For Hauerwas, politics is about sharing of common goods, about non-violence and "a positive conversation about the sort of society we want,"[27] rather than about participating in the political power struggles of the present world order. It is an alternative politics, rather than theology taking sides with the alternatives existing within the present political power game.

I must confess my intense admiration for Hauerwas's intensely ecclesiological emphasis, which to me represents the full flowering of the Anglo-Saxon Free Church tradition from which I come. Where I find myself on less certain ground is to know whether in a society like my own we can in fact draw such a sharp distinction between church and society, or churchly and worldly responsbility, as Hauerwas seems to imply, and whether one can distinguish the theological politics of the church community quite so neatly from the political ethic of the wider community. For instance, how is a state governor, a government minister, or a senior civil servant who is a Christian (or a Jew or a Muslim, for that matter), to regard his or her secular responsbility in the light of his or her faith? Does that faith give directions for behaviour in the corridors of power as well as in the intimate circle of the gathered community of the church? Are we not all, each of us, still citizens of this world as well as of the kingdom of God? Hauerwas evidently does have public concerns and does address ethical issues relating to wider society, such as *in vitro* fertilization and the use of children in medical experiments. But he argues by relating such issues to the kind of community that the church should be, rather than to the world as it can be. Evidently he is prepared to make concessions for the church's addressing of public policy, but I am not clear whether I have yet found his theological rationale for doing so. It seems to me that the claim of the secular order upon the attention of Christians can be sustained without diminishing the central place of the church. As Bonhoeffer put it, the penultimate sphere has its proper place. The fact that there is an ultimate word does not completely displace the penultimate word. The sphere of the "things before the last," i.e. worldly responsbility, is not to be prematurely written off before

25. Stanley Hauerwas, *In Good Company: The Church as Polis* (Notre Dame: University of Notre Dame Press, 1995), 54.
26. Ibid., 56.
27. Rasmussen, *The Church as Polis*, 188.

"the last things," the word of judgement, salvation and the life everlasting. Indeed, without the preservation of the "things before the last" there would be nothing for the ultimate to come to.[28] Even Jesus Christ needs his forerunner, John the Baptist.

Hauerwas's retrieval of the church as a distinct, gathered community of worship and communal virtue is superb and timely. But its own logic demands in turn a careful strategy of how the church may address the world—without saying too much or giving the impression that it knows best how to run the world, while saying enough to prompt reflection and decision. That, again, is what "middle axioms" sought to provide.

Modest but Meaningful—and Widely Usable

We have noted earlier[29] the controversy surrounding the formulation of the Preamble to the European Constitution, and the impossibility of finding agreement on whether it should make explicit reference to God, Christianity, or any overtly religious affirmation, hence its eventual, rather colourless recognition of diverse cultural, religious and humanist elements in the European heritage. That at least is consistent with what is stated, soon afterwards, to be the values shared by the member states of the European Union: "respect for human dignity, liberty, democracy, equality, the rule of law and respect for human rights" in a society "of pluralism, tolerance, justice, solidarity and non-discrimination." But while the rather heated public controversy about the Preamble was going on, a rather different project was being quietly pursued by the organisations representing the concerns of the churches to the European institutions in Brussels, the Church and Society Commission of the Conference of European Churches (CEC) and its Roman Catholic partner, the Commission of Episcopal Conferences in the European Union (COMECE). Between them, the two organisations deftly negotiated for the insertion into the actual text of the Constitution an article on "the Status of Churches and Non-Confessional Organisations" which, after affirming the Union's respect for the status under national law of churches, religious associations and philosophical organisations, states: "Recognising their identity and their specific contribution, the Union shall maintain an open, transparent and regular dialogue with these churches and organisations."[30] Quite apart from the fact that the Preamble has no legal status vis-à-vis the Constitution, this is arguably far more significant than any specifically religious statement in the Preamble would have been, for it encodes into the actual practice of the European Union a place for dialogue with the churches and other faith groups, with no restric-

---

28. Bonhoeffer, *Ethics*, 146-170.
29. See above in this chapter.
30. *Treaty Establishing a Constitution for Europe* (Luxembourg: European Communities, 2003), 43. This clause was retained in the version of the Lisbon Treaty which came into force in 2009.

tion on the agenda for such dialogue. This is far in advance of the situation of church and governmental relations within any of the member states themselves. It opens the way for the churches, on a basis of equality, without special privileges but recognised rights of access, to contribute to the discussion of major issues of public policy. It is, one might say, an invitation for the production, debate and testing of middle axioms within the context of the pluralist and democratic society that is still emerging in post-Cold War Europe in process of integration.

A contemporary close approach to the "middle axioms" approach can be found in a recent report on poverty in Europe by church-related organisations in Brussels, including the Church and Society Commission of the Conference of European Churches, COMECE, Caritas Europa, and Eurodiakonia. Presented in the European Parliament on 1 October 2010 and titled "Do Not Deny Justice to Your Poor People," it makes 14 recommendations on reducing poverty in Europe, but not before having set out the following basis:

> Poverty takes away the means and possibilities for those individuals affected to participate fully in society. It places them in vulnerable and other stigmatised positions. As Christians, we consider every human being to be created in the image of God, endowed with inherent dignity. We consequently advocate that every human being should be able to live in dignity, holistically and to autonomously develop their capacities, to contribute to and participate in society. We hold as guiding principles "the universal destination of goods" to serve all humankind (including future generations), and equally accountability of goods and services for all and the social function of every form of private or corporate ownership.[31]

Illustrated thus, middle axioms are an attempt by Christians and their faith- community to live positively in their social environment and to serve the public good: to live there, in the secular *oikoumene*, as well as in the familiarity of their inner life and tradition. They constitute a recognition that in fact the Christian community *is* part of that *oikoumene* and belongs to it, as much as any "secular" group. Moltmann is right: the church *does* always belong within the context of the world, whether it likes it or not. That, too, is a message which today is being voiced ever more strongly and with a particular tone from Asia, Africa and Latin America. It is the necessary unity of a whole community facing injustice, poverty and the end-processes of the globalized market economy, not to mention violence, which is the primary concern in such contexts, and in which alone any talk of Christian unity has any relevance. A young

---

31. The report may be found at http://www.ceceurope.org/fileadmin/filer/csc/Social_Economic_Issues/Poverty_Report_Final.pdf.

Indonesian theologian, Beril Huliselan, argues powerfully for ecumenism needing to be established in the reality of the contemporary life of people as a manifestation of the incarnation whereby God actualizes himself. Ecumenism as traditionally meant—not to mention traditional church structures themselves—means nothing to desperate people on the ground who in the absence of anything better are turning to local healers or shamans, or to the so-called prosperity gospel. He writes:

In light of God's self-actualisation in Christ, ecumenism should not be seen as a movement that tries to bring some established fixed forms or structures (the "unity movement"). On the contrary, ecumenism is a consciousness leading us to seek for its contextual realisation in different moments of history. There is no single established form of unity that has to be concretized in history. Every part of history, each place in each era, will have its own contextual unity, and every form of contextual unity should be criticized according to the spirit and purpose of unity itself: that is, with a sense of the unity of all humankind that includes concern for social and political *diakonia*, practical witness, the dignity of the person and human rights, the sanctity of life, family values, education, justice and peace, health care, the preservation of creation and, last but not least, interreligious dialogue.[32]

Huliselan's call for context-specific, time-limited projects of unity and witness manifests the desire for incarnate faithfulness to the particular piece of the *oikoumene* within which one is set, in contrast to attempts to set up some universal ecumenical structure or doctrinal system which can only be external to the particular contexts or arbitrarily imposed upon them. While wholeheartedly agreeing with this, I would make two points. First, incarnation is incarnation of something or rather Someone *other* than the context itself. It is not just an affirmation of the context, but of the entry into it and identification with it, at greatest cost of love ("He came down from heaven . . ."). It is God's own act of living in more than one place at once. Second, "a sense of the unity of all humankind," if it is indeed to serve as basis of critique of the contextual unities, needs some kind of methodology for its implementation. At the very least, this will mean an interrelating and dialogue between the contexts: in other words, living in more than one place at once, the irrepressible dynamic of ecumenism, and for this some kind of instrumentality is needed.[33] But what is perhaps most

32. Beril Huliselan, "The Ecumenical Movement in the 21st Century: Bringing Ecumenism Down to Earth," *Ecumenical Review* Vol. 60 No. 3 (July 2008), p217. For a slightly more critical view of Huliselan's language. see below, chapter 12 p000.

33. "The Unity of the Church and the Renewal of Human Community" was a major study programme of the WCC Faith and Order Commission in the 1980s and 1990s as called for by the 6th Assembly of the WCC, Vancouver 1983.

striking in Huliselan's cataloguing of the elements that make for contextual unity and therefore the church's agenda therein, is their close resemblance in kind to Oldham's middle axioms which as we have seen are "an attempt to define the directions in which, in a particular state of society, Christian faith must express itself. . . are not binding for all time, but . . . provisional definitions of the type of behaviour required of Christians at a given period and in given circumstances." They define "the forms in which at a given period and in given circumstances the Christian law of love can find most appropriate expression." The temporal provisionality of middle axioms does not mean a tentativeness or uncertainty. Far from it, they indicate what must *urgently* be aimed at *here and now,* without losing the sense that there will be other "heres and nows" and that the final home is "the city that is to come" (Heb. 13:14).

Middle axioms as a concept and praxis therefore have an almost limitless applicability even today. They express the ecumenical dynamic of a faith never being content to be self-enclosed within the safety of the church and ecclesiastical structures, but taking the risk of living in the "there" of society where the presuppositions of faith may not be shared but a common humanness certainly is. They are important since many churches even today do not habitually find it easy to engage with the public domain and the formulation of public policy. They would prefer either to be able to control and dominate it entirely as in the old Christendom, or to leave it to its own devices. An all-or-nothing approach. Or, if they cannot translate readily the whole of their beliefs and values into public policy they feel discouraged and withdraw from the scene, or loudly condemn it from a distance. Or they may give the appearance of engaging with the public domain but only over a very narrow range of issues, usually to do with personal morality. Or they may engage with politics only in attempts to ensure what they perceive to be their own interests and rights as religious entities. Worse still, they may opt for that political leadership which they feel will offer the churches themselves the most patronage, support, and protection. Or they may give the appearance of political engagement but only in the sense of trying to decide which of the existing political options on offer they should support. But there are real questions that would stand exploring in contemporary society and with which theology is specially suited to engage. For example, what does it really mean to "represent" people? Therein lies an agenda where theology should be capable of revealing translation into axioms that help society discover what its next steps should be. We do not need grand blueprints of utopia. Provisional sketch-maps for the next steps will normally be enough. Middle axioms can help to convert the passionate vision of prophecy into that much neglected other biblical category of *wisdom* and as such, modest but meaningful, they have a relevant future throughout the *oikoumene.*

Chapter 12
Who Are We?

Continuing Ecumenical Quest

The stories, episodes and people recalled and discussed in the preceding chapters illustrate in their very different ways what it means to "live in more than one place at once." That, I suggested in the first chapter, is central to what "being ecumenical" is all about.

Living in More than One Place at Once

Being ecumenical is not first and foremost a matter of structures and organisations, though these certainly come into it. It is about living relationships. It is being called into a new community in the making, in which one realises that one's present abode is not the only place to be; that there are other places from which to view the world, and from which the world might look rather different; that there are other traditions than one's own and which can lend a new perspective, whether of challenge or enrichment or both, to one's beliefs; and that there are features of the landscape in our world which need not be assumed as fixed and final, that there is another vantage point, that another world is possible. The modern ecumenical movement exhibits the capacity for what Miroslav Volf calls "double vision," seeing the social world from *there* as well as *here*.[1] That is what those first peace-building British and German pioneers sought to do in their exchange visits in 1908-09, creating the opportunities for each of their countries to be seen from the other side of the North Sea; and moreover in a world of imperial rivalry and naval races, to dare—however ingenuously in hindsight—to glimpse an alternative world. That is what started to happen at Edinburgh in 1910, as it began to dawn on the western missionary churches and their leaders that if there was indeed to be *one* mission it could no longer be *their* mission alone. The great rediscovery of the German Confessing Church at Barmen

---

1. Miroslav Wolf, *Exclusion and Embrace: A Theological Exploration of Identity, Otherness and Reconciliation* (Nashville: Abingdon, 1996), 250.

in 1934 was not just for themselves but the whole Christian world, that in whatever context the church lives, whether "here" or "there," whichever cultural forms it takes and whatever political allurements attract it or oppressions intimidate it, its central attachment is to Jesus Christ alone and it is in *his* light that we shall see light, in each "here" and "there." Indeed it is through that defining attachment to Christ that there comes the freedom truly to live in more than one place at once. It was the great gift of a figure like George Bell to be English and Anglican to his roots yet—set free by such vision—able to step outside the safe precincts of Canterbury or Chichester and stand alongside his threatened brothers and sisters whether in Germany, Eastern Europe, or Asia and Africa. To live in more than one place at once is what J.H. Oldham and his collaborators were venturing upon as they recognized the end of the old Christendom and began reimagining themselves in the new society that was emerging, a society outside traditional Christian governance, one with which faith had to learn fresh ways of creative engagement. That was closely akin to the project of those members of the German resistance who saw that what was at stake for Europe and the world had an importance far transcending any national, denominational or sectarian interest. In turn, how to live in more than once place at once is what the churches of Europe have been challenged to learn and relearn in the aftermath of the Second World War. The forty-plus years of Cold War dared the churches to be a fellowship of both sides of the Iron Curtain and not simply of either "West" or "East," and no less in the emergence of a "new Europe" they have been learning how strange even their present contexts are—contexts in which they nevertheless belong together.

These are but a few points on the swirling current of the modern ecumenical movement which has been characterized by a sense of adventure on the part of churches and Christians discovering each other, becoming conscious of belonging to a bigger community than presently embodied in any of their own traditions, and seeking a unity which is intended to be a sign and instrument of the unity of the whole human family in the purpose of God. It is a movement of repentance, renewal, and risk: repentance at past divisions, renewal in the Holy Spirit as the bond and re-creator of unity, and risk in common witness and service in the world. As such, however, it is now more readily talked about it as a piece of history than a present-day phenomenon. We have already in chapter 1 rehearsed the metaphors for the present scene: ecumenical winter, desert, doldrums and so on. Those of us still describing ourselves as ecumenical enthusiasts perhaps resemble the two disciples on the Emmaus road: "We *had* hoped..."). If so, then like those disciples we need to be both re-immersed within the total biblical perspective as portrayed in chapter 3 and made to look again at "the things that have taken place in these days," the story in the light of the risen Christ.

A Story Unknown—or Disowned?

The modern ecumenical story, even if it is known at all (which is questionable even as far as many church leaders are concerned), is evidently not owned by the churches by and large today. In Britain at any rate, indifference, introversion, and a drear acceptance of "denominational structures as they are" hold sway. The British missiologist Kirsteen Kim identifies one of the key factors in the British ecumenical movement since the 1960s: "A great deal of effort was put into working for unity but this became detached from mission as a result of postcolonial criticism and the pressures of secularization, which militated against explicit Christian confession on grounds of tolerance."[2] This detachment from mission, however, is not just a trait of "ecumenicals." It runs along with an increasing British insularity and parochialism at many levels of life, and what another missiologist calls "a contemporary British lack of engagement with the world church" and the new global mission consciousness.[3]

It is indeed a real question, that if the quest for visible Christian unity—in Britain at any rate—has slowed down, what is the connection with the (perhaps equal) hesitancy over mission? It is tempting to look for a simple cause-and-effect relationship: "Churches that have lost their sense of missionary calling are unlikely to see their need for greater unity," it will be said. But the equation might be more two-way than that, certainly when we raise it to the international level. Churches which are losing their sense of belonging to the body of Christ in the whole *oikoumene*—as is increasingly evident with the British churches—will be increasingly starved of the missionary vision, confidence and imagination that are currently animating so many other parts of the Christian world. Not that we are lacking in forms of activism that can be labelled as "attempts at mission." But how much of it is really enabling an engagement of our society and culture with Christ as distinct from safeguarding church life against the advance of "secularism"? How far is even the concept of "church planting," so much in vogue at the moment, any more than an exercise in placing new oases in the wilderness rather than irrigating the desert as a whole? Of course there are the experiments at "fresh expressions"—well and good, but fresh expressions of *what?* Perhaps the quest for Christian unity will only be re-enthused when Christians and churches move beyond their comfort zones into the uncharted wilderness where they know they simply cannot go it alone, where they will need a mutual resourcing of wisdom, practice and spirituality far beyond what they look for at present.

---

2. Kirsteen Kim, *Joining in with the Spirit: Connecting World Church and Local Mission* (London: Epworth, 2009), 267.
3. K. Cracknell, review of Kim, *Joining in with the Spirit*, *Theology* 114, no. 2 (March-April 2011): 139.

If we are indeed on the Emmaus road of disappointed hopes then it is a question of whether and how the story can be retrieved and re-owned as *our* story to be continued by us, in a new Easter encounter, just as the two disciples were given a new reading of the old scriptural story by the as yet unrecognized Christ. Hearts may then be set burning within us again (Luke 24:32), all passion rekindled. But the story itself has first of all to be told and made known again, and it is hard to imagine how anyone who reads it as an adventure of repentance, renewal and risk can fail to be moved by it and *want* to be part of its continuing into new chapters. And it really will be new: history cannot just be re-run like an old video. In the words of George Bell's hymn it will be a matter of "new lamps ... lit, new tasks begun."[4] But in its future orientation towards a new community it will continue in the same spirit of repentance, renewal, and risk, and of learning to live in more than one place at once. Before we can retrieve the story, however, there needs to be more diagnosis of why it no longer excites. What has happened in our life as western churches to make us no longer do not feel grateful heirs of our recent parents in the ecumenical faith, nor responsible for the future they glimpsed?

Identity: The Contemporary Obsession

A major feature of the church scene today is the growing preoccupation of churches and denominations with their own identity, the search by each for a secure plot on which to build their designer-home in accordance with what they think is their distinctive and unique architecture of the spirit. It is a return to the apparent safety of living in only one place at once. This will be a highly contested assertion—or at any rate there will be those who recognise the picture but see it in a much more positive light. It is certainly undeniable that virtually every Christian tradition has in recent years devoted major effort to studies on its identity: What does it mean to be Anglican ... Methodist ... Reformed? And so on. That in itself is understandable, especially in contexts of increasing plurality and the growth of new religious movements both Christian and non-Christian. It is still more to be expected where the place of the churches in relation to government, to society and to each other has drastically changed, as happened in eastern Europe following the dramatic changes of 1989-91.[5] A not dissimilar scenario emerged in South Africa after the end of apartheid. Churches that had previously been bound together in the common struggle in many cases retreated from ecumenism into a more denominationalist mode, isolationist not only from each other but to some extent from society too. Such recovery phases

---

4. See above, chapter 7.
5. See above, chapter 9.

may be inevitable and necessary—as interim measures. What is not quite so understandable is why the churches in much more stable environments such as Britain should also have followed this pattern, unless it is symptomatic of a much wider cultural crisis prompting "identity" to become the key issue at every level, from the national and ethnic communal plane to the individual. In which case churches and religious communities no less than others are simply being enmeshed in these questions too. The likelihood then is that in following this trend the churches, for all their vociferous denunciations of "secularism," are in fact simply reflecting and conforming to the age rather than countering it.

"Who am I?" is indeed the defining questioned of our age, whether for individuals seeking to trace their family tree[6] or a nation struggling for independence from a more powerful neighbour. It may be that "Who am I?" is simply the badge of post-modernity where the individual, the particular, the singular, the fragment, has primacy over the corporate, the general, the supposedly seamless garment of the universal; where the "grand narrative" has given way to the particular story, however fragmentary or incoherent, as the locus of meaning in life. Some will argue that post-modernity is essentially the ideology of free-market capitalism which trades on the view that essentially we are unique individuals marked by freedom of choice to select whatever particular goods we wish for our personal consumption. The question arises no less at the corporate level, especially in an age of the breakdown of imperialisms, or whenever suppressed communities reject the definitions imposed on them by the hitherto powerful and affirm their own identities, whether as black, women, gay, differently abled, or young. That is a prerequisite of justice. Equally, we know that the assertion of a unique identity can take demonic form and produce such dangerous myths as "national destiny" or "racial purity" and result in hideous projects like ethnic cleansing.

Identity is a genuine issue where people feel that they are not recognised for who they are under repressive systems whether of gender control, racial oppression, or repressive cultures other than their own. But does anyone seriously pretend that at the present time the distinctives of any one church are under threat by another church, or by that chimera of anti-ecumenical anxiety, a "super-church" being created by the World Council of Churches? The churches' concern for identity, rather, arises from within: internal disputes about what is the authentic tradition of one's church (especially as regards authority systems), together with a competitive anxiety to be taken seriously in the public market-place of religious goods. We can therefore

---

6. See for example the popular British TV series "Who Do You Think You Are?" which no doubt has equivalents in other countries.

also expect to see, manifest at the ecclesiastical level, what Sigmund Freud called "the narcissism of minor differences."[7]

The Anglican theologian Paul Avis justly writes: "The problem of identity is one that troubles both individuals and institutions, including churches, but to become obsessed by it would be neurotic."[8] I judge that the neurosis really has taken hold and some therapy is needed. This is not to deny that the "Who am I?" or "Who are we?" question is natural and important, but simply to keep it in proper perspective. It is not that the identity question is illegitimate, but rather that it is not the ultimate question, the be-all and end-all question, certainly not within a Christian eschatological framework. Imagine how the great final vision of the end (Rev. 6:9-12) would read if the Apocalypse was rewritten according to our present concerns: "After this I looked, and there was a great multitude that no one could count, from all tribes and peoples and languages, standing before the throne and before the Lamb, robed in white, with palm branches in their hands. They cried out with a loud voice, saying, "Who are we? What does it mean to be English, or Chinese, or Anglican, or Lutheran..." It hardly has the same ring with those who are so lost in wonder, love and praise as to declare only that salvation belongs to their God, and to the Lamb. Moreover, identity always has a final elusiveness about it, which means that over-insistence on it condemns us either to self-delusion or disappointment. Paul Avis again puts it well: "Identity is not so much a 'given' as a quest,"[9] never settled once for all: "It belongs within an unfolding narrative quest for meaning."[10] Moreover, even suppose we did arrive at a clear, if provisional, grasp of our identity as a person or community, what are we then to *do* with it? That is a still more important question.

Not "Who?" but "Whose?"

By now, someone is probably wishing to remind me that no less a person than Dietrich Bonhoeffer while in prison wrote one of his most moving poems, titled "Who Am I?" True, but far from just validating the identity question, that poem also subverts it. Bonhoeffer describes the two seemingly contrasting personas that he wears: on the one hand the outwardly calm, confident, and cheerful man who steps from

---

7. I owe this reference to Freud to Peter Baldwin. *The Narcissism of Minor Differences: How America and Europe Are Alike* (Oxford: OUP 2009). Freud saw this "narcissism," an exaggeration of imagined distinctives, as a trait of individuals under the stress of unresolved inner tensions and consequently uncertain of their status and identity in relation to others.

8. Paul Avis, *The Identity of Anglicanism: Essentials of Anglican Ecclesiology* (London: T. & T. Clark, 2007), 31.

9. Paul Avis, *Reshaping Ecumenical Theology: The Church Made Whole?* (London: T. & T. Clark, 2010), 64.

10. Ibid., 144.

his cell on his way to interrogation sessions "like a squire from his manor"; and on the other, the inwardly fearful, tormented, and helpless individual longing for release and freedom. Who am I, he asks, this or the other? He concludes:

> Who am I? They mock me, these lonely questions of mine.
> Whoever I am, thou knowest me; O God, I am thine![11]

This conclusion is not a mere pietistic flourish, but a statement that profoundly undermines conventional notions of identity. Such notions assume that identity is a matter of the circumscribed self, a kind of content of my own possession, held safe and secure by my own independence. Not so. Bonhoeffer sees identity not just as being and having, but as relational, as *belonging to* another outside of ourselves. He thus puts the emphasis neither on the *I* nor the *am* but on the *Who?* transmuted into *Whose?*[12]

No one has subsequently developed a relational understanding of identity so fully, nor pressed its implications so radically, as Miroslav Volf, his analysis all the more cogent for being forged in the context of the Balkan conflicts:

> The self is dialogically constructed. The other is already from the outset part of the self. I am who I am in relation to the other; to be Croat is, among other things, to have Serbs as neighbours; to be white in the U.S. is to enter a whole history of relation to African Americans (even if you are a recent immigrant). Hence the will to be oneself, if it is to be healthy, must entail the will to let the other inhabit the self; the other must be part of who I am as I will to be myself. As a result, a tension between the self and the other is built into the very desire for identity.[13]

We might paraphrase Volf by saying that to have an identity entails, in contrast to a closed-in self, the open self: a self open to others and finding the answer to the "Who?" question to include the others to whom one relates in particular ways. In Christian terms, the supreme exemplar of this kind of identity is Jesus Christ himself, who neither overrides or suppresses the particular identities of members of his body, the church, nor stands in aloof detachment from them in order to let

---

11. Dietrich Bonhoeffer, *Dietrich Bonhoeffer Works*, vol. 8, *Letters and Papers from Prison* (Minneapolis: Fortress, 2010), 460.

12. There is, as we have noted above in Chapter 6, a strong affinity here with the first thesis of the 1934 Barmen Declaration in its affirmation of Jesus Christ as "the one word of God which we have to hear, trust and obey in life and in death," where the German verb "to hear," *hören*, is very close to *gehören*, "to belong."

13. Volf, *Exclusion and Embrace*, 91.

them pursue their individualistic ways. Rather, at the eucharist, in Volf's words, "the one bread stands for the *crucified* body of Jesus Christ, *the body that has refused to remain a self-enclosed singularity, but has opened itself up so that others can freely partake of it.*"[14]

A self-enclosed singularity is decidedly what Christ is not. But it is what much of church self-understanding has become, so deeply have the churches in the West, however loudly they proclaim their opposition to the secularism of the time, drunk in the spirit of the post-modern age. It is small wonder that little ecumenical progress is now being made if the churches imagine that they can first define their distinctive identities and *then* go on to being "ecumenical." Ecumenism will then always be an optional afterthought instead of an imperative. One even wonders to what extent churches seek—consciously or unconsciously, but nevertheless intentionally—to clarify their identities in ways that will effectively *prevent* closer relationships with others or at any rate justify their continued detachment. Identity in ecumenical context therefore has to be re-construed so as to include, from the very outset, how this particular church or tradition sees the others, what are its relationships of interaction and interdependency, and how it sees itself as sharing in the building of that greater unity. This in turn entails a massive re-think of the total backdrop against which churches and Christians see their respective identities. For if the identity of any person or community is not self-enclosed but involves relationships with others, that means that there is an overall identity within which our particular identities only truly make sense. And if as Archbishop Rowan Williams says, "Christian identity is to belong to a place that Jesus defines for us,"[15] then our identity is really out of our hands, as Bonhoeffer saw. It is found only in relation to something much bigger and more dynamic. Therein lies the contemporary problem for churches and the ecumenical movement. What is this larger identity?

Our Story and the Larger Story

It has become a truism today to say that the identity of a person or community is expressed in narrative form: memory is the basis of our identity and consciousness of selfhood. Who we are is bound up in what we believe to be our story, whether the personal or familial experiences that have "made me what I am" or our national history of triumphs and defeats, cultural achievements and political outcomes that "define our way of life." The same applies even more to religious communities; how

---

14. Ibid., 47. (Emphases mine.)
15. Rowan Williams, "Christian Identity and Religious Plurality," address given at ninth assembly of the World Council of Churches, Porto Alegre, 2006. See official Assembly Report *God, in Your Grace*, ed. Luis N. Rivera-Pagán (Geneva: WCC Publications, 2007), 181.

readily we refer to these as not only having but *being* "traditions"! Nor does this apply only to those churches which claim a continuous history reaching back two millennia and who emphasize "tradition" as itself being a medium of truth. Indeed, we find a marked emphasis on "story" precisely among the relatively more recent appearances in Christian history and in minority communities determined to stake their claim to a distinctive place on the Christian scene. The American Mennonite Alan Kreider writes passionately: "Every Christian tradition can repent by finding new life in its own story, which it will share with other Christians as it listens to their stories. We Mennonites must not jettison our stories. We must tell our origin stories—the Anabaptist stories that demonstrate the movement's charisms and embody its witness to the deep DNA of God's liberating metanarrative. We must also find imaginative ways to tell our long haul stories—the Mennonite stories across time and around the globe that show how these charisms have shaped communities."[16] Kreider's reference to "God's liberating metanarrative" is of course a passing riposte to the post-modernist denial of any such grand narratives in favour of particular narrative fragments, but it requires some more serious attention. The relation between the particular story and the metanarrative is not just one of coexistence, but is quite complex in its reciprocity. It is not enough simply to claim that one's particular story somehow embodies or reflects the metanarrative, for it might be that what *we*, from the perspective of our particular tradition, call the metanarrative of God's liberating love, or the gospel of Jesus Christ, is simply the projection onto the big screen of our particular story, the grand magnification of our narrative fragment. How then do we escape from our own subjectivity and—assuming we wish to—apprehend an overall narrative transcending as well as including our particular story? This is the ecumenical challenge, which certainly involves the sharing of stories between Christians. But the very recognition that others too are Christians implies an acknowledgment of an authoritative and originating truth that questions the completeness and finality of our own embodiments of this truth. That must lie in the biblical narrative of creation, reconciliation, and redemption, culminating in the life, death, and resurrection of Jesus Christ and the gift of the Spirit and summarised in the Trinitarian faith of the ecumenical creeds. It is the Trinitarian life of God, drawing into itself the life of the world, in the unswerving purpose of the Father, at the utmost cost born by the incarnate Son, and in the overflowing joy of the Spirit, which is the overarching narrative, the total context in which we live and move and have our being. Graham Ward, concluding his study of the relation between the incarnate Christ and human

---

16. Alan Kreider, "Revisioning Identity: Mennonite Reflections on Narrative," *Questions of Identity: Studies in Honour of Brian Haymes*, ed. Anthony R. Cross and Ruth Gouldbourne (Oxford: Regent's Park College, 2011), 229.

history and culture, writes of the triune God's self-revelation as "a continuously unfolding process" within the horizon of the end-time:

> This unfolding process is the *dunamis* [power] of love itself and therefore the content of such revelation is a getting to love, a pedagogy of adoration, a plotting of praise, a liturgy not an intellectual property. As such our creative storytelling takes place within the operation of God's triune loving; we exist in God's endless impartations of himself.[17]

If however there is an overall narrative which tells us what the story is actually all about (or, as we have heard Paul Avis put it, "an unfolding narrative quest for meaning"), what is really going on, then there are potentially huge bearings on how we read our particular story and perceive its meaning. Our identities are not just carried within our particular stories, or in the particular role we act out. Our particular story, and therewith our identity, is affected and maybe challenged and reshaped by the larger story within which we now see we have a calling and *role* to fulfil.[18] What we think of our identity, and what matters in our life, should be conditioned by what we understand to be the grand narrative into which we are being drawn. If we think the story which carries our identity is about the conquest of the world by our particular version of what is right and good; or about making our church and our leadership of it to be a sure success story; or about securing our own church's power and privileges over against others; or even just about preserving safe and sound our "tradition" in its purity and distinction from all others... then it will come as a shock to discover that through the gospel we are given a quite different title and storyline to follow. Its key-word is *grace*, which points us once again to an identity which has very

---

17. Graham Ward, *Christ and Culture: Challenges in Contemporary Theology* (Oxford: Blackwell, 2005), 247.

18. An illustration: I recently tried an experiment with a group of ordinands on retreat in Australia. In a session on the theme "How do you read yourself?" we explored the notion of each of our lives being a story which could be the subject of a book or a film. People were then sent away for half an hour by themselves to reflect on what their own main story-line would be, and what would be the title of the book or film. Each person, however, had also been given an envelope which they could open at the end of their time of reflection, and they found within it the title of an actual novel, biography or film, selected purely at random (*Pride and Prejudice, The Idiot, Reach for the Sky, Wild Swans, The God of Small Things, The Sound of One Hand Clapping*, to name a few). On seeing this new title, they were invited to imagine that this was now the theme and title of their story: how did they now view it, what new evaluation of their experiences did suggest, did some things now seem more and some less important, what kind of new identity did they feel it gave them? Many confessed to a quite revelatory new view of their life-story and of who they might be.

little to do with what we are in ourselves, what distinguishing marks we may carry as individuals or communities, but rather with what we, or rather who, we *belong to*. More than fifty years ago the Scottish theologian Ronald Gregor Smith wrote of his youthful interest in the conversion stories of significant figures in Christian history:

> I began to see that the broad similarity between, say, the life of St Augustine and the life of John Wesley was that their interests, their thought and their energy came at the conversion to be gathered up, concentrated, and then to live in a new direction, into a new life which involved nevertheless more than just a moral change. I found myself forced to the conclusion that these lives could only be understood properly in terms of something that was *not themselves*, and not even their achievement, but something objective and solid, which I ended by calling a *structure of grace*. They were embedded in a new ground, they were entangled *in a new web, a community of relations* which gave all that they did and were a new meaning.[19]

Understanding ourselves to be caught in that web of grace, to be agents of grace ourselves, is how our true identities are shaped. On earth it means being caught up into sharing the life of the suffering God, becoming the church existing for others, and so being drawn into the life of the Triune God. As that life means an endless reciprocity, of mutual indwelling (*perichoresis*) between Father, Son, and Holy Spirit, so it must also be for the members of the body of Christ. Their communion with one another and with the Triune God forms a whole. Ecumenism is therefore inherent in Christian faith, not a supplement to it. That means, inescapably, the readiness to consider whether for the greater adoption of *that* central identity some aspects of what we consider to be our particular identities needs to be given up—and maybe some aspects of our individual or corporate selves that we have hitherto ignored or disparaged can be seen in a new and positive light. The brokenness of earthen vessels becomes the medium of transcendent grace (2 Cor. 4:7), as do all the seeming weaknesses, afflictions, failures and ambiguities of the apostolic life, summed up as "dying, and see—we live" (2 Cor. 6:9). Ecumenism therefore is not a matter of the deadening hand of formal inter-ecclesiastical exchanges, negotiated compromises and ambiguously worded "agreements" on doctrine and church order, nor even the relatively exciting (to those participating in them) processes of bilateral theological dialogues. It means, rather, developing the actual experience, at every level, of living, working, witnessing and worshipping together to the point where certain things no

---

19. R. Gregor Smith, *The New Man: Christianity and Man's Coming of Age* (London: SCM, 1956), 12. (Emphases mine.)

longer matter as once they seemed to, for the sake of the pearl of still more superlative price, namely, even more communion than is at present realised. As the Anglican theologian Nicholas Sagovsky puts it:

> What this means for the Church can only be spelt out in terms of a practice which incorporates a doctrine, not a doctrine from which a practice can be derived . . .
> The unity of the churches will not come through the steady flow of ecumenical agreed statements that spell out the virtues of *koinonia*, though they have their part to play. The way forward must include the practice of a common life, which provides a context for the continuing theological debate.[20]

But if there is to be a common life, who are to be the main participants in it?

Clericalisation: A Trend to Be Reversed

One of the most conspicuous developments in recent church and ecumenical activity has been a creeping *clericalisation*. Ordained clergy of all denominations were of course prominent in the earlier ecumenical movement and essential to it, and Bishop Bell is only one outstanding example here. But no less significant were lay leaders: John R. Mott and J.H. Oldham were the pre-eminent driving forces up until the formation of the WCC, and we have also brought onto the stage J. Allen Baker, Eduard de Neufville, Madeleine Barot, and Kathleen Bliss to represent a host of people many of whom (like their ordained colleagues) were first nurtured in the Student Christian Movement and World Student Christian Federation.[21] We have noted, too, Oldham's strategy of recruiting the "best minds" to look long, hard and deep at the ethical challenges of social life, which meant in practice utilising lay, i.e. non-ordained, people with the requisite knowledge and expertise in politics, social planning, applied science and international affairs, to do the spade-work of Christian social thinking. This insistence on the role of "experts" was but one part of Oldham's heavy emphasis, in the work surrounding the 1937 Oxford conference on "Church, Community and State," on the role of the laity as the main bearer of Christian mission and witness. In one of the preparatory reports for Oxford he states:

> If the Christian faith is in the present and future to bring about changes ... in the thought, habits and practices of society, it can only do this through the living,

---

20. Nicholas Sagovsky, *Ecumenism, Christian Origins and the Practice of Communion* (Cambridge: Cambridge University Press, 2000), 207.
21. See Robin Boyd, *The Witness of the Student Christian Movement: "Church Ahead of the Church"* (London: SPCK, 2007).

working faith of multitudes of lay men and women conducting the ordinary affairs of life. The only way in which it can affect business or politics is by shaping the convictions and determining the actions of those engaged in business and politics. It remains inoperative and unproductive, except in so far as it becomes a principle of action in the lives of those who are actually carrying on the work of the world and ordering its course in one direction or another.[22]

Far from being a matter of leaving individual lay persons to do their own thing in the secular world, Oldham envisaged creating a sense of *a common life* of Christians even as they were disperse in society, with appropriate firms of support and education for their formation. This was to find expression in his "Moot," the wartime and post-war *Christian News-Letter*, and the Christian Frontier Council.[23] In the 1950s and 1960s the laity movement was dynamically led by figures like Mark Gibbs of the Audenshaw Foundation and Ralph Morton of the Iona Community, who co-authored their invigorating studies on the laity *God's Frozen People* and *God's Lively People*, not to mention Kathleen Bliss and her *We the People*.[24] It was a notable emphasis, too, in the first decades of the WCC under such leaders as Hendrik Kraemer and in a number of countries especially Germany with its Evangelical Academies and the biennial *Kirchentag* which now draws some 100,000 people to each event. Essentially, the laity movements have sought to develop the latent ecumenism that *already* exists in the factory, the school, the hospital, the laboratory and anywhere else in the community where people associate and work together irrespective of their denomination. As has been said, Christians already have a common life from Monday to Saturday—it is only on Sundays that they are divided up.

By contrast, today in Britain, whenever "church" is mentioned, it is now once more primarily the clergy as its public representatives and spokespersons who come into the public mind. The situation is made worse by the mores of today's celebrity culture, which imagines that it is only envisage high-status individuals who will have anything interesting to say, rather than looking for what might be inherently interesting and worthwhile to hear irrespective of its source. The result can be a quite serious over-exposure of a few church leaders, generally archbishops and bishops, who are continually expected to pronounce on issues as "authorities," well-informed or ill-informed, without any hint being given of a wider collective wisdom and responsibility in the

---

22. J.H. Oldham, in *The Church and Its Function in Society*, ed. J.H. Oldham and W.A. Visser 't Hooft (London: George Allen and Unwin 1937), 117.
23. See above, chapter 8.
24. See Mark Gibbs and Ralph Morton, *God's Frozen People* (London: Collins, 1964) and *God's Lively People* (London: Collins, 1971) and Kathleen Bliss, *We the People* (London: SCM, 1963).

church as a whole, out of which they may or may not be speaking. Along with this runs the anxiety of some church leaders and clergy to be active on their own account. They have to be seen to be doing something in the hope that this will increase the visibility of the church, although this in fact leaves most of the church out of account. "Why," complained a cathedral chancellor to me a year or two ago, "does every bishop seem to want to have a 'bishop's initiative' on something—youth, or housing, or the environment or whatever? Why can't he just be a *bishop*?" A good question, which applies not only to bishops and not only to Anglicans. It is good to have an initiative, so long as it enables and encourages the initiative of the whole membership of the church, the *laos* of God. Clerical hyperactivism can disable and demotivate instead of inspire the people.

It might be thought that this concern for the role of laity reflects the socially oriented Life and Work stream of ecumenism rather than Faith and Order, where of course differing understandings of ordained ministry have long been wrestled with. But one should take note of the most widely received and discussed ecumenical document of modern times, the 1982 Faith and Order text *Baptism, Eucharist and Ministry*,[25] The first section of the chapter on "Ministry" is a substantial exposition of "The Calling of the Whole People of God." Here it is affirmed that in a broken world God calls the whole of humanity to become God's people, and for this purpose Jesus Christ is sent, and through his death, resurrection and the gift of the Holy Spirit there is laid "the foundation of a new community" built up continually by the Gospel and the sacraments: "The Holy Spirit unites in a single body those who follow Jesus Christ and sends them as witnesses into the world. Belonging to the Church means living in communion with God through Jesus Christ in the Holy Spirit."[26] In this communion "all members of the Church are called to confess their faith and to give account of their hope" in witness to the good news of the kingdom, through caring love and sharing in the struggles for justice and peace in the world.[27] Only then, out of this communal understanding of the church as the body of Christ, are the questions of diverse gifts of ministry, and the contemporary questions about the ordained ministry and the ordering of the communal life, to be addressed. It has to be said that in practice this primacy of the whole people of God in the understanding of the church is far less apparent now than in former years. Ecumenical issues and dialogues are focused ever more narrowly on who may or may not be ordained, which ministries may or may be mutually recognised, and ecumenical relations themselves

---

25. *Baptism, Eucharist and Ministry*, Faith and Order Paper No. 111 (Geneva: WCC Publications, 1982).
26. Ibid., 20.
27. Ibid., 20.

are seen as primarily involving relations between the clergy, as if the whole of ecumenism was both *about* and in *the hands of* the ordained. This applies at all levels: I recently encountered in England a situation where the local "Churches Together" had been shut down by the clergy as unnecessary, on the grounds that they themselves met together regularly.

Where Does Theology Come From?

Clericalisation—or the de-laicising of the church—is genetically close to another virus. This one infects how theology is done in the church, and the source materials for that theology. It is being raised especially in ecumenical contexts. To take a specific example, mixed marriages of Roman Catholics and partners of other Christian traditions have long presented acutely difficult problems of pastoral care and church discipline, and nowhere more painfully so than in the question of shared communion.[28] On the Catholic side, the official position remains that Catholics may not receive communion in the church of their non-Catholic spouse, and conversely the non-Catholic partner may not receive communion in the Catholic Church with their partner. Special permission may be granted by the bishop, but this seems to be far from consistent from diocese to diocese (an ecclesiastical version of the "postcode lottery"[29]). What is increasingly causing pain and frustration, however, is the situation facing the children of such marriages who as they approach adulthood do *not* wish to have to make the choice between Catholic and non-Catholic loyalty, and in some cases are tempted to throw over any church attachment at all on account of such seeming intransigence and hypocrisy. A whole generation is in danger of being lost, sacrificed on the altar of ecclesiastical rectitude. It has to be asked: in formulating the discipline and practice of the church, what account is being taken of the experience and lived reality of its lay members? Does truth only come from the inherited tradition and established codes? What might the Spirit now be saying, as experienced by the (very) faithful in their daily lives? If the answer is that at church leadership level "We have not yet reached sufficient agreement on communion" then the response must be "*Find* that agreement, *now*—or else... you are failing in your mission." Or maybe the people will simply take the law (or rather the gospel) into their own hands and trust that the rules will eventually catch up with the reality of apostolic life.

---

28. Here I reflect my impressions gained while attending the annual assembly of the Association of Inter-Church Families at Swanwick, England, in August 2010.

29. "Postcode lottery" is a currently popular term in Britain denoting how the quality of public services such as health care and education can vary enornmously and apparently randomly according to where one actually lives.

It is not only, however, Roman Catholic hierarchical discipline (and perhaps Anglican inertia) that causes such problems. Complaints are heard from within Local Ecumenical Projects (LEPs)[30] that the denominational bureaucracies (including Free Church ones) seem unable to cope with the emergence in the LEPs of a membership which, nurtured from the cradle in such communities, is thoroughly ecumenical in its consciousness and which does not wish to be formally attached to any one denomination at the expense of the rest. Not far removed from this is the rather patronising criticism of the large numbers of lay people who, in an increasingly geographically mobile society, seem able to migrate from one denomination on to another quite happily, looking to find congenial worship and community (and, not least, effective Christian nurture for their children) wherever it can be found in their new location. "Non-theological church membership," sniff the denominational purists, without considering that this phenomenon of the increasing porousness of denominational walls may itself be of prime theological significance.[31]

"For it has seemed good to the Holy Spirit and to us..." (Acts 15:28). So the apostles and the elders in the mother church of Jerusalem learnt to accept that things were happening on the gentile frontiers of the church's mission which the previously established rules had not envisaged and the inherited practices could not cope with. Theology was no longer being handed down from on high, but was being learnt from where the gospel was being shared and lived in new contexts. Not that the gentile mission was entirely free to do as it wished. The blessing of the Jerusalem council was necessary, for the unity of the church was vital. But Jerusalem had the humility to learn from the margins. Today, no less, both in the churches themselves and the ecumenical movement, lay people must be accepted not just as recipients of teaching but—through their own experience, expertise and aspirations—sources and resources for the churches' mission in the world. A lot of recent ecumenical talk, it must be admitted, has also failed here, subtly infiltrated by clericalism even as it celebrates and affirms "theology of the people" and "ecumenism on the ground." For example the language, so familiar in ecumenical circles, about the need to "do theology from the bottom upwards" in contrast to "theology from on high" or "top-down theology," itself perpetuates the hierarchical attitudes it claims to subvert.[32] Rather

---

30. Later renamed Local Ecumenical Partnerships.

31. For an account of how transfer (or disregard) of denominational loyalties and identities is proving a positive factor in the renewal of mainline Protestant congregations in the USA, see Diana Butler Bass, *Christianity for the Rest of Us: How the Neighborhood Church Is Transforming the Faith* (HarperSanFrancisco 2006).

32. See for example the articles in *Ecumenical Review* 60, no. 3 (July 2008) by Beril Huliselan, "The Ecumenical Movement in the 21st Century: Bringing Unity Down to Earth"; and Chad Rimmer, "Proposals for Ecumenism in the 21st Century: Towards an Ecumenical Theology of

than "above" and "below" it would be better to speak, respectively, about "hinterland" and "frontiers."

Dialogue: Words Alone?

If, as has been noted several times in this book, there is at present no single agreed goal of the ecumenical movement, it is at least gratifying that not all have given up on the quest. We can be sure that theological *dialogues* between the churches and traditions will continue, and it is to be hoped moreover that their undoubted fruits of convergence will be harvested.[33] A crucial question for the further journey is, however, just what is involved in this great, endlessly repeated term "dialogue"? If it is simply a never-ending exchange of views on theological and practical issues that is of itself unlikely to produce really new results. There will be, at best, an elegant dance in which participants move around, perhaps successively exchanging partners but finally ending up exactly as before albeit with a reverential bow to one another as the music ends. We may perhaps understand a little more of what one another's "positions" are, but the positions are unlikely to have changed, though we might hope for yet another consideration of what "reconciled diversity" might offer. We shall therefore need to look more seriously into what kind of *logos*, speaking, must now make up truly ecumenical dia*logue*.

At this point we may note a term that has now come into vogue in ecumenical discourse, at least in Europe, and mainly from the Roman Catholic side: "spiritual ecumenism." This term betokens a welcome recognition that prayer and spirituality must be at the heart of ecumenical encounter and endeavour, and not just abstract theological discussion and reorganization. It might also, however, arouse suspicion that an emphasis on the "spiritual" is being offered as a diversion from tackling the thorny, divisive issues of ecclesiology, ministry, and sacraments. One cannot but notice, for example, that in gatherings of one of the most attractive and popular movements drawing Catholics and other Christians together in Europe today, the Focolare movement, there is joyous and wholesome celebration that communion in Christ is real despite all doctrinal differences—while at the same time there seems to be a studied avoidance of the question "If this is so, then why cannot we celebrate the eucharist together?" The implication of such an attitude would seem to be either that we *should* be at the Lord's table together here and now, or that the question of eucharistic communion does not really matter so much after all—a position which it is hard to credit being held by the many Catholic bishops who identify with Focolare!

the Wilderness."
33. See especially Walter Kasper, ed., *Harvesting the Fruits: Basic Aspects of Christian Faith in Ecumenical Dialogue* (London: Continuum, 2009).

Such questions can only be answered by delving further into what the actual content will be of the spirituality which impels more creative dialogue. Prayer, yes; "exchange of gifts," yes. But is this as far as we can get towards "the practice of a common life," an actual *koinonia*, which, as we noted with Nicholas Sagovsky earlier, must be the context for continuing theological dialogue?

"Dialogue," as is well-known, has its origins in the Greek *dia*, "through," and *legesthai* "speaking" or *logos*, "speech" or "word." It is conversation, through-speech. But is there not also a dimension to the New Testament understanding of *logos* which should haunt and disturb us? *Logos* according to the Scriptures is ultimately Jesus Christ, and *ho logos sarx egeneto*: the Word became flesh (John 1:14). Dialogue where *logos* simply remain *logos*, speaking, is no longer enough in the light of this gospel of incarnation. The Scottish poet Edwin Muir had in his immediate sights the hyper-Calvinist highland church where in doctrinal polemic

The Word made flesh is here made word again,
A word made word in flourish and arrogant crook.[34]

But there are collateral implications wider than Protestant verbosity, and ecumenical discourse too must heed the warning. The churches must take the risk of making experiments in sharing their actual ways of being and acting as church. For example, could not the churches, meeting in conciliar fellowship, jointly commission an "order" of persons to whom would be assigned the mission of sharing for a time in the life of churches other than their own, experiencing from within and to the full the liturgical, pastoral, diaconal, and missionary life of those churches, and then bringing their experiences and reflections into the on-going ecumenical dialogues? The integrity of the different churches would be maintained while at the same time a form of *koinonia* would be enabled that could fructify ecumenical encounter with quite unforeseen possibilities. At the very least, it would be an exercise in living in more than one place at once, and of bringing double vision into where there is very little vision of any sort just now. So why not a new word for a new chapter on the story?

Unfortunately we do not at the moment have a word for what I am suggesting so let us invent one, based on how John the Evangelist continues immediately after saying the Word became flesh: " . . . and lived among us" (John 1:14). Here the Greek word for "lived", *eskēnōsen* literally means "pitched his tent." An allusion may be

---

34. Edwin Muir (1887-1959), "The Incarnate One," in *The Penguin Book of Religious Verse*, ed. R.S. Thomas (London: Penguin, 1963), 55.

intended to a parallel with God dwelling among the Israelites in the tent (*skēnē*) of the tabernacle in the wilderness (Ex. 25-30), but in any case the image is deeply suggestive of "living in" and sharing all the conditions of skin-thin tented life and human vulnerability. To live authentically in response to such incarnate love will mean a parallel readiness to pitch one's tent where others are, even to exchange tents if called for. This would mean going beyond dialogue to—let us invent the new word —diaskeny, exchange of living or residence. That could be a way of realising something of my dream: "a ballet of communities of love indwelling each other, drawing from each other, giving to each other, suffering with each other and rejoicing in each other in a way that spills over to embrace the entire world in its need and suffering and divisions."

Of course we do not know for certain where this will lead us, but such inability to predict is, paradoxically, often the sign that we are on the right path. So let there be diaskeny, endlessly manifesting the ecumenical dynamic of living in more than one place at once.

Index

Action of Churches Together in Scotland, 12 16n

Africa, Christianity in, 84

Althaus, Paul, 64

Amsterdam World Conference of Christian Youth 1939, 4

Anglo-German church peace exchanges 1908-09, **57-76**, 195

Anglo-German relations prior to 1914, 58, 66

Angola, Portuguese atrocities in, 30

Associated Councils of Churches of British and German Empires, 69-71, 74

Atkins, Martin, 13 n18

Aubrey, M.E., 96

Audenshaw Foundation, 207

Avis, Paul, 200, 204

Azariah, Samuel, bishop, 85f, 86 n27, 98 n13

Baillie, John, 126, 128, 130, 137, 184

Baker, Joseph Allen, 59-66, 68, 69, 71, 73, 74, 75, 206

Balfour of Burleigh, Lord, 80

Baptism, Eucharist and Ministry, 8, 208

Baptist Missionary Society, 30

Baptists, British, 15, 28f, 96

Barmen Synod 1934, 91-105

Barmen Theological Declaration, 92f, 95f, 102, 104

Barot, Madeleine, 3f, 5, 21, 206

Barth, Karl, 52, 81, 92, 93, 96f, 98, 101f, 103, 104, 117, 126, 136f, 185

Bauckham, Richard, 161

Bede, 28,

Bell, George, bishop, 6, 75, 94, 95, 96, 99, 102, **107-124**, 196, 198

Benedict XVI, Pope, 13, 178

Beveridge, William, 128

bird-watching, 29

Black-led Churches (Britain), 12

Bliss, Kathleen, 113, 127, 206, 207

Bloch, Ernst, 188

body of Christ, 51, 86f, 115, 124, 153, 158, 172

Boegner, Marc, 102

Boesak, Allan, 179

Bonhoeffer, Dietrich, 5f, 31, 75f, 95, 96, 97, 100, 101, 101f, 104, 105, 111, 112, 116f, 122, 122f, 145, 159, 173, 185, 190, 200f, 202

Bonhoeffer, Klaus, 122

Borgman, Albert, 167

Bornholm, ship, 142

Bourne, Francis, archbishop, 62

Boyle, Nicholas, 164

Brent, Charles, bishop, 81

British Council of Churches, 12, 14, 34

British role in world, 139

Brunner, Emil, 185

Caligiorgis, Metropolitan Jérémie, 150

Cambridge Intercollegiate Christian Union, 32

Cambridge University, 31-34, 64

Cambridge Word Alliance conference 1931, see World Alliance.

Campbell-Bannerman, Henry, 62

Caritas Europa, 192

Carnegie, Andrew, 72

Centesimus Annus, 187

Charta Oecumenica, 149-151, 151 n17, 152f

Cheng Ching-yi, 85

Chernobyl disaster, 146

China, 27f, 85

Christ, lordship /kingship/sovereignty of, 115-119, 124

christendom, 131, 131 (new), 138 (post-), 182, 196

Christian Aid, 112

Christian Frontier Council, 130, 138, 207

Christian News-Letter, 129f, 138, 140, 207

church in relation to society, 132f, 189f

Church of England, 9, 11, 13, 14, 15, 17f, 62, 95f, 110, 123

Church of Scotland, 9, 128, 184

Commission on "The Interpretation of God's Will in the Present Crisis", 184

Church of South India, 9f, 86

Church Peace Union (USA), 72

Church Struggle (German), 91-105, 108, 110

Church, Confessing, see Confessing Church

Church, German Evangelical, 91f

Church, Reich (Germany), 94, 94 n4, 100, 101

churches of North America, 71f

Churches Together in Britain and Ireland, 12 n16, 14

Churches Together in England, 12 n16, 14

churches, in Germany East and West, 145

CIMADE, 4

civil society, 135, 160, 186

Clarke, Fred, 127, 128, 139

Clegg, Cecelia, 170-171

clericalisation, 206-209

Clifford, John, 63, 65, 72

climate change, 163

cold war, 141f, 143, 160, 196

Commission of Episcopal Conferences in the European Union (COMECE), 191, 192

communion, 159, 205 See also *Koinonia*

communities, Christian, 159

community, general, **157-175**, 177

community, Christian, 32f80, 86, 158; 173; 172. See also body of Christ, koinonia, sharing

Conference of British Missionary Societies, 87

Conference of European Churches (CEC), 24, 26, 34, 141f, 145, 147

Church and Society Commission, 191, 192

Conference on Security and Cooperation in Europe (CSCE), 145

confessing belief, 103, 105

Confessing Church (Germany), 8, 75, 92, 97, 196

and ecumenical movement 101, 105.111

Confessing the One Faith (Faith and Order study), 143, 143n, 147

consumerism, 164f

contextualisation, 193

Council of Catholic Episcopal Conferences in Europe (CCEE), 142 145, 147

Council of Churches for Britain and Ireland, 12 n16, 34

creation, 146

creation, biblical narrative, 38f

Cromwell, Oliver, 136

Cuthbert, Saint, 28

Cytun (Wales), 12 n16

Darlington, 26f

Davidson, Randall, archbishop, 62, 70, 71, 73, 80, 87, 109

Dawson, Christopher, 127, 130

de Blank, Joost, 33

de Gruchy, John, 180

de Neufville, Eduard, 61, 66, 68, 73, 206

democracy, 160

dialogue, 211-213

diaspora/dispersion, Jewish, 43f

Dibelius, Otto, bishop, 113, 116

Dickinson, W.H., 69, 70

Diognetus, Letter to, 6

dispersion, Christian, 50

Dryander, Ernst von, 63
Dudzus, Otto, 104f
Duncan Jones, A.S., 66
Durham Cathedral, 28

economics, 134, 184
ecumenical peace council, 75, 100
ecumenical formation, writer's experience
   of, 26-34
ecumenical movement:
   and prophecy, 35, 124
   commitment to, 23-35
   criticisms of, 9f, 23
   current difficulties in, 13-14, 124, 138, 197
   renewal of, 21f, 34f, 198
   self-criticism by, 35
   understandings of, 6-7
   and Confessing Church, 101f
   Ecumenical Patriarchate, 1920 Appeal, 8
ecumenical, meaning of, 6-7
ecumenism:
   biblical basis, **37-54**
   contextual realisation, 193
   relational, 195f
Edinburgh Faith and Order conference
   1937, see Faith and Order
Edinburgh World Missionary Conference
   1910, 7, 22, 34, 35, 77- 89, 91
   commemoration of 2010, 15, 78f
   continuation committee, 78, 81, 87, 97, 110
   significance in ecumenical history, 77f,
      83, 84, 87
education, 129, 139
Edward VII, King, 64
Edwards, Jonathan, 13 n18
Ehrenberg, Hans, 98
Eiche, Die, 71, 72, 72 n29
Eliot, T., 126, 128, 129, 135
empire, 124. See also imperialism
environment, 146. See also climate change.
eucharistic communion, 7, 211
Eurodiakonia, 192
Europe:
eastern, 34, 147
   post-1945 reconstruction, 112f, 124

European unity and churches, 113
   current negativity to, 124
   cold war division, 141, 160
   end of cold war division, 146
European Court of Human Rights, 185
European Ecumenical Assemblies: Basel
   1989 145; Graz 1997 148; Sibiu 2007, 151
European ecumenical encounters:
   Chantilly 1978, 143
   Logumkloster 1981, 143
   Riva del Garda 1984, 142-145, 148
   Santiago Compostela 1991; 148
   Assisi 1995, 148
   Strasbourg 2001, 149f
European Treaty, preamble, 178, 191
European Union, 141, 152, 191
Evangelical academies, 207
evangelicalism, 16f, 78f
exile, Jewish, 42f, 47

Faber, General Superintendent, 63, 65, 68
Faith and Order movement, 8, 23, 34, 77, 84,
   88, 99, 100f, 110, 208. See also Lausanne
   conference 1927
   Edinburgh conference 1937, 143, 102,
      111, 121
Fanø conference (Life and Work and World
   Alliance) 1934, 75, 99f, 111, 145
Federal Council of Churches of Christ in
   America, 72
Fenn, Eric, 127, 130
Ferdinand, Archduke, 72
Fisher, Geoffrey, archbishop, 122
Focolare movement, 211`
Forrester, Duncan, 181
Forster, E.M., 167
Free Churches (British), 11, 13, 62, 96, 109,
   123
Free Churches (German), 64
freedom, post-Enlightenment, 134; western,
   160
freedom, religious, 94, 96, 117f;
Freud, Sigmund, 200
Fukuyama, Francis, 160f
fundamentalism, 21, 180

gender issues, 17, 124
George VI, King, 133
"German Christians", 91f, 100
German missions – in first world war, 87f;
    under Nazi revolution, 97f, 100
German resistance, 112, 122, 139f, 196
Gibbs, Mark, 207
Glasnost, 143, 146
globalization, 163, 173, 192
Glover, T.R., 116
Goodwill, 73. See also *Peacemaker, The*
Gorbachev, Mikhail, 143 n3, 146
grace, 204f
Graham, Billy, 30
Graham, James (Marquess of Montrose), 140
Great Britain, ecumenism in, 11-12
Gurs refugee camp, 3, 21

Hague Peace Conference 1907, 59, 60f, 76
Hanson, R.P.C., 143
Harnack, Adolf von, 70, 73
Harvey, Barry, 172
Hastings, Adrian. 11, 13
Hauerwas, Stanley. 189-191
Hayward, M.C., 84 n22
Headlam, Arthur C., bishop, 100
health, 165f
Heckel, Theodor, bishop, 100, 101, 102
Helsinki Final Act, 145
Henderson, Ian, 9
Henriod, Henri Louis, 75, 107f, 121
Henson, Hensley, bishop, 115, 116, 120, 121
Hetherington, Hector, 127, 128
Hickman, Rebecca, 181f
Hitler, Adolf, 91f, 108, 110, 134
Hodges, H.A., 126, 135, 139
Hodgson, Leonard, 100f
Holiness Churches (Britain), 12
hope, 144
Horne, Charles Sylvester, 66, 67
Huddleston, Trevor, 33
Huliselan, Beril, 193f
Hull, John, 15 n20
Human Rights, Universal Declaration of, 186
Hume, Basil, Cardinal, 13

identity, 19, 20; 169 (communal); 198-200
    (as contemporary issue); 200-202 (as
    relational); 202-205 and narrative
imperialism, 58, 87
incarnational theology, 193f, 212f
India, 85f (missions and)
individual freedom, 160
Inge, W.R., 66
institutions, 18f, 34
interchurch families, 209
interfaith relations. 17, 124, 124 n27
International Missionary Council (IMC), 74
    n32, 77, 83, 84, 88, 97-99, 121
International Review of Missions, 81
Iona Community, 207
Iraq, 34
Iredale, Eleonora, 127, 128
Irenaeus, 51
Irish Council of Churches, 12 n16
Irish Inter-Church Meeting, 12 n16
Islam, 17, 180

Jehle, Herbert, 4, 5, 21
Jenkins, Daniel, 127
Jeremiah, 42
    Jesus, ministry of, 47-49, 158
Jerusalem, 41-45
Jerusalem, New, 52f.
Jewish thinking, 12, 137f,
Jews, Nazi persecution of, 138
John Paul II, Pope, 9, 13, 146, 187
John XXIII, Pope, 123, 142, 187
Jones, Evan, 66
Josephus, 43
justice, 119f, 123, 188, 192, 193
Justice, Peace and the Integrity of Creation
    (JPIC), 8, 75

Kaftan, Julius, 63
Kent, John. 9f, 14
Kim, Kirsten, 197c
King, Martin Luther, Jr, 33
King's College, Cambridge, 32, 64. See also
    Cambridge University.
kingdom (reign) of God, 47-49, 50, 53, 115
    (and church), 130

Kirchentag, 207
Koinonia, 158f, 172, 206, 212
Kraemer, Hendrik, 207
Kreider, Alan, 203
Kreisau Circle, 139f
Küng, Hans, 17

laity, role of, 69, 137, 206-209
Lake, Frank, 33
Lambeth Conference Appeal 1920, 8, 109
Lang, Cosmo Gordon, archbishop, 96, 107f
Lausanne Faith and Order conference 1927, 77, 99
League of Nations, 186
Ledger, Christine, 167, 171
Leibholz, Gerhard, 120
Leo XIII, Pope, 187
liberation theology, , 186, 187
Liechty, Joseph, 169-171
Life and Work movement (Universal
    Christian Council), 8, 74, 77. 83, 84, 88,
    99f, 110f, 117 145, 208
    Oxford 1937 conference "Church,
        Community and State", 77, 100, 102,
        111, 119, 121, 126, 137, 158, 173-
        175, 182f, 206f
    Stockholm conference 1924, 74f. 77 ,
        83, 110
Lilje, Hans, 103, 104
"Lima Text", see *Baptism, Eucharist and
    Ministry*
local ecumenical projects/partnerships, 210
Löser, Werner, 143
Löwe, Adolf, 127, 138f
Lund principle, 8
Lynch, Frederick, 72
Lytham St Annes, 28f

Mackinnon, Donald, 127
Macleod, George, 33
Makarios, Archbishop, 122
Mannheim, Julia, 129
Mannheim, Karl, 127, 128, 130, 133, 134f,
    136, 137, 138f
Marshall, Newton H., 63, 70

Marty, Martin E., 23
Marx, Karl, 137
Maury, Paul, 103
Men Without Work report (1938), 128
Methodist Church, British, 15
Metropolitan Free Church Federation, 60
Metz, Johann Baptist, 187
middle axioms, 139, **177-194**
migration, 152, 163
Míguez Bonino, José 186
Milbank, John, 189 n24
Miller, Alex, 127, 137
missionary agenda, 80 (post-Edinburgh), 83
Mission-Shaped Church (2004), 15
Moberly, Walter, 126f, 128f, 133, 136,
Moltke, Helmut von, 140
Moltmann, Jürgen, 187f, 189, 192
monasticism, 159
Moore Ede, W., 71, 72
Moot, the, **125-140**, 183, 207,
Morton, Ralph, 207
Mott, John R., 78, 80, 86 n27, 206
Muir, Edwin, 212
Müller, Ludwig, 92, 94 n4, 100
Munich crisis 1938, 134
Murry, John Middleton, 126, 130, 133, 136, 137
mysticism, 169

natural law, 135-137, 181, 184
Nazi policies, 121
Nazi revolution, 91f, 97f (consequences for
    German missions)
Nelidoff, A.I., 60
Newbigin, Lesslie, 35
Niceno-Constantinopolitan Creed, 143
Niebuhr, Reinhold, 127, 188f
Niemöller, Martin, 29, 33, 92, 113, 118
non-governmental organisations, 186
Northampton, Marquis of, 65
Northern Ireland, 169-171, 180
"Not Strangers but Pilgrims Inter-Church
    Process", 11-12

O'Connor, Murphy, Cardinal, 13 n18
Oakeshott, Walter, 127, 128

Octogesima Adveniens, 187

Oesterley, W. O. E, 66

oikoumene, 6, 21, 28, 52, 86, 123, 125, 165, 192

Oldham, J.H., 34f, 74 n32, 78, 80, 81, 82f, 86
    n27, 87f, 98, 102, 108,112, 124 n27, **125-
    140**, 180, 182f, 185, 187, 196, 206f

Oldham, Mary, 127, 130

"order", J.H. Oldham's idea for, 137f

orders of creation, 184f

Orthodox Church, 13, 32, 110, 114;
    Russian, 146; Synod 147, 148. See also
    Ecumenical Patriarchate

Oud Wassenaar conference, see World
    Alliance.

Oxford Conference 1937, see Life and Work

Pacem in Terris, 187

Pakenham, Frank, 127f, 138

Pastors' Emergency League, 92, 99

Paton, William, 98, 133, 140

Paul, 50-52, 109, 158, 197

peace as ecumenical issue, 57-76, 112, 123

Peacemaker, The, 70, 71. See also *Goodwill*.

penultimate sphere of ethics, 190f

Perestroika, 143, 146

Philo, 43

Pius XII, Pope, 112

Planning for freedom, 134f

Polanyi, Michael, 127, 128

political theology, 187f

Populorum Progressio, 187

post-modern context, 18f

poverty, 192

Programme to Combat Racism (WCC), 8

proselytism, 147

Protestant Synod, 147

psalms, spirituality of, 41-47

public policy, **177-194**

race, racial justice, 33f, 83, 86 (relationships),
    87, 92 (Nazism and German church)

Raiser, Konrad, 24

Rawls, John, 181

reconciliation, 50, 74 n32, 87f, 113; 123, 144,
    148f, 179

Reeves, Ambrose, 33

Regent's Park College, Oxford, 34

religion – "organised", 133, 181 (as private
    opinion)

Rerum Novarum, 187

"responsible society", 139

Richter, Julius, 63, 81, 81 n12

risk, 140, 168

river chart, 7, 77, 79

Robertson, Edwin, 116

Robinson, John, 33

Roman Catholic Church in Britain, 12, 13,
    14, 15, 62

Roman Catholic Church, 8, 9, 10, 13, 15f;
    147 (European Synod); 186f (social
    teaching)

Rominger, Roberta, 13 n18

Rowntree, Joseph, 62

Rushbrooke, J.H., 63, 70, 73

Ruskin, John, 166

Russell, David S., 5, 21

Sagovsky Nicholas, 206, 212

salvation history, biblical, 39-41

Sanneh, Lamin, 84

Schönfeld, Hans, 102

Second Vatican Council, 142
    Decree on Ecumenism, 8, 123f

sectarianism, 21, 169-171 (Protestant-
    Catholic, Northern Ireland)

secular sphere, church and, 118f, 128

secularisation, 130, 178

sexuality issues, 17, 124

sharing as service, 51f. See also body of
    Christ, community.

Shaw, Gilbert, 127

Siegmund-Schultze, Friedrich, 64, 68, 71,
    72, 73, 73 n29, 108, 121

Simpson, John, 166

Smith, Ronald Gregor, 205

social breakdown, 162

social ethics, 130

social gospel movement, 178

social imaginary. 30, 53

social values, 131f, 135-137

sociality, 162-164

society, nature of, 160 See also civil society.
   church and, **125-140**
   "Christian", 132
   "responsible", 139

Soden, Hans von, 64

Söderblom, Nathan, archbishop, 74f, 83, 109f, 116

South Africa, 34, 179, 180

Spiecker, E. A., 67, 68, 70

spirituality, 168f

Stalin, Joseph, 134

state, 119 (absolutisation of);

Stewart, James, 33

Stockwood, Mervyn, bishop 33

Strabo of Cappadocia, 43

Student Christian Movement (Cambridge),
   33, 206

Student Missionary Volunteer movement, 78

Stuttgart Declaration 1945, 8, 113

Swanwick Declaration 1987, 12

Sword of the Spirit movement, 112

Tanner, Mary, 20

Tawney, R.H., 183

Taylor, Charles, 30, 49

technology, 166f

Temple, William, archbishop, 83f, 108, 112,
   122, 128

Thatcher, Margaret, 160

theology, sources of, 209-211

Thomas, William, 63, 71

Tolstoy, Leo, 168

totalitarianism, 119, 132 134f, 137, 146, 184
   See also state.

triune God, 205

Troeltsch, Ernst, 157. 159

Trott, Adam von, 140

Truth and Reconciliation Commission
   (South Africa), 179

Tutu, Desmond, archbishop, 166, 179

Tveit, Olav Fyske, 79

Ubuntu, 161

United Nations, 163, 185, 186

unity of churches, 7, 9f, 80f, 88, 89, 109-114,
   123, 124, 173, 206f

University Teachers' Group, 138

Ut Unum Sint, 9

Versailles Treaty, 88 (on missions)

Vidler, Alec, 126, 128, 129, 133, 136f, 138

Visser't Hooft, W.A., 35, 103f, 111, 114, 137, 139

Vlk, Cardinal Miloslav, 150

Volf, Miroslav, 195, 201f

Wakefield, H. Russell, 63

war, first world:
   outbreak 72f
   responses of German and British church
      leaders 73
   consequences for post-Edinburgh
      western missions, 81f
   legacy of bitterness, 110

war, "just", 120

war, second world
   churches and, 111
      refugees, 112
      bombing of civilians, 112
      post-war reconstruction in Europe,
         112f, 120
   international ecumenical links in, 140
   Oldham and war aims, 184

Ward, Graham, 203f

Warnock, Mary, 181 n7

Weatherhead, Leslie, 33

Westcott, B.F., 58

Wilhelm II, Kaiser, 58, 66, 67, 81

Williams, Rowan, 13f, 164, 202

Winnington Ingram, Arthur, bishop, 65

Woods, Theodore, bishop, 110

Wordsworth, William, 147

World Alliance for Promoting International
   Friendship through the Churches, 57,
   58f, 78, 99f, 110
   formation, 71-73;
   and first world war, 73;
   work following war, 74.
      Oud Wassenaar conference 1919, 74,
         75, 109
      Cambridge conference 1931, 75

World Congress of Faiths, 124 n27.

World Council of Churches (WCC), 4, 8, 9,
    13, 23, 24, 34, 75, 77, 147, 207
    formation 111, 121, 126
    inauguration 113f, 121, 147, 207
    1st assembly Amsterdam 1948, 8, 77, 113
    2nd assembly Evanston 1954, 113
    3rd assembly New Delhi 1961, 114
    4th assembly Uppsala 1968, 139
    6th assembly Vancouver 1983, 75, 145

World Student Christian Federation
    (WSCF), 4, 103f, 206
worship, Anglican, 29, 32
worship, Free Church, 29, 32

Yoder, John Howard, 189
Yugoslavia, 147 (break-up of former)

Zizioulas, Metropolitan John, 173